Mastering
Human Resource Management

Palgrave Master Series

Accounting
Accounting Skills
Advanced English Language
Advanced English Literature
Advanced Pure Mathematics
Arabic
Basic Management
Biology
British Politics
Business Communication
Business Environment
C Programming
C++ Programming
Chemistry
COBOL Programming
Communication
Computing
Counselling Skills
Customer Relations
Database Design
Delphi Programming
Desktop Publishing
Economic and Social History
Economics
Electrical Engineering
Electronic and Electrical
    Calculations
Electronics
English Grammar
English Language
English Literature
Fashion Buying and
    Merchandising
    Management
Fashion Styling
French

Geography
German
Global Information Systems
Human Resource
    Management
Information Technology
Internet
Italian
Java
Management Skills
Mathematics
Microsoft Office
Microsoft Windows, Novell
    NetWare and UNIX
Modern British History
Modern European History
Modern United States History
Modern World History
Networks
Organisational Behaviour
Pascal and Delphi
    Programming
Philosophy
Physics
Practical Criticism
Psychology
Shakespeare
Social Welfare
Sociology
Spanish
Statistics
Strategic Management
Systems Analysis and Design
Theology
Visual Basic
World Religions

www.palgravemasterseries.com

Palgrave Master Series
Series Standing Order ISBN 0–333–69343–4
(outside North America only)

You can receive future titles in this series as they are published by
placing a standing order. Please contact your bookseller or, in case of
difficulty, write to us at the address below with your name and address,
the title of the series and the ISBN quoted above

Customer Services Department. Macmillan Distribution Ltd,
Houndmills, Basingstoke, Hampshire RG21 6XS, England

Mastering

Human Resource Management

Kelvin Cheatle

Business Series Editor
Richard Pettinger

palgrave

First published 2001 by
PALGRAVE
Houndmills, Basingstoke, Hampshire RG21 6XS and
175 Fifth Avenue, New York, N.Y. 10010
Companies and representatives throughout the world

PALGRAVE is the new global academic imprint of
St. Martin's Press LLC Scholarly and Reference Division and
Palgrave Publishers Ltd (formerly Macmillan Press Ltd).

ISBN 0–333–79280–7

This book is printed on paper suitable for recycling and
made from fully managed and sustained forest sources.

A catalogue record for this book is available
from the British Library.

10   9   8   7   6   5   4   3   2   1
10   09 08 07 06 05 04 03 02 01

Printed and bound in Great Britain by
Creative Print and Design (Wales), Ebbw Vale

In loving memory of Phyllis Florence Lillian Cheatle, always in my heart

Contents

List of Figures   xi
Selected Reading List   xii
Preface   xv
Acknowledgements   xvi

1 Introduction to management   1
  1.1   Introduction   1
  1.2   Role of human resource management (HRM) in organisations 2
  1.3   Understanding the role of HRM in your organisation   4
  1.4   Activity   5
  1.5   Checklist   6

2 The legislative and good practice framework   7
  2.1   Introduction   7
  2.2   Employment law   7
  2.3   Case law   9
  2.4   Codes of practice and regulations   9
  2.5   Organisational employment rules   10
  2.6   Checklist   11

3 Contract of employment (1)   12
  3.1   Introduction   12
  3.2   Legal framework   12
  3.3   Types of contract   17
  3.4   Forming the contract of employment   23
  3.5   Varying the contract   25
  3.6   Problem areas   27
  3.7   Activity   29
  3.8   Checklist   29

4 Contract of employment (2)   31
  4.1   Introduction   31
  4.2   Legal grounds for terminating the contract of employment 31
  4.3   Handling dismissals   33
  4.4   Unfair grounds for terminating the contract of employment 36
  4.5   Unfair, constructive and wrongful dismissal   39
  4.6   Tribunals and courts   42
  4.7   Tribunal powers and remedies   45
  4.8   Periods of notice and associated provisions   47
  4.9   Post-termination restraints and termination agreements 49

	4.10	Problem areas	50
	4.11	Activity	52
	4.12	Checklist	52
5		**Recruitment, selection and retention**	53
	5.1	Introduction	53
	5.2	Legal framework	54
	5.3	Codes of practice	55
	5.4	Preparing to recruit	55
	5.5	Recruitment strategy and practice	60
	5.6	Selection techniques	64
	5.7	Retention	71
	5.8	Problem areas	74
	5.9	Activity	76
	5.10	Checklist	76
6		**Pay and benefits**	77
	6.1	Introduction	77
	6.2	Legal framework	78
	6.3	Pay and pay systems	82
	6.4	Holidays	91
	6.5	Pension arrangements	92
	6.6	Sickness and sick pay	96
	6.7	Maternity rights and benefits	98
	6.8	Other benefits	100
	6.9	Problem areas	101
	6.10	Activity	103
	6.11	Checklist	103
7		**Personnel information systems and workforce planning**	105
	7.1	Introduction	105
	7.2	Legal framework	106
	7.3	Categories of employee data	107
	7.4	Types of personnel information system	109
	7.5	Data applications	115
	7.6	Workforce planning	118
	7.7	Problem areas	122
	7.8	Activity	124
	7.9	Checklist	125
8		**Equal opportunities**	126
	8.1	Introduction	126
	8.2	Legal framework	127
	8.3	Codes of practice	130
	8.4	Good practice	130
	8.5	Sex discrimination	133
	8.6	Race discrimination	134
	8.7	Disability discrimination	136
	8.8	Sexual orientation and ageism	139
	8.9	Other statutory rights	141

	8.10	Problem areas	142
	8.11	Activity	144
	8.12	Checklist	145
9	**Training and development**		146
	9.1	Introduction	146
	9.2	Legal framework	147
	9.3	Training cycle	148
	9.4	Vocational education and NVQs	153
	9.5	Induction and mandatory training	153
	9.6	Management development and professional training	154
	9.7	Appraisal and performance management	159
	9.8	Problem areas	162
	9.9	Activity	164
	9.10	Checklist	164
10	**Employee relations**		166
	10.1	Introduction	166
	10.2	Legal framework	167
	10.3	Trade unions and staff associations	169
	10.4	Consultation, negotiating and bargaining	171
	10.5	Disciplinary, grievance and disputes procedures	174
	10.6	Problem areas	179
	10.7	Activity	181
	10.8	Checklist	181
11	**Redundancy, reorganisation and transfers**		182
	11.1	Introduction	182
	11.2	Legal framework	183
	11.3	Handling redundancies	188
	11.4	Reorganisation and managing internal change	190
	11.5	Transfers of employment	192
	11.6	Problem areas	196
	11.7	Activity	198
	11.8	Checklist	199
12	**Health and safety and risk management**		200
	12.1	Introduction	200
	12.2	Legal framework	201
	12.3	Enforcement of health and safety in the workplace	204
	12.4	The essential framework	206
	12.5	The management of health and safety at work	207
	12.6	Health at work	211
	12.7	Problem areas	215
	12.8	Activity	217
	12.9	Checklist	217
13	**Employee support and welfare**		219
	13.1	Introduction	219

13.2 Legal framework 220
13.3 Occupational health services 222
13.4 Counselling services 223
13.5 Stress management 224
13.6 Employee support measures 226
13.7 Problem areas 227
13.8 Activity 229
13.9 Checklist 229

14 New developments 231
14.1 Introduction 231
14.2 EU directives: the Social Chapter 232
14.3 Other employment law developments 236
14.4 Key case law and HRM developments 239
14.5 The future? 241
14.6 Activity 243
14.7 Checklist 243

Index 244

⩔ List of figures

2.1   The legislative and good practice framework   10
3.1   Contract and written statement clauses   13
3.2   Qualifying periods for employment rights   21
3.3   Model outline contract of employment   24
4.1   Handling dismissal: a model approach   34
5.1   Model outline job description   58
5.2   Person specification for healthcare assistant grade "A"   59
5.3   Range of recruitment methods   61
5.4   Model interview assessment grid   68
5.5   Overview of recruitment and selection process   70
6.1   Components of the pay package   85
6.2   Salary structure: the NHS Trust   89
6.3   Types of pension scheme   97
7.1   Model specification for a computerised HR system   114
7.2   Statistical analysis of absence trends   116
8.1   Model equal opportunities questionnaire   135
8.2   Equal opportunities policy framework   144
9.1   Outline training process   149
9.2   Model training plan: accountancy firm   151
9.3   Model health and safety training programme   152
10.1 Hierarchy of disciplinary sanctions   176
10.2 Disciplinary flowchart   177
10.3 Model grievance procedure   178
11.1 Redundancy payments statutory ready reckoner   185
11.2 Model approach to handling redundancy   191
11.3 *TUPE*: a methodical approach to handling transfers   193
12.1 Systems approach to health and safety management   208
13.1 Network of employee support and welfare provision   229

◼ ⌄ Selected reading list

Mastering Human Resource Management is designed to be a general introduction to the wide-ranging subject of Human Resources. For those who wish to further their studies and gain a more in-depth knowledge of specific issues the following short reading list will be of assistance. In all cases the latest editions should be consulted.

Codes of Practice
Commission for Racial Equality, *Race Relations Code of Practice*
Department of Health, *Code of Practice for Staff Working in Children's Residential Care*
Disability Discrimination Act, *Code of Practice in Disability Matters*
Equal Opportunities Commission, *Sex Discrimination Code of Practice*
Health and Safety Executive, *Five Steps to Successful Health and Safety Management*

Guides
ACAS, *Consultation, Bargaining and Negotiation*
——, *Discipline at Work*
——, *Disciplinary Practice and Procedures*
——, *Grievances in Employment*
——, *Time Off for Trade Union Activities*
——, *Contracts of Employment*
Incomes Data Services, *Trade Union Membership*
Industrial Society, *Appraisal and Appraisal Systems*
——, *Effective Discipline*
——, *Managing Change*
——, *Motivation*
——, *Salary Management*
——, *Selection*
——, *Training Your Staff*

Reference Works
Armstrong, M., *Human Resource Management* (London, Kogan Page)
Cheatle, K., *A Code of Employment Practice* (London, NCVCCO)
Handy, C., *Understanding Organisations* (London, Macmillan)
Morris, S., *Discipline, Grievance, Dismissal* (London, Industrial Society)
Nicholson, M., *Mastering Business Administration* (London, Macmillan)
Pettinger, R., *Effective Employee Relations* (London, Kogan Page)
——, *Managing the Flexible Workforce* (London, Technical Communications)

——, *Mastering Basic Management* (with Eyre, E; London, Macmillan)

——, *Preparing and Handling Industrial Tribunal Cases* (London, Technical Communications)

Slade, E., *Employment Handbook* (London, Tolleys)

Stewart, V. & A., *Practical Performance Appraisal* (London, Gower HMSO)

Warner, N. & Associates, *Choosing with Care* (London, HMSO)

Periodicals

Institute of Personnel and Development, *People Management* (London, Centurian Press)

Various, *Employers Law* (London, Reed)

——, *Personnel Today* (London, Reed)

☑ Preface

The world of Human Resource Management has never been so complex and challenging as it is today. No matter how accomplished or experienced, all students and practitioners in the world of Human Resource Management constantly struggle to keep up-to-date and come to terms with the growing complexity of their subject. The reason for the shifting nature of the subject is not simply that employment law changes with great regularity, overlaid as it is by a plethora of European Union directives, and weekly changes in case law determined by employment tribunals and courts. Overridingly, the subject is endlessly dynamic and fluctuating because of the nature of its business – put simply it is about managing people, and people are the most difficult of all resources to harness and come to terms with.

This book is aimed at both the student and the practitioner of Human Resource Management or as an accessible reference book for the busy manager, trade union official or employees who wish to access material in a simple, straightforward form. It focuses very much on establishing the legal framework that organisations and individuals need to be aware of and seeks to outline good practice guidance in each of the main aspects of Human Resource activity. For economy of space, some highly technical subjects within the Human Resource field can only be covered in overview or summary terms and there are many specialist reference and text books in the market that will help the interested reader gain more in-depth understanding of these special interests. My aspiration in writing this book is, above all, to provide clarity and accessibility and to focus on practical approaches which are readily applicable in the workplace.

KELVIN CHEATLE

◼ ⩗ Acknowledgements

In writing a text of this nature, one inevitably draws on the wisdom of others and in my case the experience drawn from twenty years of HR practice and development.

I am therefore grateful to Board colleagues, the staff and senior managers of Broadmoor Hospital; Pricewaterhouse/Coopers, the RPS/Rainer Organisation, the many voluntary and charitable organisations I have worked with and for over the years, and all my old friends on the local government circuit. There are many excellent examples of good HR practice in these organisations from which one can draw material for *Mastering Human Resource Management*. Equally, bad experiences provide major learning opportunities and I have seen enough to fill another text book! Indeed I can honestly say that, as a "victim" on one major occasion, this kind of poor practice has driven me to write a book that I hope will in some small way help improve HR Management standards across the board.

My particular thanks to Richard Pettinger, Anne Spence, Gina Short, Lord Norman and Lady Suzanne Warner, Dr Julie Hollyman and John Cheatle.

With love and thanks also to, Sarah, Emily, Liz and the Moody Blues for their inspiration and support.

The authors and publishers wish to thank The Controller of Her Majesty's Stationery Office for permission to the Crown copyright material – Fig. 12.1 from the front cover of *Five Steps to Successful Health and Safety Management*, HSE, IND(G) 132 LC100 7/93. Every effort has been made to trace all the copyright-holders, but if any have been inadvertently overlooked the publishers will be pleased to make the necessary arrangement at the first opportunity.

KELVIN CHEATLE

▼ 1 Introduction to human resource management

1.1 Introduction

As we enter a new millennium, one could be forgiven for thinking that with all the attendant media hype and the huge growth in public interest, managing information technology resources was the biggest preoccupation of organisations and businesses, small or large, public or private. Yet, walk into any one of these concerns and ask the Managing Director or the Chief Executive where their biggest problems and their largest challenges lie, and they will invariably tell you that it rests with the management of their workforce – the Human Resources that are usually the most expensive and critical part of their activity. The purpose of this book is to provide the student of Human Resources, the manager who has to handle staffing problems regularly, or the practising personnel officer who needs to develop technical expertise to advise others, with a clear frame of reference. It seeks to summarise the key principles of UK and European Law; to place these in a clear business context so that the principles can be readily understood without drowning in a sea of employment law terminology; to discuss good practice that can be readily accessed and applied to most working situations; and to explore the day-to-day problem areas that will be experienced in managing people, for which some solutions are posed.

Above all else, of course, managing people is a dynamic, endlessly changing, complex, and sometimes a downright frustrating business. But as writers such as Handy, Peters, Maslow and others have ventured in their more philosophical works of the twentieth century, there is no substitute for adopting a rational and technically sound approach to managing people just as one would any other key organisational resource. That is not to say that people can be depersonalised; indeed the complexity of human behaviour and emotions is all the more compelling reason for a clear structure to surround the way we tackle the issue of harnessing this our most valuable, and yet most perplexing, resource. Each chapter of this book strives to provide clarity of reference for the reader by adopting the following basic structure:

An introduction to the legal framework

Although this is not an employment law manual, a clear understanding of the legal framework within which each aspect of Human Resource activity operates is essential to the development of good practice. Be it recruitment, selection,

redundancy or health and safety, a brief distillation of the key legislative requirements is the foundation upon which each chapter is built.

Good practice guidance

Whilst there are many types of HR practice to meet different organisational circumstances, there is a body of received wisdom about what constitutes good
practice which underpins the principle of being a good employer and acting
safely and reasonably towards employees in the organisation's interests. Examples of good practice are given under each chapter heading.

Problem areas

What are some of the typical problems a manager or personnel professional
might come across in handling, for example, a complaint about a lack of equal
opportunities in the recruitment and selection process? These questions are
asked, and model solutions posed, to provide a way through the employment law
and practice maze.

Activities and checklist

To aid the budding student or practitioner, or merely the interested line manager,
a checklist of the key points is provided at the end of each chapter with some
suggested activities to aid studying and learning.

1.2 Role of human resource management (HRM) in organisations

Increasingly, in both the UK and Europe at the beginning of the new millennium,
successful organisations are tying Human Resource Management (HRM) closely
to the fundamental business practices that manage the rest of their activities.
Thankfully, the days when Personnel Management was an administrative afterthought are largely gone, although the nature of the function will depend on the
type of business it sits in, the size and complexity of the business activity, and the
culture and traditions of the organisation.

The largest private and commercial organisation will usually have a Human
Resource Director on its main Board either as a stand alone role or as part of a
broader Resources directorate or function. The director will in turn manage a
large and often powerful function dealing with every aspect of people management from "hiring to firing". In this kind of organisation, HRM is at the centre of
business decision-making; the managing director or chief executive will work
closely with the HR director on key business decisions involving him or her at the
outset of policy-formulation, not as an afterthought, or only to be included when
things go wrong. This is the essence of *strategic human resource management*,
and it will be found in major UK and European companies from Ford to ICL, and

from Virgin to Marks and Spencer. To justify its existence this branch of management requires more than just effective management of a collection of HR-related functions. In business jargon, it needs to be seen to be "adding value" to the organisation's bottom line, its profitability or effectiveness. It is highly influential in affecting key business decisions and forming strategies about new products and markets. It helps secure Human Resources in the right quantity and of the right calibre to bring these strategies to fruition. It provides effective in-house management and regulation of the resources so that they are nurtured and developed and, most importantly, retained within the organisation. This, therefore, is very much the progressive arm of HR Management and it has been so influential in the late twentieth century, that it now is a regular feature of the most modern forward thinking public sector organisations including local government, health, government agencies and many other statutory functions. Indeed, such is the importance attached to people-management issues that HR directors are increasingly being seen as the natural material for future chief executives and often act as formal deputies. This would have been unheard of twenty years ago; the Director of Operations or a Finance Director would traditionally have been seen as the chief executive's right-hand person. But growth in stature of the function and its role has led to this important elevation.

Not every organisation, of course, has the resources, the culture or the type of business that allows HRM to have such an important strategic role. In many organisations a huge turnover in staff, the large numbers they employ, or the homogeneous nature of the business means that very often what is needed is a much more regulatory HR function. This is the essence of *operational human resource management.* In this kind of organisation HRM is not involved with strategy or the policy agenda, but is more concerned in making sure that the organisation's Human Resources are properly resourced and function correctly. It was typical of many large manufacturing industries in the last quarter of the twentieth century, and is now prevalent in many types of service sector particularly those where specialist skills are not in high demand. It also exists in some parts of the retail sector and the more traditional areas of public sector management and is still found in local government, health and central government organisations. At its heart is the need for organisational efficiency and good systems management be it in Recruitment, Health and Safety, or Training.

Although Personnel Management textbooks talk about the history and development of HRM during the twentieth century, few comment on the policing and welfare roles which were identifiable steps in the development of the function in the 1960s and 70s. These roles still exist and they perform a valuable function for small public and private concerns providing effective personnel administration but having little influence in the key strategic or operational decision-making of the organisation. The policing functions are important of course because they allow the organisation's management to exercise control normally maintained through very clear procedures for recruitment, discipline and training and they often are accompanied by a welfare role, especially in the smaller types of organisation where more sophisticated counselling and support services will not exist. Therefore the Personnel Officer or Manager will be seen as the natural port of call for staff to take their problems. The *Welfare and Control* brand of HRM is thus still alive and well early in the new century and well suits many types of private and public concern as it meets their essential modest needs.

It is important to understand these differing types of HRM function, because they say much about the essence of mastering Human Resources in an organisation. Above all else HRM needs to be fit for purpose and needs to work with the grain of the organisation not against it or in spite of it. Organisations as diverse as British Leyland (in the 1970s) and the Royal Opera House (in the 1990s) have tried using their Personnel or HR functions as a way of achieving major organisational change in often confrontational circumstances. The results have sometimes been disastrous both for the individuals concerned and the organisation as a whole because in these contexts HRM has been used "against the organisational grain". But at its best, tied closely to the core organisational values and working sympathetically with the majority of the workforce, HRM can be a very powerful tool for effecting change and achieving organisational success. From British Telecom to the Metropolitan Police, there are many examples of huge transformations in organisational practice being led and supported by an effective HR function and there is a large body of evidence in these of HRM adding huge organisational value to the benefit of all.

1.3 Understanding the role of HRM in your organisation

Trying to identify the role of HRM in your organisation, and recognising some or all of the above descriptions, is an essential precursor for developing sound HRM. Attempting to develop *strategic human resource management* in a voluntary organisation of less than 100 employees may be worthy but this is hardly likely to meet the organisation's core needs and is most unlikely to be affordable. The following is a list of questions to help ascertain the role of HR within the organisation and to think about its development as a tool for organisational success.

QUESTIONS

1 Is the business or organisation you work in largely people-centred?
   If most of the goods and services provided by your organisation are delivered through people rather than goods, products or technology then the answer is likely to be yes, although the organisation need not be a particularly large employer.
2 Have the skills required of the individuals working in the organisation changed significantly over the last ten years?
   If the answer is "yes", then there is likely to be a need for a proactive HR Management capability to influence recruitment and employee development.
3 Are the skills the organisation employs plentiful in supply or relatively scarce?
   This question is important because it will distinguish something about the nature of the workforce as opposed to its size. For example, an employer of a 1000

staff of a relatively low skill requirement and homogeneous in nature will require a very different kind of HR function to that of 250 staff in a scarce skill category.

4 Does your organisation operate from more than one location?
This again will say something about the nature of the HR role with single site operations tending to be less complex than multi-site operations.

5 Does your organisation employ more than one category of employee and with a range of terms and conditions of employment?
Generally speaking, the more categories of employee and the more types of contract they are employed on, the more complex and demanding the HRM will be.

6 To what degree is the workplace unionised and what is the history and tradition of industrial relations?
The Labour Government's employment rights legislation introduced in 1999 will offer the opportunity for much greater trade union representation to small and medium-sized companies in the new millennium (see Chapter 10). The handling of industrial relations is an important facet of HRM. Much will depend on the number, nature and power of trade unions and 'staff side' organisations and the tradition of their activity in the organisation.

7 Does the organisation train its own staff?
Most organisations engage in some kind of employee development or training but the degree to which the organisation invests in staff training will in turn say much about the HR role within it.

8 What is the public profile of the organisation you work in?
Some public and many large private concerns have the potential for a high profile and the need to regulate organisational behaviour and that of its employees will again say much about the kind of HR role that is required.

Answering positively to six or more of the above questions is likely to dictate that the organisation you work for has a *strategic HR management* need within it. Answer "yes" to between four and six of the above questions and the HR Management profile for your organisation is much more likely to be *operational*. Answer positively to three or less and you are likely to require no more than a *welfare and control* function. What your organisation has in place, of course, is a different matter altogether and one that will provide interesting material for discussion and debate.

1.4 Activity

Using the questions posed above in section 1.3, produce a profile for the role of HRM within your organisation. Compare and contrast it to the kind of function that exists. Is there a good match? If not, in what aspects do you believe it to be deficient?

1.5 Checklist

▶ Mastering Human Resource Management is often the key to business and organisational success as people are increasingly an organisation's most expensive, valuable and challenging asset.

▶ A good grasp of the essentials of employment law provides a clear framework for understanding the subject properly.

▶ There is a body of HR practice, which is largely regarded as good practice, which needs to be understood.

▶ Good HRM practice is often about solving different people-related problems and examples are given.

▶ Understanding the different types of HRM role in organisations is an essential platform for this work.

▶ A simple diagnosis of the nature of your organisation and its HRM needs, contrasted with what already exists is a helpful starting point.

☒ **2** The legislative and good practice framework

2.1 Introduction

The legislative and good practice requirements in HRM can be a mystifying and complex array of statutes, directives, codes of practice and case law that even the most experienced manager or personnel practitioner finds difficult to comprehend. The aim of this chapter is to simplify this labyrinth of regulations as far as possible and to provide a framework that enables the manager, personnel officer or lay person a window through which to clearly view good Human Resource practice. In most organisations, four elements will determine the rules under which the organisation's Human Resources will be engaged, deployed and terminated.

2.2 Employment law

This is the body of statute which lays down the main legal requirements for employment in the United Kingdom, now reinforced by European Union (EU) directives and legislation. The great bulk of the legislation dates from 1945 onwards, with a major explosion in the 1970s and again in the 1990s. EU directives, adopted by the UK government, either have themselves been enacted through primary legislation or are embodied by regulations into already existing laws. Most employment provisions are mandatory (that is they must be followed to ensure legal practice) but sometimes are discretionary or enabling (that is they do not prescribe but rather encourage certain actions). By and large the law does not distinguish between types of organisation, be they statutory, commercial or voluntary. Indeed exemptions from the law are usually given only by virtue of size and resources (organisations employing less than twenty people is a typical threshold) or by specific functions (for example the armed forces or security services) but even these exceptions are now being eroded by EU directives and key rulings from case law. The following are some key pieces of employment legislation from the last thirty years which can be regarded as fundamental to HRM at the beginning of the millennium.

KEY POINTS

▶ The *Data Protection Act 1984* – provided regulation for the first time to govern the keeping of computerised records, updated by the *Data*

Protection Act 1998 which covered computerised as well as manual record keeping.

▶ The *Disability Discrimination Act 1995* – replaced the *Disabled Persons Acts 1944 and 1958*, bringing disability on to the same discrimination footing as that provided by the *Sex and Race Discrimination Acts* (see Chapter 8).

▶ The *Employment Protection Act 1975* – introduced the first proper regulatory framework governing redundancy and employment protection rights updated by the *Employment Protection (Consolidation) Act 1978* which extended the concept of unfair and constructive dismissal and the use of industrial tribunals in dealing with such employment related litigation.

▶ The *Employment Rights Act 1996* (updated by the *Employment Relations Act 1999*) providing a clear strategy framework for trade union recognition and further rights at work for employees.

▶ The *Employment Tribunals Act 1996* – updated the rules governing the operation of industrial tribunals (with a consequent renaming) and their powers.

▶ The *Equal Pay Act 1970* – provided in law for the first time the concept of equal pay for work of equal value.

▶ The *Factories Act 1961* – together with *The Offices, Shops and Railways Premises Act 1963* – provided the regulatory framework for basic health and safety provisions in the workplace updated and underpinned by the *Health and Safety at Work Act 1974* which in turn has been updated by various EU regulations.

▶ The *National Minimum Wage Act 1998* – provided the first ever framework for a national minimum wage in the UK economy.

▶ The *Public Interest Disclosure Act 1998* – introduced in law for the first time the concept of whistleblowing in the workplace and legal protections for employees who do so.

▶ The *Race Relations Act 1976* – introduced the statutory framework as we know it today to outlaw direct and indirect discrimination in the workplace related to race, culture and ethnic origin.

▶ *Sex Discrimination Act 1975* – as with the *Race Relations Act* provides a statutory framework for outlawing direct or indirect discrimination on grounds of gender or marital status. Updated by the *Sex Discrimination Act 1986*.

▶ The *Trade Union and Labour Relations (Consolidation) Act 1992* – provided further controls and limits on the rights of trade unions.

▶ The *Trade Union Reform and Employment Rights Act 1993* – provided further trade union reforms and also consolidated how TUPE would operate in terms of employment rights in the workplace. TUPE relates to the transfer of undertakings regulations concerning business and organisational transfers.

This is by no means an exhaustive list but covers some of the important pieces of employment legislation that have a bearing on HRM at the beginning of this millennium.

2.3 Case law

Case law describes decisions made by courts and tribunals that affect the way legislation is implemented and interpreted and it creates precedents in UK common law and has been particularly important in employment law matters. Each decision of an employment tribunal sets a precedent for and is binding on each successive case heard at a tribunal and may be referred to by either party in this context. This is why employment tribunals have increasingly become a more formal or legal process for redress in employment matters over the years. Case law and employment law terms abound and some will be referred to throughout this book. Some keynote cases are worth mentioning in this introduction however.

- ▶ *Polkey v. Dayton Services Ltd* (1988)
  This case created a key precedent: in every case of dismissal, employers must strive to follow a fair procedure.
- ▶ *Holmes v. Home Office* (1984)
  Established that employers must not create indirect requirements for work which are discriminatory (in this case refusing a woman with children the right to work part time).
- ▶ *Walker v. Northumberland County Council* (1995)
  The outcome suggests that employers must take reasonable steps under health and safety legislation to protect employees from stress which has a detrimental effect on their health.

2.4 Codes of practice and regulations

The practical application of much of the employment law in the UK has been assisted by the creation of Codes of Practice and regulations which provide a framework for interpreting how employers are to meet the legal obligations set out by the statutory framework. Formally issued codes of practice will normally be taken into account by courts and tribunals in judging cases before them and examples include those issued by the Commission for Racial Equality (to support the *Race Relations Act 1976*), the code issued by the Equal Opportunities Commission (to support the introduction of the *Sex Discrimination Acts 1975*) and more recently regulations published by the Government to enact and enforce the EU *Working Time Directive 1998*. Statutory instruments, provisions or regulations are used by the government to update and enact changes in primary legislation and examples here often concern EU directives, with those relating to Health and Safety being a prime example where the primary legislation of the *Health and Safety at Work Act* remains intact, updated by new regulations.

2.5 Organisational employment rules

The final layer in this body of legislative and good practice framework concerns the rules that the organisation itself introduces to build on statutory provisions. The simple rule of thumb here is that individual employers and organisations can establish their own regulations provided they meet the minimum standards dictated by statute and so long as their own in-house rules do not break the law in any way. So, for example, most organisations have remuneration policies to reward their employees far in excess of those laid down by the national minimum wage and provide holiday entitlements in excess of those prescribed by the EU *Working Time Directive* (1998). Many organisations' provisions for parental leave will also go considerably beyond that required by the minimum statutory framework. Once this body of rules is developed and exists (usually as expressed terms in the Contract of Employment – see Chapter 3) they become legally enforceable and form another cornerstone of the legal and good practice framework. It is thus possible to track through the various stages of primary legislation, codes of practice, employment case law and employer's own terms and conditions of employment to see how provisions can be enhanced and developed on any individual aspect of Human Resource Management. Figure 2.1 provides an example of how this framework operates in practice.

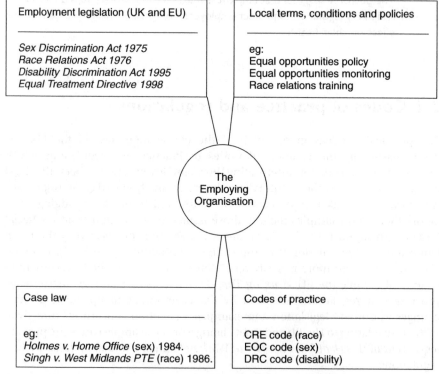

Figure 2.1   The legislative and good practice framework example: equal opportunities

2.6 Checklist

▶ The legislative and good practice framework consists of employment law, EU directives, codes of practice, regulations and case law.

▶ Some of the benchmark laws of the last thirty years are highlighted.

▶ Case law created by courts and tribunals makes precedents which may be referred to in legal proceedings.

▶ Some of the major codes of practice include those issued by the Equal Opportunities Commission and the Commission for Racial Equality.

◼ ◿ **3** Contract of employment (1)

3.1 Introduction

The Contract of Employment is arguably the most important document in the whole sphere of HRM as it underpins the legal relationship between the employer and employee. The contract is a promise, or a set of promises, that the law will enforce. Superimposed on the contractual terms and conditions between the employer and employee are a large number of statutory rights and restrictions, and, in most workplaces, a number of terms and conditions reached through collective agreement in the workplace normally with staff or trade union representatives. However, the essential contractual nature remains and it is to the common law rules governing the formation of contracts that one must first turn to determine whether a valid employment contract has indeed been made and properly exists.

In the next two chapters we shall examine all aspects of the contract of employment: how a contract may be created; the legal terms within it including common law duties; the legal framework that underpins the creation of the contract of employment; the different types of contract of employment that exist; patterns of work that can be reflected within the contract of employment; and how a contract may be legally varied. Issues relating to the termination of the contractual relationship and associated legal processes are examined in Chapter 4.

3.2 Legal framework

A contract of employment may be either written or oral or a mixture of the two. This means that its form may range from a document drawn up by solicitors and signed by both parties to an informal discussion between employer and employee. However, the complexity of the modern employment relationship means that the written form is much more common today and will have to rely on various legal requirements, even though the law itself does not require a written version to exist.

Employment Rights Act 1996

Under this piece of legislation provisions previously included in *the Contracts of Employment Act 1975,* and the *Trade Union Reform and Employment Rights Act*

1993, have been updated and consolidated. The legislation says that a *written statement* of particulars must be given to an employee not later than two months after the beginning of their employment. Certain of the particulars must be included in the single document. These are:

- the names of the parties;
- date when employment and continuous employment began;
- particulars of remuneration;
- particulars of hours and holidays;
- job title and description;
- place of work.

If employment ends within the two month period, a statement must still be given unless the employment lasted for less than one month in total. The Act goes on to detail the particulars which the written statement must include and these are referred to in section 3.4 and summarised in Figure 3.1.

Common law duties

There is a body of statute drawn from English common law which imposes various duties on both the employee and the employer within the employment contract.

Standard contract clauses

The law requires every contract statement to:

Identify the parties involved
Specify the date when employment began
Specify the date when continuous employment began, taking into account any employment with a previous employer that is relevant
State the rate of pay and pay intervals
State entitlement to holiday, bank holidays and holiday pay
State hours of work including any contractual overtime commitment
Contain the job title or brief description of the job
Specify the place or places of work

Written statement clauses

In a separate document from the main contract, known as the written statement (or staff handbook) the following must be stated:

Rules on sickness and sick pay
Details of pension or pension schemes
The length of notice the employee is entitled to receive and to give
Any collective agreements relating to terms and conditions of employment
For temporary contracts, when the contract will expire
A note on grievance and disciplinary policies (procedures should not be included)
The organisation's health and safety policy
Any other provisions the employer wishes to state (e.g. code of conduct, ancillary benefits, etc.)

Figure 3.1 Contract and written statement clauses

These other common law duties can be summarised under two headings.

For the employer

▶ Pay: the employer will provide for work done under the terms of the contract.
▶ Health and safety: before the *Health and Safety at Work Act 1974* there already existed a common law duty on employers to provide a healthy and safer environment for employees.
▶ Mutual trust and confidence: the employer must do nothing to undermine the mutual trust and confidence of the employment relationship.
▶ Indemnifying: the employer must indemnify the employee against any cost or expenses involved in him/her performing his/her job of work.

For the employee

▶ Service: the employee is personally contracted to provide work (as opposed to a company with a contract for service).
▶ Competence: it is implied in the contract that the employee is competent to do the job.
▶ Care: the employee must exercise as much care as possible in undertaking their duties.
▶ Fidelity: employees must act in good faith, show honesty and not work against the employer's interests.
▶ Loyalty: employees must not divulge confidential information learned through their employment.
▶ Obedience: employees have a commonlaw duty to obey lawful and reasonable instructions from their employer.
▶ Mutual trust and confidence: the employee must also maintain the relationship by acting reasonably and cooperatively.

Statutory provisions which may not be excluded from the contract of employment

As well as common law duties which are binding on all contracts of employment, there are a number of pieces of primary legislation from which both employee and employer *may not contract out* of no matter what the nature of the agreement between them. These are largely the discrimination acts: *Sex Discrimination Act 1975*, the *Equal Pay Act 1970*, the *Race Relations Act 1976*, and the *Disability Discrimination Act 1995*, which are binding on both parties no matter what the nature of the employment relationship (see Chapter 8 for more details). However, there are also provisions within other pieces of legislation that must be enforceable in the contract of employment, and these include the *Trade Union and Labour Relations (Consolidation) Act 1992*, relating to trade union membership and rights; and the *Health and Safety at Work Act 1974* relating to the duties of both employees and employers (see Chapter 12 for more detail).

Unfair Contract Terms Act 1977

The effect of this Act is to render certain types of contractual term *unenforceable* in law and makes others unenforceable unless they satisfy a test of reasonableness laid down in the Act. In essence this technical piece of legislation states that neither a contract term nor a notice within it may validly exclude or restrict liability for death or personal injury resulting from negligence; the formation of a secondary contract between employer and employee (perhaps in the form of a second employment for the individual concerned) may not take away rights or exclude provisions contained in a primary contract of employment; and other provisions relating to employers' overall responsibility for the safety and protection of employees within their employment.

The Employment Protection (Consolidation) Act 1978

The *Employment Protection (Consolidation) Act 1978* is updated by the *Trade Union Reform and Employment Rights Act 1993* and the *Employment Rights Act 1996.* The *Employment Protection (Consolidation) Act* is a benchmark piece of legislation which re-enacted a fundamental right originally created by the *Industrial Relations Act 1971* concerning the right of employees not to be unfairly dismissed. Since this came into force an employer who dismisses an employee without good reason or without following a fair procedure lays themselves open to a claim for *unfair dismissal.* When such a claim is brought, the employer has to establish the reason for the dismissal. An employment tribunal will then consider whether the dismissal was fair in all the circumstances, neither party having the evidential burden in this inquiry. If the dismissal is held to be unfair, the employer can be ordered to re-engage, reinstate or pay compensation to the employee. The parties to a claim of unfair dismissal are known as the applicant (usually the employee) and the respondent (usually the employer).

The legislation also introduced the concept of *constructive dismissal*, where an employee resigns their employment but claims they were effectively forced to resign because their employer fundamentally breached their contract of employment and made their ongoing employment untenable. The concept of *wrongful dismissal* provides another slant on the unlawful termination of the contract, on this occasion where the employer has breached the terms of the contract usually by failing to follow procedures or by failing to give proper notice required to terminate the contract of employment. These termination provisions are dealt with in Chapter 4 in more detail as this is one of the most difficult aspects of managing the contract of employment.

The *Employment Protection (Consolidation) Act,* and the updating pieces of legislation that followed it, also contain important provisions relating to the employer's right to *vary* the contract of employment. The legislation states that the employer needs to demonstrate that either they have a condition within the contract of employment that allows them to vary it (so-called flexibility clauses); or can demonstrate that they have gained the employee's or representative's agreement to vary the contract (so-called consensual variation); or, if they have to impose a variation of contract, have a sound, economic, technical or organisational reason for doing so. It should be noted that where a variation in the contract of employment is imposed (a so-called unilateral variation) or where the original contract is ended and a new one enforced, the employee may have the right to submit a claim for breach of contract, unfair dismissal, or even constructive dismissal. These issues are dealt with in more detail in section 3.5 below.

The Redundancy Payments Act 1965

The *Redundancy Payments Act 1965*, is updated by the *Employment Protection Act 1975*, the *Employment Protection (Consolidation) Act 1978*, and the *Employment Rights Act 1996*.

This legislation has a bearing on the contract of employment in that *redundancy*, is one of the legal grounds on which a contract of employment may be ended. Provisions are referred to in Chapter 4, but are covered more extensively in Chapter 11 of this book. This later chapter on Managing Redundancy, Reorganisations and Transfers, also contains detailed reference to the provisions of the *transfer of undertakings* regulations, which govern the transfer of the contract of employment from one employer to another.

Custom and practice

All of the above legal provisions can be found in various pieces of legislation on the statute book and will feature in the contract of employment either as expressed, incorporated or implied terms or as a common law duty. But the last aspect of the legal framework we need to consider are those practices which are common and clearly embedded in the working relationship between the employer and the employee: these are often referred to as *custom and practice*. What this term really means is that although there is no statutory provision for its existence, the contract of employment can include custom and practice in its implied terms as long as it is *certain, reasonable and notorious*. A typical example of this concerns working patterns. Although the contract and the written particulars may be silent on the patterns of work in operation in the workplace, custom and practice may dictate a certain pattern of working that applies within an organisation.

So if, for example, we take the practice of a small engineering firm working a 39-hour week where there is customarily a 4.30 pm finish on Fridays, this would constitute custom and practice because it is certain (because it always happens then); reasonable (because both employee and employer adhere to and follow the practice); and notorious (it is well known by all parties that it happens). One of the difficulties in ascertaining custom and practice is that by definition they relate to a set of unwritten rules that operate. So the key is do they pass the above test? If they do, then they are likely to constitute reasonable custom and practice and are an implied term of the contract of employment.

3.3 Types of contract

Employment patterns in the world of work have changed beyond recognition over the last twenty-five years and the types of contract of employment that exist to reflect these different types of employment are many and varied. There are a number of considerations to be made in determining the type of contract that may be used to describe an employment relationship:

Contract of employment or for service?

Given the huge growth in self-employment in the 1980s and 1990s, a number of tests have been used by Tribunals and the Inland Revenue to try and determine whether or not a contract of employment or a contract for service exists. Some of the factors which will help determine this are illustrated in the following questions:

1　Does a master servant relationship exist? (that is does the employer dictate when and how the employee will do their work?) If the answer is yes there is likely to be a contract of employment in existence.
2　Does the employee work a regular pattern at the employer's request? Again, an affirmative answer will usually dictate that a contract of employment exists.
3　Does the support for the employee's work derive from the employer's resources? If the employer provides an office space, secretarial support, information technology and other equipment and aids, then it is most likely that a contract of employment exists.
4　Does the employee work for a variety of employers and can the employee operate flexibly between them? Whilst contracts of employment may be obtained with a multiplicity of employers, the ability to flexibly juggle work and manage one's own time usually dictates a contract for service exists as opposed to a contract of employment.

Tenure

The concept of a job for life, where an employee worked for one employer from school or university leaving age through to retirement is now very much a rarity and contracts of employment have changed to reflect this. Whilst permanent contracts of employment still exist, they do not imply that employment will be for working life. The following categories of employment tenure need to be considered in determining the duration of the employment contract.

Permanent

A permanent employee is one who is wholly engaged to work for an employer and is part of their permanent establishment or payroll. It means there is an intention to employ them for the foreseeable future in continuous work and accrues various employment rights and costs. A permanent employee may work varying numbers of hours (see below).

Temporary

As the name implies, a temporary employee is engaged for a specific period of time or to undertake specific work. A tenure will normally have a prescribed end date or duration. Whereas temporary employees are usually engaged to cover absences or to do specific pieces of work, a fixed term employee will be engaged for a specified period to undertake specified pieces of work with a given end date. Traditionally, temporary employees are used to cover seasonal and lower graded forms of work. Fixed term contracts are usually issued to senior professionals and managers on a time limited basis.

Casual

Often used as an interchangeable term with temporary, casual employees do not form part of the establishment of the workforce and are engaged as and when to assist an organisation with peaks of work or to cover absences. These typically will be students working for summer vacations or to assist organisations with seasonal peaks and troughs of work.

Hours of work

The hours of work to be performed by an employee also go some way to dictating the type of contract of employment.

Full-time

Full-time means an employee is contracted for full-time hours of work that apply within that organisation. Typical full-time working hours in the UK range between 35 and 40 per week and are now limited for most categories of employees by the working time directive which came on to the statute book in 1998 and prescribes a maximum 48 hour week. (See Chapter 6).

Part-time

The definition of a part-time contract used to be someone working less than a specified number of hours in a working week. But the term now specifies an individual who works anything less than the full-time contracted hours for the organisation. The use of part-time working has increased particularly as employment rights for this category of employee have grown (see below).

Term time

This was a category that used to apply to those who used to work in the Education Service, particularly school meals workers, but now is a term used much more broadly to describe those employees who work only when their children are not on holiday and it now covers many types of industry and organisation. Whilst some paid holiday is usually a feature, pay for the whole of school children's holiday periods does not usually apply.

Zero hours

Much derided in the 1990s for encouraging poor employment practices, zero hours contracts were introduced by fast food and retail outlets which basically gave them the flexibility to use employees as and when they wished with no minimum working hours requirement in the contract of employment.

Total or flexible hours contracts

The reverse of zero hours, the total or flexible hours contract will simply specify the total number of hours of work required by an employee in a given period (normally a year) which can then be worked flexibly by arrangement rather than being prescribed in daily or weekly patterns. It has become a particular feature of working in the information technology industries.

Patterns of work

Patterns of work also go towards determining the type of contract offered. They can be summarised as follows:

Shift work

Many service, production and manufacturing industries still operate on shift patterns and cover everything from retail to the health service. Shift patterns can cover hours of work from a long day (normally 12 or more) or the full 24-hour period and will normally rotate over a prescribed pattern (days, evenings and nights for example on a 3-week rotating cycle).

Fixed patterns

Fixed patterns still apply in many industries and jobs because they require individuals to be at a place of work for prescribed periods of time. They typically apply in parts of retail and many office regimes where a traditional 9 am – 5 pm Monday to Friday culture still applies.

Flexible patterns

Very much a feature of the 1990s consultancy style of operation, flexible patterns allow individuals to work largely when they choose providing they complete the jobs or tasks required of them and are often associated with total hours contracts. They are particularly a feature of work, given the growth of tele- and home-working and the use of information technology to support this, which does not require an individual to be at a desk for a particular given period during a day.

Employment rights

One of the most welcome trends of employment legislation in the 1990s was to erode the differences between employment rights for *part-time* and *full-time* workers and to accord much greater status to *temporary, fixed term* and *casual* employees. This section deals with some of the differences in the employment rights within these categories of employee which will dictate the type and nature of the contract offered.

Previously, under the provisions of the *Employment Protection (Consolidation) Act 1978*, those employed under a contract which normally involved less than 16 hours work a week, were excluded from the right to having a written statement. Only if an employee had been continuously employed for at least eight but not less than 16 hours a week for more than 5 years would they become entitled to a written statement not later than 13 weeks after the end of the 5-year period of employment. The provisions of the *Employment Rights Act 1996*, removed these barriers and draws no distinction between part-time and full-time working in terms of entitlement to a written statement other than the provisions about a period of continuous employment (8 weeks) as the threshold for issuing a written statement.

This welcome change has also triggered the creation of other facilities that favour the part-timer and gives them equal rights on the same footing as the full-time employee. Pension rights, previously the domain only of the full-time permanent employee, have now also become available to part-timers, the rationale being that it should make no difference about the length of work in which the employee is engaged, rather that the responsible employer will allow them to make provision for their retirement at some stage in the future. It is particularly significant to note that part-time exclusion provisions are likely to be discriminatory given the proportion of women who work part-time hours in the UK economy.

EXAMPLE

> Indeed the change in the law was precipitated by a legal case, *R v. Secretary of State for Employment, Ex Parte Equal Opportunities Commission*, which meant the government had to introduce the Employment Protection (Part-time Employees) Regulations 1995 as a precursor to their incorporation into the Employment Rights Act. The effect therefore is that periods of part-time employment, irrespective of the number of hours worked, will count in the computation of continuous employment.

Figure 3.2 shows a table of qualifying periods for entitlements to statutory employment protection rights that are built into the law, and as will be seen, no distinction is made between part-time and permanent employees. As this shows, one of the biggest changes in recent years has been the reduction in the qualifying period for continuous service which an employee needs to bring a claim of unfair dismissal against their employer. The previous provisions of the *Employment Protection (Consolidation) Act* stated that this had to be a minimum of two years.

Employment rights	Qualifying period
Maternity rights	None
Minimum statutory notice	1 month
Unfair dismissal	1 year
Redundancy payment	None
Redundancy consultation rights	3 months (if a fixed term contact)
Statement of particulars	2 months

Figure 3.2 Qualifying periods for employment rights

EXAMPLE

In a landmark test case, *The Secretary of State for Employment Ex Parte Seymour Smith and Another,* the Court of Appeal held that the qualifying condition for unfair dismissal claims of 2 years' continuous employment indirectly discriminated against female applicants, so that this qualifying condition was declared to be incompatible with the EU's equal treatment directive.

Despite the Court of Appeal's finding, the case rumbled on through the House of Lords and the European courts for a further four years and the confusion created was only finally resolved when the government reduced the qualifying period to bring such a claim to one year as part of the provisions of the *Employment Relations Act 1999.*

As is dealt with later in this chapter, this reduction in qualifying period and the increase in the compensation limits available to applicants is likely to greatly increase the amount of business being heard by employment tribunals in the future. Further information relating to the rights of part-timers is included in Chapter 14, New Developments, with information on the EU *Part-Timer Workers' Directive 2000.*

For *temporary* and *seasonal* workers, the rights accorded to part-time workers through recent changes in UK and European Law have generally been beneficial to them as they accrue the same rights as other employees, provided they meet the minimum service entitlements outlined above. It is therefore possible that a temporary employee may accrue sufficient qualifying employment to present a complaint of unfair dismissal now that the qualification period is reduced to one year, and provided they can show continuous employment for that duration. It will, therefore, no longer be sufficient for employers to offer a number of temporary rolling contracts that accrue to more than one year's continuous service, as the individual will be able to claim continuous employment rights.

Indeed, the practice used by some less reputable employers to employ temporary workers for short periods of time, then to insist on a break in employment and re-engage them may also fall foul of the law as tribunals will look at the total employment package and will be suspicious of such dubious practices. This does not mean that temporary replacement employees cannot be fairly terminated at the end of their employment. Provided that their contract of employment makes it clear that they have been taken on in place of a permanent employee (either on grounds of sickness absence, pregnancy or for some other purpose) and provided that the dismissal is effected to allow the permanent employee to resume their work and that the dismissed employee is treated fairly and reasonably in terms of the contractual arrangements, then such replacements can be sought legally.

Many temporary workers are engaged via *Employment Agencies* and concerns over some of the employment practices used by such agencies have led to more statutory control in recent years. Persons who carry out employment or employment businesses are regulated by the Secretary of State for Employment, who can prohibit individuals from carrying out such businesses where there is concern about the practices contained therein. Such prohibition may stop an agency from practising for up to a period of 10 years. These regulations provide for written statements of terms and conditions about the business to be given to workers, protect the workers' right to take direct employment with the hiring employer, and restrict the use of agency labour for strike breaking. Since 1998, such agency workers are of course also protected by the provisions of the *National Minimum Wage Act* and are afforded all the other statutory rights that fall to permanent employees, including protection against discrimination. It is important to note here that the hiring employer has a vicarious responsibility and liability for the actions of agency staff whom they engage.

EXAMPLE

> So, for example, in the case of *Denham v. Midland Employers Mutual Assurance 1955*, the main employer, not the agency, were held liable for personal injuries sustained by the applicant during the course of their employment. This clearly shows, therefore, that protection both from discrimination and under the Health and Safety legislation will fall to the primary employer, although the direct agency employer will also have similar responsibilities as well as complying with the controls on agency employment.

Seasonal and *casual* workers too can enjoy all the normal employment protection rights outlined above, provided they have the necessary qualifying periods of employment. Where such an employee is dismissed when the seasonal demand has ended, the fact that they were only taken on as a seasonal worker does not automatically make the dismissal fair. As with temporary employees, much will depend on the contract they are issued with and the reasonable actions of their employer in terminating their employment. It therefore follows that a seasonal worker must be given at least the statutory minimum period of notice required to terminate their contract of employment. If the period of unemployment between seasons is short and the employee is habitually re-engaged, their continuity of employment may be preserved and continuous employment shown as required by the law. Employers should therefore take as much care to comply with all the applicable employment rules regarding seasonal staff and casual employees as they do with their permanent workforce.

3.4 Forming the contract of employment

So now that we have a grasp of the legal framework that governs contracts of employment and have examined in detail some of the characteristics of employment that will dictate the kind of contract to be offered, how do we go about creating a model contract of employment? An important consideration here is at what point the contract of employment is created as mention has been made of the existence of verbal contracts before they are confirmed in writing. In essence, a *verbal contract* is created at a point where an offer is made and acceptance is given. This will usually happen immediately after a job interview when a candidate will be told that they are offered the job, subject to various references and checks, and at which point they usually tender their verbal acceptance of it. At this point the contract is created, albeit in an embryonic form, and legal redress is available to challenge and support it, although the offer can be withdrawn by the employer and the acceptance by the employee. The point at which some written confirmation of the contractual offer comes into being is usually at the point of an offer of employment which is usually a precursor to the creation of the formal contract of employment and the written terms and particulars. The formal offer will usually include the job title, the name of the employer and employee, some details of the remuneration and a commencement date for continuous employment. It will usually refer to a full written contract being in preparation or to follow within a prescribed date (and this must be within 2 months of commencement of employment as outlined above). A model outline contract of employment is included in Figure 3.3.

As contracts of employment are made up of a variety of terms and conditions which set out the respective obligations of the parties, it is important at this point to examine some of the component parts that will be used in forming the contract of employment. The main components are *expressed terms; implied terms; incorporated terms;* and *statutory terms.*

Expressed terms

Expressed terms may be oral or written. However, whatever form they take they are terms which have to be spelled out in detail and there is a statutory requirement under the *Employment Rights Act* as referred to above to provide written statements to employees who have been engaged for more than 8 weeks.

Implied terms

As the name suggests these are terms which are not spelt out in so many words but are implied in the contract of employment. This may be because they are too obvious to need recording or because they are necessary to give business efficacy to the other terms of the contract or because they form part of the custom and practice arrangements referred to above. The common law duties referred to in section 3.3 form part of the implied terms and conditions of employment in a normal business contract as do custom and practice requirements.

```
                                                    The Zanco Company Ltd
                                                         24 High Street
                                                            Anytown
                                                              UK
Mrs J Snowdon
"Driftwood"
Hodge Avenue
Anytown
UK                                                        3 May 2001

Dear Mrs Snowdon

                    Appointment of Part-Time Receptionist

Following your recent interview I am writing to offer you an appointment as a part-time recep-
tionist with this company.

Subject to completion of references and health checks, the appointment will start on 27 May
2001. This is a permanent post for 25 hours per week, Monday-Friday 9 am–2.30 pm, with
a 30-minute lunch break. Continuous employment will commence on 27 May 2001.

The total pay for the post is £20,000 per annum, pro rata 25 hours per week, paid monthly
in arrears. You will receive 20 days paid holiday a year, rising to 25 after 5 years' service,
plus 8 paid bank holidays, which will be determined by the company from time to time.

You will be based at our Headquarters at 24 High Street, but may be asked to travel to our
other site for which travel expenses will be paid.

Some other terms and conditions of employment including a note of overtime, disciplinary
and grievance arrangements are included in the attached written statement of particulars.

We look forward to working with you; please sign and return the attached copy of this letter
if you wish to accept the appointment on the terms stated.

Yours sincerely


John Hayward
Personnel Manager
```

Figure 3.3   Model outline contract of employment

Incorporated terms

The parties may also agree to incorporate other terms into employment contracts from other sources. These will include collective agreements with trade
unions, work rules and disciplinary procedures and codes. The incorporation
of these terms may be either expressed or implied. It is clearly better employment practice to express incorporation into written terms and conditions of
employment rather than relying on implied terms as this can create grounds for
dispute.

Statutory terms

Finally, a number of terms are either imposed or implied by statute into employment contracts as they exist under primary legislation. This includes, for example, the discrimination body of legislation, including *Sex and Race Discrimination*, *Disability Discrimination*, and the *Equal Pay Acts*; it includes the *National Minimum Wage Act*; and the key provisions relating to contracts enshrined in the *Employment Rights Act.*

Thus, having mapped out the territory for the contractual provisions, the employer can now go about preparing a contract of employment that reflects these terms, and identify those elements that suit their particular circumstances.

Once the contract has been created and exists in written form there is usually a requirement for a written acceptance of it and a copy placed on the employee's personnel file for future reference. Everything in the employment relationship will then flow and connect back to this important piece of documentation. It will be the reference point for pay, hours of work, holiday, sickness, pension, disciplinary and grievance matters and is a key reference document.

3.5 Varying the contract

Given that employment is a dynamic relationship with changing employment circumstances, contracts will rarely stay the same for the duration of their existence. There will be times when usually the employer, but sometimes the employee, will seek to vary the contract of employment for good reasons. Again, statutory provisions provide protection for employees, in ensuring that employers follow proper procedures when seeking to vary a contract of employment, and provide clear remedies when they do not. This is a critical area of good HRM practice. So many of the cases that come before courts and employment tribunals are to do with the attempts by employers to change the contract of employment without following such guidance. This will often result in a claim by an employee for breach of contract, unfair or constructive dismissal or even wrongful dismissal. Some key principles apply.

The employer must have good reason to change or vary the contract

Employers cannot act on a whim in seeking to vary the contract of employment. The *Employment Protection (Consolidation) Act* originally specified that employers needed to demonstrate sound *economic, technical or organisational reasons*, for wanting to change a contract of employment. An *economic* reason might be that a downturn in their business means they can no longer afford the rates of pay they were previously providing and they are seeking to reduce rates of pay so as to stay in business and sustain employment. It does not mean that in wishing to increase profit margins as a benefit to shareholders they can unilaterally cut rates of pay. A *technical* reason will usually be to do with circumstances beyond the organisation's control, created by a change in markets or the law, which affect the business. So, for example, the introduction of the minimum wage legislation in 1999 would have meant the rates of pay for some low-paid employees were automatically changed and their contracts varied to their benefit, as a result. An *organisational* reason is usually to do with the way the business or organisation configures its work and may affect locations and terms of conditions that are embodied in the contract of employment. They can often be linked to an economic reason, so, for example, a company with many retail outlets may rationalise its business for economic reasons and change its organisation accordingly, requiring the relocation of employees if they are going to remain in employment.

The *employer* must act reasonably, following reasonable procedures, in seeking to vary the contract

This means that having established that there are proper *economic, technical* or *organisational* (ETO) *reasons* for changing a contract of employment, the employer needs to consult with the employee or their representatives on the reason for the change and the impact it will have on them. This will often result in the original employer proposal being modified or renegotiated to the employees' benefit, or the timescale for change being modified. Many productivity deals in manufacturing industry in the late 1990s resulted in major changes in contracts of employment but were negotiated with trade unions and staff associations on behalf of employees to ensure that businesses survived and jobs were retained.

There are no prescribed procedures or timescales for undertaking this consultation process. But courts and tribunals in judging claims brought by employees, concerning breaches and variations to their contracts of employment, will look at each case on its merit based on the resources of the organisation, the changes involved and the imperatives for them. Only the most dire and exceptional circumstances would justify an imposed variation of contract without consultation and would only usually be as a result of economic necessity or as a result of an urgent change in legislation. So the key message to employers here is consult and consult early both on the reasons for change and how you want to achieve it.

Unilateral variation

Where employee and employer fail to reach an agreement about a change to a contract of employment, the employer is faced with two choices: they can either *impose* the contract as it is, giving notice to terminate the old contract and suffer the legal implications of effecting the change; or, more likely, they can *unilaterally* impose the new term as a fait accompli. Employers beware: the introduction of new contracts or indeed variations must be undertaken by providing due notice (usually the notice period described in the original contract or 90 days) and leaves the employer open to a claim of unfair dismissal, constructive dismissal or breach of contract on behalf of the employee as the original contract has effectively been ended or unilaterally varied. So although attempts at negotiating revised contracts may fail for a variety of reasons, good practice will require the employer to show that they have sound reasons for needing to change the contract and have made every effort to act reasonably in trying to reach agreement on the revised terms.

To add to the employer's burdens, they must also make sure they continue to comply with the implied common law requirements in the contract of employment and, for example, do not discriminate against one group of employees in favour of another and fall foul of the discrimination legislation; do not in changing the contract of employment endanger the employee's health and safety at work; and do not fundamentally undermine good faith, fidelity and trust in the employment relationship. So even though an employer may have a sound reason for needing to change a contract, and even though they may have sought to gain agreement to this change by reasonable measures, a claim for unfair or constructive dismissal brought by an employee in these circumstances may still succeed if the court or tribunal believes the change is so fundamental as to make the original contract untenable.

However, a well-organised case for an ETO reason may well succeed.

EXAMPLE

> In *Tiochta & Scott v. Courtaulds Clothing 1984* a dye works employing 90 employees was faced with closure because of heavy losses. Following negotiations with the union over a lengthy period of time the company imposed new wage rates by terminating all contracts of employment with proper notice and offering new ones. Two of the workforce claimed unfair dismissal, but even though their wages were cut by £69 and £30 per week respectively the tribunal found the dismissals were not unfair as the company had no real choice.

3.6 Problem areas

QUESTION:
I have just started doing some work for a medium-sized company on legal matters and they have asked me to take a contract for service on a self-employed basis. I am a little concerned as a friend was recently challenged by the Inland Revenue who said the service he was providing of a similar nature was in fact as an employee. What should I say to the company concerned?

ANSWER:
The test of whether or not a contract of employment or contract of service exists and your status as a contractor who is legitimately self-employed or otherwise would depend on a variety of tests that have been developed by courts over the years and referred to earlier in this chapter. Put simply, if you run your own business and can pick and choose when you do your work and how you do it, and have your service bought in by the company for a specific purpose, whilst you work for a range of other people, then you are more likely to be self-employed than not. However, if you are performing work that

would normally be carried out by an employee, working in a way and a pattern dictated by the employer, on their premises using their equipment, and you do not work for other people normally, then you are almost certainly going to be classified as an employee.

The opportunity you have described sounds more like a contract of employment than a contract for service and there are risks to both yourself and the company in accepting such an offer. First, for yourself the risk comes largely from the Inland Revenue who if they catch up with you and determine you are an employee, can ask you to pay back Tax and National Insurance on that basis. Similarly, the employer may be liable to such an Inland Revenue judgment and may be subject to a fine or even prosecution for engaging your services on an illegal basis. So, the advice is that you have a discussion with the organisation and try to get them to clarify their offer either by confirming you as an employee through the offer of a proper contract of employment, or properly describing your services in the contract for service provided you can satisfy the other conditions referred to above.

QUESTION:

We are undergoing a major reorganisation at work, and as a result my job title, the department I work in and whom I report to, and my terms and conditions of employment are proposed to be changed by my employer. We currently do not have trade unions in the workplace but I am very unhappy about the proposed changes and the lack of consultation accompanying them. The company's position appears to be very much take it or leave it; what can I do if I am unhappy with the position they are planning to impose?

ANSWER:

Essentially, the company must first have good grounds on which to seek to vary your contract of employment (so-called economical, technical or organisational reasons) and assuming they do so must then act reasonably in trying to effect these in their change of contract of employment for you. This requires consultation with you in trying to gain your agreement before they get to the position of imposing either a varied contract or cancelling your old one and offering you a new one. There are a number of things you can do if you are very dissatisfied with the position. First, you can go to the company and complain about the lack of consultation and attempts to agree the changes with you or your workplace representatives. You can point out the legal requirements placed on them (described earlier in this chapter) and, even if they do have sound reasons for effecting the change, the need for them to try and gain your agreement to do so. After all the original contract of employment is based on a consideration by both parties; it therefore follows that any changed or renewed contract should be on a similar basis.

Assuming your complaints fall on deaf ears, there are a number of forms of legal redress ultimately open to you. If the company seek to impose a varied contract, it would be open to you to resign immediately and claim constructive dismissal quoting the adoption of an unfair procedure by the employer as a fundamental breach of your contract of employment or the fact that the terms and conditions of that employment have been fundamentally altered by the employer through imposition. You could also consider taking a claim for a breach of contract whilst you remain in employment, on which you would need to take appropriate legal advice. Alternatively, if the employer cancels your old contract and offers you a new one, you can simply refuse to accept it and upon the termi-

nation of your old contract claim unfair dismissal. From the employee's point of view, cases of unfair dismissal are often easier to prove than constructive dismissal, because the act of dismissal clearly is on the part of the employer and all the employee is required to show is that this has happened and the grounds for it were unfair or a reasonable procedure was not followed. From your description of your case, it sounds as though the employer has not followed a reasonable procedure, even though they may have reasonable grounds for seeking to change your contract. Of course, you, your colleagues or even your workplace representatives in the absence of a trade union may jointly approach the employer and tell them that if they continue to pursue this course of action they are at risk of such a legal challenge, and this of itself may be enough to force them to change their ways.

3.7 Activity

Your company is undergoing a major reorganisation, and as a result you need to relocate a group of sales staff to a new base twenty miles away and alter their working hours to match those of colleagues at the new site. Assuming there is no flexibility clause in their existing contracts of employment how would you go about introducing this change without causing major difficulty?

Outline the steps you would take and the legal grounds you would rely on. If at the end of the process the staff refused to transfer, what would you do?

3.8 Checklist

▶ The contract of employment is the document that underpins the fundamental employment relationship between employee and employer and it is the most single important piece of documentation in Human Resource Management.

▶ The law relating to what constitutes a contract of employment and the provisions that must be included in written particulars has gradually been evolving and has become more onerous for employers in recent years.

▶ The law distinguishes between the employed and the self-employed and a contract of employment and a contract for service.

▶ A contract is made up of expressed, implied, incorporated and statutory terms which include common law duties placed on both employee and employer.

▶ Contracts can be verbal, in writing or both, but written particulars must be provided in all cases of employment in excess of 8 weeks.

▶ Contracts can be constructed dependent upon different patterns of work (shift, flexible or fixed), the hours the employee works (full-time, part-time or term-time) or their tenure (permanent, casual/temporary or fixed term).

▶ The law now does not distinguish between full-, part-time, permanent or sessional employees in terms of employment rights. All that matters for the purposes of accruing employment rights is the period of continuous employment.

- ▶ Once created, the contract of employment can only be varied by agreement, or if there are sound economical, technical or organisational reasons for the employer seeking to change it without the employee's agreement.
- ▶ An imposed variation, either by cancelling the old contract and creating a new one, or imposing a varied contract, leaves the employer open to a claim of unfair or constructive dismissal, or even breach of contract. There must be proper grounds for varying the contract and a reasonable procedure must be followed.

▼ 4 Contract of employment (2)

4.1 Introduction

The legal framework governing the termination of the contract of employment is covered as part of the legal context in Chapter 3.

In this chapter we will examine all issues relating to the termination of the contract, including: good practice guidance; procedural advice; the legal remedies available to address unfair dismissal; and the powers and jurisdiction of employment tribunals.

Alongside the handling of contractual variations outlined above, the other area that is most likely to bring the employee and employer into conflict and lead to recourse to a court or tribunals is when the contract of employment is brought to an end for one reason or another. In this section we will consider the legal grounds on which termination may be sought, those grounds which are clearly not lawful, and some of the important legal and good practice considerations.

4.2 Legal grounds for terminating the contract of employment

It is potentially fair to terminate a contract of employment on a number of grounds provided the decision to terminate was a reasonable one in the circumstances and was carried out in line with a fair procedure. A dismissal is potentially fair if there is a fair ground for it.

Lack of capability or qualifications

If the employee lacks the skill, aptitude or physical health to do the job for which he/she is being paid then there is a potentially fair ground for terminating the contract.

Misconduct

This category covers the range of behaviours that are examined in detail in considering grievance and disciplinary matters in Chapter 8, and include disobedience, absence, insubordination and criminal acts. It can also include illegal forms of industrial action.

Redundancy

Where an employee's job ceases to exist it is potentially fair to dismiss them on grounds of redundancy (see Chapter 11)

By reason of statutory prohibition

What this means is that where an employee cannot continue to remain in employment without breaking the law they can be fairly dismissed. Almost invariably the operation of this category exists for drivers who have been disqualified from driving for a period, although dismissal on these grounds will not automatically be fair.

Some other substantial reason

The most intangible category is introduced in order to cater for genuinely fair dismissals that are so diverse that they cannot be realistically listed. Examples include reasons of security or commercial information. But again the reason must be substantial and a proper procedure followed.

Voluntary resignation

This is where the employee brings the contract to an end of their own volition.

It is worth examining each of these grounds in more detail. In terms of *lack of capability* or *qualifications*, the tests here will relate to skill, aptitude or health. Dismissals on ground of incapability require very careful handling because in most cases the issues will be progressive rather than instant. Such gross incapability is only likely to occur where a very bad match is made at the appointments stage between an individual's skills and the requirements of the job, or where the needs and demands of the job change substantially during employment, or where the individual's performance deteriorates drastically. In such situations it may be possible to dismiss fairly on grounds of gross incapability quickly. However, in all other situations good practice begs that the employer must give the opportunity to the employee to:

- understand the *gap* between their performance and that required and the reasons for it.
- have the opportunity to *improve* with regular reviews.
- have the opportunity for the employer to provide them with *training* and *support* to help their improvement.
- receive *warnings* if they fail to improve as required.

This suggests a process that will take weeks and months rather than a few days and the reasonable employer will be expected to show they have demonstrated with a fair capability procedure if they wish to dismiss on these grounds. Even so, clear evidence of the action the employer has taken to support the individual will be required in such a dismissal, and the employer will also be expected to have considered finding suitable alternative employment for the individual that matches their skill. After all, the law will reason here, the employer took the decision to engage in the first place and therefore has a duty to try and support ongoing employment.

In relation to *misconduct*, to warrant a fair dismissal, misconduct must be extremely serious, or if not extremely serious repeated on one or more occasions. However fair the procedure adopted, a single incident or, for example, bad time-keeping will not in most cases be considered sufficiently serious to justify dismissal. Equally, the fact that an employee has recently been given a disciplinary warning may make it more reasonable to dismiss. For a dismissal to be held as fair it must be a reasonable sanction for the offence concerned and other possible penalties should be considered. It is important to consider all the circumstances of the individual case and not simply to impose an inflexible policy.

More details are given in Chapter 10 about issues relating to disciplinary and grievance procedures, and these are based on good practice guidance issued by ACAS. In terms of gross misconduct (that is those grounds that will automatically lead to dismissal if proven), it is normal for an employer's disciplinary procedure to give an indicative list of the grounds that will be deemed liable for a charge of gross misconduct. These will relate to the particular circumstances of employment, but would typically include issues such as theft, dishonesty, fraud, violence or threatening behaviour, insubordination, or failure to comply with a reasonable management request.

4.3 Handling dismissals

A model approach to handling dismissal is summarised at Figure 4.1 but it is crucial, even if there are proper grounds for a dismissal relating to misconduct, for employers to follow a fair procedure that will include a proper investigation of the facts; the opportunity for the employee to answer the charges and to defend him/herself; a fair and impartial disciplinary hearing process; and consideration of the reasonableness of the employer's decision to dismiss taking account of all the circumstances and evidence available to them. Clearly, this is very difficult HRM territory for any employer to engage in because we are talking about the cessation of employment and often the loss of livelihood with all its serious implications. The law is therefore rightly onerous and requires consistently good HR Management to ensure that such serious matters are properly managed and conducted.

The reduction in the qualifying period for bringing a claim of unfair dismissal to one year has been accompanied by provisions in the *Employment Relations Act 1999* to increase the statutory limit for compensation up to a maximum of £50,000. As this is for the basic award only, and other forms of compensation may be made (see below for details) it becomes all the more important for employers to get decisions about dismissal on any grounds as correct as they can given all the information available to them. The law will take a very dim view of the irresponsible employer who uses flimsy evidence and unfair procedures to dismiss individuals on grounds of misconduct and the financial penalties can now be severe.

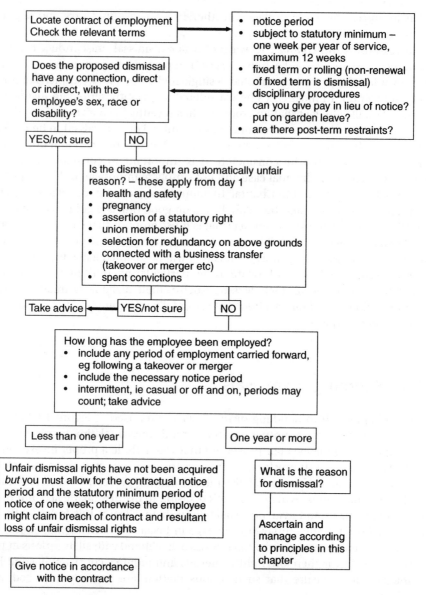

Locate contract of employment
Check the relevant terms

- notice period
- subject to statutory minimum – one week per year of service, maximum 12 weeks
- fixed term or rolling (non-renewal of fixed term is dismissal)
- disciplinary procedures
- can you give pay in lieu of notice? put on garden leave?
- are there post-term restraints?

Does the proposed dismissal have any connection, direct or indirect, with the employee's sex, race or disability?

YES/not sure | NO

Is the dismissal for an automatically unfair reason? – these apply from day 1
- health and safety
- pregnancy
- assertion of a statutory right
- union membership
- selection for redundancy on above grounds
- connected with a business transfer (takeover or merger etc)
- spent convictions

Take advice ← YES/not sure | NO

How long has the employee been employed?
- include any period of employment carried forward, eg following a takeover or merger
- include the necessary notice period
- intermittent, ie casual or off and on, periods may count; take advice

Less than one year | One year or more

Unfair dismissal rights have not been acquired *but* you must allow for the contractual notice period and the statutory minimum period of notice of one week; otherwise the employee might claim breach of contract and resultant loss of unfair dismissal rights

What is the reason for dismissal?

Ascertain and manage according to principles in this chapter

Give notice in accordance with the contract

Figure 4.1 Handling dismissal: a model approach

The provisions relating to the handling of *redundancy* are discussed in detail at Chapter 11 of this book. The termination of the contract of employment on grounds of redundancy may be a fair ground for termination provided that the redundancy is genuine, proper notification and notice periods have been given to the employee and trade union representatives, and the procedure for handling the redundancy is fair. It should be noted here that whilst there may be a genuine ground for redundancy, employers who fail to adopt a proper procedure can suffer financial penalties through the employment tribunals in the same way as those who do not follow a correct procedure in the handling of dismissal on grounds of misconduct or incapability.

Dismissals by reason of statutory prohibition

This means in essence that the grounds for dismissal are because the employer genuinely believes that they will be breaking the law by continuing to engage an employee. Whilst this is a potentially fair ground for dismissal, for example where a particular job category is abolished as a result of changes in the law, upon the death of an employer in a small family firm, or because the employee cannot comply with statutory provisions (the example of an HGV driver who loses their licence on grounds of disqualification or for medical reasons as quoted above) the employer will be required to follow a fair procedure. In these cases employers should discuss the matter with the employee and their representative to explore the scope for resolving the problem, and in appropriate cases seek to provide redeployment if at all possible. Provided these measures are complied with, dismissal by reason of statutory prohibition may be judged to be fair grounds for terminating the contract of employment.

Dismissal for some other substantial reason

This is specified in the *Employment Rights Act* as a potentially fair ground for dismissal and a list of examples can be provided.

1 Because of the *necessary reorganisation* of the business. Under these grounds, the original employment will be effectively ended, although again the employer will be expected to follow a good and fair procedure.
2 For an *economic, technical or organisational* reason entailing changes in the workforce, particularly relating to a transfer of an undertaking under the TUPE legislation.
3 On the expiry of a *fixed term contract* when it is shown that the contract was adopted for a genuine purpose and the fact was known to the employee and it was also shown that the specific purpose for which the contract was used has ceased to be applicable.
4 The imposition of a *sentence of imprisonment* on an employee which whilst it may not directly involve a workplace related act may effectively mean that they cannot comply with their contract of employment and are deemed to have frustrated it, thus bringing the employment to an end.
5 Dismissal of *temporary* or *replacement* employees who are legitimately engaged to cover for employees who are sick, suspended on medical grounds, or absent due to pregnancy.

Voluntary resignation

Finally, whilst not an act of termination by the employer, the contract of employment can of course be brought to a close by the employee on grounds of voluntary resignation. Such a resignation may not be expressed in a formal way and indeed there is no requirement that it must be in writing unless this is made clear in the contract of employment. Indeed, it may be reasonable for an employer to judge that an employee has effectively resigned if they simply cease to come to work for a protracted period and the employer has done all they can to try and ascertain their whereabouts. Nonetheless it is important that the employee's intention to leave is communicated to the employer even if this is by default.

Although, strictly speaking, employees too are bound by the minimum notice requirements contained in the contract of employment (see below) it is for employers to enforce these, because if the employee leaves the only sanction the employer has is to refer to this in any subsequent reference or to deduct pay for periods not worked. Although, in theory at least, the employer could sue the employee for breach of contract, the costs and work involved normally make this a fruitless exercise.

Another form of resignation is where both employee and employer agree to terminate the contract by agreement. Where such a mutual agreement can be proven, the employee is effectively denied any employment protection rights in courts and tribunals on grounds of unfair, wrongful or constructive dismissal. Examples of this form of mutual agreement and resignation will include an employee overstaying their leave (where they stay on a period of leave without agreement for a period that is such that will deem it reasonable for the employee to be considered to have resigned); or on grounds of voluntary redundancy and early retirement where the contract of employment is brought to a close on mutual grounds by form of resignation where the employment has come to a normal close.

There are also circumstances in which an employee agrees to resign rather than face a dismissal on grounds of misconduct or incapability and this is discussed in more detail in Chapter 10. Employers beware however: a resignation can sometimes be a precursor to a claim of constructive dismissal by an employee where they will seek to demonstrate that their resignation was enforced as the employer had fundamentally repudiated one or more core terms of their contract of employment (see below).

4.4 Unfair grounds for terminating the contract of employment

Having considered some of the grounds on which the law may consider it to be fair to terminate a contract of employment, provided there is a genuine legal reason and that a fair procedure has been followed, we must now turn our attention to those grounds on which the law will judge it to be automatically unfair to bring a contract of employment to a close. Most of the grounds on which a dismissal will be deemed to be unfair will also apply if they have grounds to select an individual for redundancy. These grounds can be summarised as follows:

- *Union-related* dismissals connected with membership or trade union activity in the workplace.
- *Health and Safety-related* dismissals, connected with the provisions of the *Health and Safety at Work Act 1974* and other safety issues.
- Dismissals for *asserting statutory rights*, where an individual is protected by statutory provisions but an employer takes action to terminate their contract for a reason connected with the exercising of these rights.
- *Maternity-related* dismissals.
- *Working time* cases connected to the working time regulations.
- Unfair selection for *redundancy*.
- Dismissal upon the *transfer of an undertaking*.
- For issues related to the *National Minimum Wage Act 1998*.
- Public interest disclosure cases connected with the *Public Interest Disclosure Act 1998*.

As with the potentially fair grounds for dismissal, each of these potentially unfair grounds warrants further examination.

Union-related dismissals

These will automatically be regarded as unfair if the principal reason was that the employee was a member of an independent trade union; had taken part in legitimate activities of that trade union; or was not a member of a trade union and had refused to become a member (the former closed shop provisions). So, an individual engaged in legitimate workplace activity as a trade union member cannot be fairly dismissed for this action. It also follows, that it is automatically unfair to dismiss an employee if the employee is an elected trade union or staff representative carrying out legitimate staff representation activity in the workplace on any legitimate collective workplace agreement, and in representing their trade union members or employees, or for any issue related to a transfer of undertaking or redundancy, where consultation is part of statutory provisions. It follows that employers need to be very careful in the handling of trade union representatives when they themselves are subject to disciplinary action, or where the employer believes they have breached statutory or workplace agreements relating to legitimate activities.

Health and safety-related dismissals

Similar protections relate to individuals who are asserting rights and are dismissed for health and safety-related reasons. If the principal reason for the dismissal was any reason connected with an individual carrying out legitimate activities as a health and safety representative, as a member of a health and safety committee, or representing concerns about dangerous or unsafe practices in the workplace, or for taking reasonable measures where they believe there is imminent danger or risks to fellow employee's health and safety at work, then a dismissal will be automatically unfair (see Chapter 12, Health and Safety and Risk Management for more details).

Dismissals for asserting a statutory right

It is automatically unfair to dismiss any employee where they are asserting their rights under other forms of legislation. This will include the right not to be victimised or discriminated as prescribed by the *Sex Discrimination Act 1976, Race Relations Act 1975* and *Disability Discrimination Act 1995*; the right to seek protection of their employment as prescribed by the *Employment Rights Act 1996*; the right to receive statutory minimum notice (see below); rights conferred by the *Working Time Regulations 1998;* and the rights to belong to a trade union and take part in legitimate trade union activities as prescribed by the *Trade Union and Labour Relations Consolidation Act 1992.*

Maternity-related dismissals

A woman will automatically be held to be unfairly dismissed if the principal reason for her dismissal is for a maternity-related reason. The grounds here may include any reason in connection with her pregnancy: when her maternity leave period is terminated by dismissal; where she is made redundant for any grounds in connection with her maternity; or for any other substantial reason connected with the pregnancy. These provisions are discussed in more detail in Chapter 6, Pay and Benefits.

Working time-related dismissals

Adding to the scope of automatic grounds for unfair dismissal following the introduction of the *Working Time Regulations 1998*, an employee's dismissal will be automatically regarded as unfair if the principal reason for their dismissal was their failure to comply with a requirement imposed by their employer which was in breach of the regulations; failed to sign their workforce agreement under the aegis of the regulations which again did not comply with the requirements of the regulations; and for any activity in representing the interests of other workers in connection with their rights under the working time protections. Related protection also exists for shop workers who refuse to work on a Sunday following the provisions of the *Sunday Trading Act 1994.* These provisions are now included in the *Employment Rights Act 1996* so that employees who elect not to work on Sundays are protected and any dismissal in connection with such a refusal will again be deemed to be automatically unfair.

Dismissals for redundancy

A dismissal for redundancy will be unfair if the selection is made on any of the grounds listed as automatically unfair grounds for dismissal. So it follows that in each and every case of redundancy an employer has to select fair grounds and cannot rely on anything that was otherwise deemed to be unfair as indicated by this list. Chapter 11 discusses in more detail some of the issues relating to managing redundancy properly, and also includes reference to the *Transfer of Undertakings Regulations 1981*. This states that any dismissal connected with a transfer of an undertaking is automatically unfair, unless the reason for the dismissal is for economic, technical or organisational reasons entailing changes in the workforce.

Recent legislation

The final two categories of grounds which are automatically unfair grounds for dismissal, have been created by legislation introduced at the very end of the 1990s. The *National Minimum Wage Act 1998* states that it will be automatically regarded as unfair if the principal reason for dismissal was an individual seeking to assert their rights under the national minimum wage legislation. This will mean that an employee has a right to the national minimum wage and the employer cannot take any action against them for asserting this right providing their actions are reasonable and genuine. Similarly, the *Public Interest Disclosure Act 1998* means that employees who "blow the whistle" and do so genuinely and follow reasonable actions in doing so are protected from unfair dismissal by the law.

4.5 Unfair, constructive and wrongful dismissal

Having explored the legal and illegal grounds for terminating a contract of employment, it is timely to look at the concepts of unfair, constructive and wrongful dismissal which will almost certainly arise where an unfair ground is relied on to terminate a contract, but may also be the subject of a challenge in a tribunal or a court even if the ground for termination is potentially fair. There are three main definitions to consider here:

1. Unfair dismissal: the definition of unfair dismissal under the terms of the *Employment Rights Act 1996*, is dismissal on grounds that are unfair (see above) or where a fair and reasonable procedure has not been followed by the employer in determining reasons for dismissal. So, it follows that whilst the grounds for dismissal may potentially be fair (for example misconduct) unfair dismissal may be proven if the employee has the minimum of continuous service required to bring a claim (one year) and can show that the employer did not follow a fair procedure or reach a reasonable conclusion given the facts of the case. It equally follows that no matter how fair and rigorous the employer's procedures, unfair dismissal will be automatically found if the reason for dismissal is one of the grounds listed above (for example for a maternity-related reason).

2. Constructive dismissal: the definition here is where an employee resigns their employment, without notice, because they believe the employer has fundamentally breached a contract of employment. To prove constructive dismissal, the employee will need to show that the breach was fundamental, and that

their reason for leaving was the employer's conduct and not some other reason, and they must leave quickly to be able to sustain that a fundamental breach of contract took place.

3. Wrongful dismissal: the definition of wrongful dismissal is quite simple; any dismissal that is in breach of the contract of employment, may give rise to an action for wrongful dismissal. The most common ground for wrongful dismissal is a dismissal without proper notice as required by the contract of employment; the termination of a fixed term contract before it is due to expire; and dismissal in breach of a contractual dismissal procedure contained within the organisation's disciplinary procedure.

Unfair dismissal

Each of these concepts are worthy of explanation in more detail to establish the differences and inter-relationship between them.

To entertain a claim of unfair dismissal the first consideration that will be considered by a tribunal is first whether the employee has the requisite service to bring an action (one year); whether they have brought their claim within the requisite period since the act or actions they complain of (normally three months but maybe longer in discrimination cases); that the individual bringing the action is actually properly described as an employee; and that a dismissal actually occurred. The latter often gives rise to much debate in employment tribunal cases as to whether or not a dismissal has actually happened.

EXAMPLE

> In the case of *Norrie v. Munros Transport* 1988 a driver who had been redeployed following a reorganisation was asked to start driving vehicles again. N refused to do the job. After attempts to persuade him a director said "the job is there for you" upon which N asked if he was being dismissed. He was told that he was not but he maintained his stance until the director said "you might as well put your jacket on". N left the premises and claimed unfair dismissal. The tribunal looked at the words used in this case but also the other circumstances and decided that there had been no dismissal. The words "you might as well put your jacket on" was clearly an expression of frustration on behalf of the director but did not in the tribunal's eyes constitute dismissal as it was obvious they were trying to encourage the man to continue working.
>
> Similarly, in *Futty v. D & D Breckkes Ltd* 1974, a fish filleter and his foreman, fed up with F's *banter*, told him if you do not like the job "f . . . off". F claimed this was a dismissal and found himself another job. The tribunal found differently. They found the use of "industrial language" justifiable in the context of a fish dock and found the words were not a dismissal but a "general exhortation to get on with the job".

Conversely, however, employers who place employees under duress and pressure to resign may be found by tribunals to have actually created the act of dismissal. Obvious examples of this are where employees are given an ultimatum of going or being pushed, or are given some incentive to resign. In these circumstances, it is possible that the tribunal will find that the employer actually terminated the contract. Cases of unfair dismissal may be brought where the contract has been terminated either with or without notice as discussed below.

Constructive dismissal

To stand the test of constructive dismissal, a number of points must be proven by the resigning employee. First, they must show that the employer's conduct was tantamount to fundamental breach of the contract of employment. The breach can either be actual or one that is anticipated because of various actions by the employer. As with other terms in unfair dismissal legislation, the issues that will be determined by a tribunal are the matters of fact and degree.

EXAMPLE

> In the case of *R F Hill Ltd v. Mooney* 1981, the employment appeals tribunal upheld a claim of constructive dismissal where the employers unilaterally altered the pay structure in an organisation and cut the wages of the employees without consulting them.

In such cases tribunals will look at the degree of changes to the contract to make a judgment whether a fundamental breach has occurred or not. So, for example, although the act of lack of consultation in cutting pay may be a breach of contract it may not be fundamental if the cut is small in relation to the total remuneration for the employee. Thus a £5 pay cut is clearly a more serious matter for an employee earning £100 a week than for one earning £500 and is therefore more likely to constitute a fundamental breach.

Other fundamental breaches of the contract may be more to do with the employer's general behaviour and their breaching of one of their common law duties enshrined in the contract of employment. So, if it can be shown that the employer has broken their own bond of trust and fidelity with the employee by their actions, then a fundamental breach may be demonstrated and constructive dismissal may apply. To prove a case of constructive dismissal, the employee will also need to act quickly and not hold on to their resignation too long or do anything else which indicates an acceptance of the changed basis of the employment relationship.

Merely to protest at the time will not suffice, and tribunals will look for actions that show that the breach of contract was so fundamental as to make the employee resign or give notice of their resignation. Failure to do so will mean that the employee is considered to have affirmed to the contract even if the basis for it has been unilaterally changed by the employer. Finally, the employee will need to demonstrate that he/she resigned because of the fundamental breach of contract and not for some other reason.

Wrongful dismissal

This is very different to complaint of unfair or constructive dismissal. The reasonableness or otherwise of the employer's actions in a case of wrongful dismissal is immaterial. All a court or a tribunal has to consider is whether the employment contract has been breached. If it has, and dismissal is the result, then it is wrongful although it is not necessarily unfair. Conversely, an unfair dismissal is not necessarily wrongful. However, if it is both wrongful and unfair there will be little point in the employee pursuing both remedies as the award of damages for wrongful dismissal takes into account the unfair dismissal compensatory award (see below).

Most cases of wrongful dismissal will relate to the way notice is used in terminating a contract of employment. Employers are only entitled to summarily dismiss an employee (that is without notice) if the employee has been guilty of gross misconduct amounting to a repudiation of their contract. In other words the employee's conduct must be so serious as to constitute a fundamental breach of the contract. Unless the act is so serious as to satisfy these conditions, then any dismissal without notice or without sufficient notice as prescribed in the contract of the employment will constitute a breach of contract and may give rise to a claim for wrongful dismissal.

Claims for wrongful dismissal may also be brought because employer's failed to comply with other contractual procedures.

EXAMPLE

> In *Gunton v. Richmond-upon-Thames, London Borough Council* 1980, *G* was employed under a contract which included a provision for one month's notice and also prescribed a procedure for the dismissal of employees on disciplinary grounds. The employers dismissed him for disciplinary reasons with one month's notice but did not follow the right procedure. The Court of Appeal held that *G* had been wrongfully dismissed. *G* was awarded damages for the amount of notice he was not provided with.

4.6 Tribunals and courts

Claims of unfair, constructive and wrongful dismissal are usually heard by Employment Tribunals, although cases of wrongful dismissal relating to a breach of contract where substantial damages are being sought can also be heard in civil courts. Industrial tribunals were first introduced as the lay court for the hearing of employment-related grievances under the *Industrial Relations Act 1971*, and were properly constituted in their modern form by the *Employment Protection Consolidation Act 1978*. Since then, the growth in the number of cases that tribunals hear has grown enormously from a low of 29,304 in 1988/89 to a peak of nearly 90,000 in 1996/97. Concern about delay, complexity and costs of proceedings has led to many proposals for the reform of the tribunal system, and indeed changes have been introduced via both the *Trade Union Reform and Employment Rights Act 1993* and the *Employment Rights Act 1996*. Following these changes industrial tribunals now become known as employment tribunals and confer additional powers to tribunals to dispose of hopeless cases and uncontested claims, to increase the reliance on the use of written evidence, extend the use of compromise agreements, and strengthen the role of ACAS (Advisory, Conciliation and Arbitration Service) in trying to broker settlements before cases come to tribunals.

Employment tribunals are administered by the employment tribunal service, a branch of the Department of Trade and Industry. They have the following composition:

- A chairman, appointed by the Lord Chancellor, who is a legally qualified QC.
- An employee's representative appointed by the Secretary of State for Trade and Industry after consultation with the Trades Union Congress.
- Persons appointed after consultation with the Confederation of British Industry (CBI) and employers' representatives.

A full tribunal consists of one member of each of the above and they sit in an informal court atmosphere to consider cases brought under the following legislation:

- *Employment Rights Act 1996*
- *Pension's Scheme Act 1993*
- *Trade Union Labour Relations Consolidation Act 1992*
- *Equal Pay Act 1970*
- *Sex Discrimination Act 1975*
- *Race Relations Act 1976*
- *Disability Discrimination Act 1995*
- *Working Time Regulations 1998*
- *Health and Safety at Work Act 1974*
- *National Minimum Wage Act 1998*
- *Public Interest Disclosure Act 1998*

Tribunal proceedings are instituted by the employee (the applicant) who completes an originating application (known as Form IT1) giving details of why they are bringing their claim, against whom the claim is made, when the actions they complain of are alleged to have taken place, and what remedy they are seeking in law. The applicant may represent themselves as this is effectively a lay court, or may be represented by a human resources advisor or a lawyer. Generally speaking, the time limit for bringing a claim is 3 months for an application based on unfair dismissal and 6 months for a redundancy application. For example in a claim alleging unfair dismissal, the time starts to run from the effective date of termination when the dismissal took place. Although claims of discrimination under the *Sex, Race and Disability Discrimination Acts* have a notional 3-month time limit, in practice courts and tribunals are much more liberal in flexing this and will often hear claims that are notionally out of time provided there are good grounds to do so. (NB: the new Race Relations Act being introduced by the government in 2001, is proposing an extension of the time limit formally to 6 months).

Once an IT1 is filed the respondent (normally the employer) must complete and return a written notice of appearance within 21 days stating whether or not they intend to resist the application and if so on what grounds they seek to do so. An extension to the 21-day time limit may be granted by the employment tribunal provided there are good grounds to do so. Before a case actually comes to a tribunal hearing, employment tribunals have powers of pre-hearing review, and various so-called interlocutory powers. The purpose of the pre-hearing review is to weed out claims that have little merit and to substantiate exactly what the issues are before a case comes to full tribunal. The interlocutory powers given to a tribunal help establish the way that a particular case will be conducted. For example a tribunal may order either the applicant or the respondent to provide further particulars for the grounds on which they intend to rely in a hearing; they may also require a party to give discovery of documents to the other side or make an order for an individual to attend as a witness. All of these powers will help establish the merits of the case to be determined at a full hearing and clarify the evidence that will be heard. Once a case actually comes to tribunal hearing, the case will be heard rather as though it were a matter being determined in a civil court of law. The usual procedure to be followed would be as described below:

1 The party on whom the *burden of proof* rests, normally the employer in an unfair dismissal claim, but (at the moment) the applicant in a discrimination claim will open the proceedings.
2 The party who opens will normally make an *opening statement*, and call their evidence which may be written and in the form of witnesses.
3 The members of the tribunal will have the opportunity to *question* the party and any witnesses they call.
4 The person defending the claim or who does not open the case, will have the opportunity to *cross-question*.
5 The whole procedure may then be *reversed*.

Documents will normally be required to be submitted in advance of the hearing under rules established by the tribunal and to help clarify what witnesses will say; witness statements may be required to be prepared by the tribunal in advance. Evidence given in person is always preferable to witness statements, simply because people can be cross-examined on what they say and documents cannot. Once all the primary evidence has been heard both parties will be asked to sum up their submission and the tribunal will normally adjourn to consider their decision.

The tribunal may reach unanimous or a majority decision, but in difficult cases they may reserve their decision. The decision may be announced on the day of the hearing, and/or written reasons may be sent to all parties after the hearing giving details of what the tribunal's decision is and the grounds for it. Tribunals are very careful in reaching their decisions and stating the grounds for it as they will need to take account not just of the evidence they have heard, but of precedents set by any previous tribunal cases, referred to by any party, that are relevant to the proceedings. They will also want to ensure that the decision they have reached is legally sound as it may be open to challenge and appeal, by either party, by a claim to the Office of the Employment Appeals Tribunals (EAT).

The EAT may review a decision made by an ET on one of the following grounds:

1 The original order was wrongly made as a result of an *error* on the part of the tribunal or its staff.
2 The party did not receive *notice of proceedings* leading to the decision.
3 A decision was made in the *absence* of a party.
4 *New evidence* became available after the conclusion of the hearing which could not have been reasonably known or foreseen.
5 The interests of *justice* require such a review.

Appeals to the EAT must be presented by notice of appeal within 42 days from the date of which the written decisions of the original tribunal are submitted to the parties. If either party is dissatisfied with the outcome of a decision of the EAT, this decision in turn may be challenged by an appeal to the Court of Appeal or later to the House of Lords, and the European Courts of Justice provided there are clear legal grounds for doing so.

4.7 Tribunal powers and remedies

There are a number of remedies available to tribunals in reaching their decisions. The main remedies can be summarised as follows:

Reinstatement

An order for reinstatement is defined as an order that the employer shall treat the complainant in all respects as if they have not been dismissed. So if a case of unfair or constructive dismissal is found in favour of the employee, a tribunal may make such an order. Whether they do so or not will depend partly on whether the complainant wishes to be reinstated, whether it is practicable for an employer to comply with such an order, or whether it would be just to make an order. So, whilst a tribunal may uphold a claim of unfair dismissal and consider a case for reinstating the employee to their former position, it may not be practicable for them to do so if the employer is very small, already has filled the post and does not have the resources to reabsorb the employee. An order for reinstatement may not, however, be complied with by an employer. If this is the case, the tribunal will normally award compensation additional to an original amount levied against the employer for refusing to comply with the tribunal's decision.

Re-engagement

If an Employment Tribunal decides not to order a reinstatement it must go on to consider re-engagement. An order for re-engagement is defined as an order that the complainant be engaged by the employer or by an associated employer in employment comparable to that from which he or she was dismissed or some other suitable employment. In considering a case for re-engagement the tribunal will consider the same factors as in the case of reinstatement. Re-engagement is often a much more practicable option where cases of unfair and constructive dismissal are proven, as it is usually easier for employers to re-engage an individual into a suitable alternative post (and indeed often better for the employee to do so) than for them to try and engage an individual back in the job from which they were originally dismissed.

Compensation

When a tribunal makes an award of compensation for unfair constructive or wrongful dismissal, the award must consist of a *basic* and a *compensatory* award. There are statutory maxima for nearly all these awards and the eligibility of the successful party for compensation will be dependent on a number of factors, including the degree to which they contributed towards the situation that arose. So therefore, although a tribunal may find in favour of an applicant on grounds of unfair dismissal, they may reduce the amount of compensation they award on the basis that the applicant contributed to the situation, or will reduce the compensation by the amount of earnings the individual has earned since bringing their case forward (so-called recoupment or mitigation of loss). The basic award is usually equivalent to the same amount as that that would be eligible under a statutory redundancy payment (see Chapter 11).

The payment depends on the basic weekly pay, length of service and age of the party. The compensatory award limit has recently been revised by the *Employment Relations Act 1999* to a maximum of £50,000. The amount of the compensatory award will be assessed depending on the immediate loss of wages since the act complained of; the future loss of earnings which will be determined by some assessment of the individual's future employability and earnings they will lose whilst they seek alternative work; loss of benefits including car, accommodation and medical insurance; loss of reputation where an applicant may receive damages as a result of a stigma attached to them following their dismissal; loss of pension rights; and loss of any statutory rights that are proven in the case before the tribunal.

Additional award

This may also be made by a tribunal where an employer fails to comply with an order for reinstatement and re-engagement. The maximum additional award is the equivalent of 52 weeks' pay, calculated on the same basis as the statutory redundancy payments. Finally, a tribunal may make a special award to employees whose dismissal is regarded as unfair for issues related to health and safety activities, or trade union activities. At the time of writing, the limit for a special award does not exceed £29,000. All of the above awards may be reduced to recoup earnings that the successful party has earned since bringing forward their case to the tribunal, and for their contribution to the issues arising in the case. Some of the most headline-grabbing awards from tribunals in recent years have arisen in sex discrimination cases, where tribunals have found wholly for the female applicant, and have determined that she has not contributed any fault in the case, and has not been able to mitigate her loss by obtaining alternative employment. In the most notorious cases, the total of the basic compensatory and additional awards has totalled over £300,000, and has brought disrepute as well as financial hardship upon the organisations deemed to be at fault.

4.8 Periods of notice and associated provisions

Statutory notice

Whatever the grounds and reasons for terminating a contract of employment the observance of agreed notice periods is an important HRM requirement. There are two aspects to consider here: first, what the law requires as a minimum statutory notice period dependent on length of service; and, what employers sometimes agree over and above this in the form of the contract of employment. To qualify for minimum notice rights, an employee must have worked continuously for one month, and is essentially entitled to one week's notice for each completed year of continuous service up to a maximum of 12 weeks' notice. Thus the entitlement for an employee who has worked for 6 years and 2 months is a statutory minimum of 6 weeks' notice. On grounds other than summary dismissal arising from a proven case of gross misconduct, the employer is duty bound to pay the employee the minimum notice entitlement or to serve and allow the employee to work such notice. So, using the above example, the statutory minimum notice that would have to be paid by the employer in lieu of notice would be 6 weeks, or as an alternative the employee would need to be served 6 weeks' notice, allowed to work this and receive remuneration for it.

Contractual provisions

These may exceed the statutory minimum requirements at the agreement of employee and employer as enshrined in the contract of employment. Generally speaking, the higher the remuneration and the more senior the appointment, the longer the notice period built into the contract. It is therefore not unusual for some chief executives or managing directors to have a one year notice period built into their contract of employment, with 6 months as the norm for senior or executive directors. Three months is the most common period for senior professionals and 4 weeks for most other salaried staff (NB noting that the statutory minimum must be complied with in all cases where this exceeds the contractual stipulation).

Notice periods

These offer a *double-edged protection* to both employee and employer. For the employee, they guarantee that unless they are found guilty of an act of gross misconduct they are given reasonable notice about the termination of their contract of employment where there are legal grounds to do so. This provides them with the opportunity to seek alternative work and to plan for the cessation of their current employment. For the employer, it gives them a reasonable amount of time in which to make provision for replacing the employee or dealing with their departure where it is at the employee's behest on grounds of voluntary resignation or retirement on grounds of ill health. Strictly speaking, the employee is required to work their notice period unless some other arrangement can be reached with the employer (see below). However, in practice employees who fail to work or serve the appropriate notice period are rarely sued by the employer for breach of contract due to the cost and time involved.

Payment in lieu

It is possible for payment to be made in lieu of notice where there is a contractual provision to do so (in which case any payments made to the employee would be subject to tax and NI deductions) or where there is an agreement between the parties not stipulated by the contract (in which case the payment in lieu may be made gross of any deductions). Payments in lieu are often used where it would not otherwise be beneficial for the employee to remain at work or where circumstances simply do not allow it. So, given the sudden closure of a business on economic grounds where a redundancy is being paid, it may simply not be possible for the employer to allow the notice period to be worked and a payment will have to be made in lieu. Similarly, if there is a consensual agreement between the employee and employer to terminate the contract, because matters are not working out for one or either party, it may be agreed that it is best for the employee to be paid in lieu of notice and not to return to work.

Garden leave

In association with these pay-in-lieu provisions, there has been an increasing tendency for employees to be asked to take so-called garden leave. The notion of garden leave (which as the name suggests allows employees to be at home or in the garden) is that the employee would continue to be paid and for the contract to remain in operation until a future agreed date, but for the employee to actually be away from the workplace. Following recent test cases, there should be an expressed condition in the contract of employment if an employer may require an employee to take garden leave at some point in the future.

EXAMPLE

In an earlier case of *Collier v. Sunday Referee Publishing* 1940, the judge determined that there was no such need for a contractual provision because "provided I pay my cook, she cannot complain if I choose to take any or all of my meals out"! However, the later case of the *William Hill Organisation v. Tucker* 1998, showed that employers were under duty to provide employees with work as part of the consideration they receive for carrying out their duties and in the absence of an expressed garden leave clause employers were likely to act in breach of contract by insisting the employee takes a period of paid leave during their notice period.

4.9 Post-termination restraints and termination agreements

The extent to which an employer can limit the activities of ex-employees is much more restricted than is the case of employees whose contracts of employment are still in existence. Whilst an employer may reasonably require an employee not to engage in competitive work, or disclose confidential information or *intellectual property* to competitors whilst they remain in their employment, it is much more difficult for them legally to do so, once the employee has left their employment. Such restrictions are likely to be regarded as restraints of trade unless the employer can show that the restriction is reasonable. The *restrictive covenants* that may be placed in the contract of employment usually relate to restraints on working for competitors or restraints on soliciting or dealing with customers. Such restraints must be reasonable given the business interests of the employer and the markets they operate in.

Even where an employee does offer a potential threat to the employer's legitimate interests, restraint that is wider than necessary to protect those legitimate interests will be unenforceable.

EXAMPLE

> In the case of *Mason v. Provident Clothing and Supply* 1913, M worked on commission as a canvasser in Islington for a draper. His contract said that he would not within 3 years of termination of his employment be employed in any similar business within 25 miles of London. M was subsequently dismissed and went to work for a competitor in Islington and the company sued for an injunction to stop him. Ultimately, the House of Lords held that the restraint was unenforceable. The company employed about 1,000 canvassers in London, based in some 15 district offices. Given that the population was then in excess of 6 million people the area of restraint was vastly larger than the area of the legitimate operations of the organisation.

Similar considerations apply to the use of confidential or "intellectual property". The law makes a distinction between the knowhow an individual builds up in the course of their employment, which is legitimately transferable with them when they seek alternative employment in the future, and that which is confidential based on the duty of fidelity to the former employer.

EXAMPLE

> In the case of *F S Travel and Leisure Systems Ltd v. Johnson* 1998, the Court of Appeal refused to grant an injunction to enforce a non-competition clause where the evidence was insufficient to show that the information obtained by the defendant, a computer programmer, was sufficiently sensitive and confidential to amount to a trade secret. The company was not entitled to control after the termination of the employment given the skill, knowhow, experience and knowledge the defendant had gained during the course of his employment as a computer programmer. However, the law would be much more likely to find in the case of the employer where it could be shown that the employee breached confidentiality which he/she was legit-

imately bound to (for example former civil servants who signed and are bound by the *Official Secrets Act* who sold state secrets for personal gain).

In more complex termination cases, sometimes when post-termination clauses are entailed, or where there is a dispute between employee and employer that is resolved by agreement, a *consensual termination* agreement may be drawn up. In this respect either party is free to terminate the contract of employment without notice, and if they do so, then all legal obligations under the contract will cease and either side will be entitled to any compensation. Often, such agreements are reached in the context of an out-of-court settlement arising from a claim to an employment tribunal. If this is done, one of two courses must be followed for any agreement reached with an employee to be binding. Either a conciliation offer must be involved, normally brokered by ACAS (often referred to as a COT 3 settlement taking its name from the pro forma used), or the conditions of a statutorily arrived-at compromise agreement must be fulfilled including the rights of the employee to have received independent advice in reaching such an agreement. If this is not done, an employee will be free to bring a claim, notwithstanding that they have received a sum in settlement. Such compromise agreements normally have a number of features in writing, including the terms of the settlement (financial or otherwise); often a confidentiality clause (banning public statements by the parties); and a statement to the effect that the matters are now concluded between the parties and no further action will be taken by one against the other. Such legally drawn-up settlements are enforced within law if either party breaches them in any way.

4.10 Problem areas

QUESTION:

I am a managing director of a small cosmetics company, and I had a very unpleasant situation to deal with at work this morning. I found a female employee in tears with a male colleague in attendance whom she claimed had just assaulted her. The chap in question has been nothing but trouble since he joined me, and such was her distress I had no option other than to call him into my office and dismiss him on the spot. It is clear in our contract of employment that assault, sexual harassment are automatic grounds for summary dismissal and I assume my actions are sound given the facts in this case?

ANSWER:

From what you have described, your actions are far from being sound, and, dependent on the length of service of the male employee, could well land you with a claim of unfair dismissal. Remember that to dismiss someone fairly, one must not only rely on fair grounds for doing so (in this case an alleged act of gross misconduct) but following reasonable procedure and reaching a reasonable conclusion given the facts before you. Although prima facie there may well have been a case of gross misconduct to answer, you have not observed any of the rules of natural justice in this case. The rules of a matter of justice say that the accused must know the case against them, must have the chance to be represented, and the chance to answer the allegations before them. It sounds in this case as if you jumped in at the deep end, accepted the female employee's version of events, failed to conduct any investigation into the facts, failed to constitute a disciplinary hearing, and terminated the male employee's contract summarily. Even if the act of assault of sexual harassment can be shown to have happened it is very unlikely that any court of tribunal will uphold your actions as a fair dismissal because of the procedure you have followed or in this case failed to have followed. What you should have done is first separate the male and female employee and commence an investigation.

If prima facie there was a case to answer, the male employee may have been suspended from work or sent home while you conducted the investigation. An independent person should have carried this out and prepared a report for you to consider. Only when you received this report could you then determine whether or not there was a proper case to answer. After all, these may have been workplace lovers having a tiff and you may have unwittingly become involved in a domestic wrangle. Even if you had determined there was a serious case to answer and the evidence supported this, you still needed to give the male employee an opportunity to represent his case and face the charges at a disciplinary hearing. Had these steps been followed, and the facts proven, it is likely that the dismissal would have been on a fair ground and would have followed a fair procedure. In the absence of this, you and your organisation are vulnerable to a challenge in the courts or an employment tribunal.

QUESTION:

I have just heard that one of our senior salesman has got a job with a competitor and I am concerned that he will sell company secrets to the competitor while he works his notice with us. Can I require him to stay at home during his notice period on garden leave, and not to have any further contact with his prospective new employer until then?

ANSWER:

Much of the answer to this will depend on what is stated in your contract of employment, and what a reasonable restriction of his future trade is dependent on your business and that of your competitors. You can certainly impose any contractual restriction you have on the selling of intellectual property rights whilst he remains in your employment provided this has been legally drawn up in the originating contract. However, this is likely to fall short of not allowing him to have any contact whatsoever to do with the new employer. In terms of the garden leave requirement, much again will depend on what is in the contract of employment. If the contract either in an expressed term or through custom and practice allows for the taking of garden leave in such circumstances, then you will be within your rights to ask him to work his notice period at home. If it does not, you will either have to allow him to continue to be in the workplace subject to the legitimate restraints on the selling of trade secrets referred to above, or probably better still to pay him in lieu of notice so there is no potential conflict of interest whilst he remains in your employment.

4.11 Activity

List five grounds on which the termination of a contract of employment may be

- fair
- automatically unfair

based on the legal requirements outlined in this chapter. Assuming the grounds for dismissal are potentially fair what an employer must do to enforce a fair dismissal – outline some of the steps they would need to take to convince a tribunal in the face of a claim for unfair dismissal, where the grounds for dismissal are potentially sound.

4.12 Checklist

KEY POINTS

▶ There is a range of potentially fair grounds on which contracts of employment may be terminated including redundancy, lack of capability or qualifications, misconduct, end of a fixed term contract, or some other substantial reason.

▶ Even if a fair ground for termination can be shown, the employer must follow a fair procedure and reach a reasonable conclusion in each and every case of dismissal.

▶ There are a number of potentially automatically unfair grounds for dismissal including reasons related to maternity, the *Working Time Directive*, the *Minimum Wage Act*, race and disability discrimination, or trade union activities.

▶ No matter how fair or reasonable the procedure or the actions of the employer, unfair dismissal will be found if the reason for dismissal is on one of these aforementioned grounds.

▶ The law provides for cases of unfair, constructive or wrongful dismissal to be heard by employment tribunals who have wide-ranging powers to hear the evidence and cases brought before them.

▶ Employment tribunals may order reinstatement, re-engagement and/or compensation to the successful party.

▶ The law prescribes various statutory notice periods that must be complied with if a case of wrongful dismissal is not to be invited and also makes provisions for pay in lieu of notice and the granting of garden leave in certain circumstances.

▶ The use of post-termination clauses in contracts of employment may be legal to protect trade secrets but not to restrain future trade or employment of the individual.

5 Recruitment, selection and retention

5.1 Introduction

Of all the traditional images of the Personnel Manager at work, none is so archetypal as that of the selection interview. Even before the development of HRM as a vital arm of business management in the 1960s, the selection interview was seen as the domain of the personnel section and where they could bring their expertise to bear. Early in the 2000s we are dealing with a much more diverse situation in terms of the total HR Management picture. First, the traditional methods and techniques of recruiting and selecting staff have been severely challenged by the massive upheaval in employment patterns in the late twentieth century. The abandonment of lifelong employment and single organisation employees means the traditional newspaper or journal advertisement is no longer enough to attract staff of the right calibre in today's competitive markets. So new techniques, some highly sophisticated and technical, have been developed to aid organisations in recruiting and selecting the right staff in the right place at the right time. The other important aspect that has changed is that recruitment and selection is no longer the sole domain of the personnel function. In many organisations recruitment and selection is now a line management function with HR expertise bought in to advise or to manage processes, but not necessarily as the sole decision makers.

So we have a slightly contradictory picture of a very diffused recruitment and selection operation with much higher levels of expertise spread over a few people. The other compelling reason for recruitment and selection (and indeed retention) to be the cornerstone of good HR practice is simply the cost of getting it wrong. In 1998 the Chartered Institute of Personnel and Development estimated that the average costs of recruiting, inducting, training and developing a basic grade professional in their first year in an organisation were between £5,000 and £8,000. The costs escalate hugely when the new recruit is tied into some professional training programme and costs in excess of £10,000 in year one are not exceptional. So this is a major investment decision for any organisation to make.

Indeed, it is for the same reasons that retention is becoming equally as important now as recruitment and selection have been for the last twenty years. Once organisations have made the investment in the individual's training, development, and support, they want to hang on to it for as long as they can assuming their investment turns out to be a good one. As an extreme example of these considerations, it was not unusual for finance houses and brokers in the City of

London in the late 1980s and early 90s, in the boom years for the City, to tie employees to companies through what were termed "golden handcuffs" which were huge bonus payments as a reward for staying loyal to the company of their choice, potentially large penalties for leaving early, and loyalty clauses to ensure valuable, confidential, intellectual property was not lost to their competitors. Although there are legal restraints on how far organisations can go to bind individuals to their contracts, as freedom of labour movement is enshrined in the EC Treaty of Rome, organisations essentially do all they legally can to encourage the highest calibre of employee to stay with the organisation through training, development, perks and benefits and building up organisational loyalty.

In this section we will examine some of the legal requirements that underpin recruitment and selection strategies; good practice in recruitment and selection; retention techniques; and some of the pitfalls and problem areas that often pervade this area of HR activity.

5.2 Legal framework

Three principles underpin most of the law in relation to recruitment, selection and retention matters. They can be defined as:

1. Objectivity: the need for those recruiting and selecting staff to demonstrate objectivity and transparency in their decision making and not to show undue favour or bias to any particular individual or group of individuals.
2. Equity: following the same procedures and adopting sound equal opportunities policies in the recruitment, selection and retention processes.
3. Fairness: as an extension of the above ensuring "a level playing field" particularly in the treatment of internal staff versus external candidates, between men and women particularly in terms of remuneration and terms and conditions of employment. These threads run throughout the main legislative framework that governs this branch of HR.

The key legislation can be summarised as follows:

Equal Pay Act 1970

This provides that men and women must receive equal pay and fringe benefits for work of equal value. The law provides that the definition will include like work (work of a broadly similar nature); equivalent rated work (where a process such as job evaluation ranks the work as being of comparable standard and weight); and equal value (equality in terms of effort, skill and responsibility).

The Sex Discrimination Act 1975 (amended 1986); Race Relations Act 1976; and the Disability Discrimination Act 1995

All three major pieces of legislation are dealt with in detail in Chapter 8, Equal Opportunities. However, they are particularly relevant to recruitment and selection decisions and make it illegal for employers to directly or indirectly discriminate against employees and potential employees on grounds of their gender, marital status, race, colour, nationality or ethnic origin and disability.

Rehabilitation of Offenders Act 1974

Under this act a person who has been convicted of a criminal offence may consider the conviction to be spent after a period of time. This means that once the offence has become spent the offender need not disclose it to any prospective employer. Under an exemption order passed in 1986 this provision does not apply to those who are convicted of offences relating to children where they apply for jobs with access to young people. In these cases the conviction remains for life. Examples of spent periods are given in the following table.

Sentence	Spent period
Imprisoned for more than 30 months	After 10 years
Imprisoned not exceeding 6 months	After 7 years
A fine	After 5 years
Conditional discharge	After 1 year

The Asylum and Immigration Act 1996

This act makes it an offence to employ a person who is not entitled under immigration rules to work in the UK. The onus is on employers to have checked that a potential employee is in possession of documentation to confirm their status.

5.3 Codes of practice

The main codes of practice which have a bearing on recruitment, selection and retention activity are those concerned with equal opportunities (on grounds of sex, race and disability). These are dealt with in detail in Chapter 8.

5.4 Preparing to recruit

Job design and job analysis

The starting point for the recruitment and selection process is not with the placing of a job advertisement. The first stage is determining what kind of work needs to be undertaken and how this should be collectively described in a job description; this applies whether or not we are looking at an existing job in an organisation (where it is prudent to check to make sure the job falling vacant is still the job the organisation requires to be done) or in defining a wholly new or substantially changed need. Job analysis is essentially the role of defining the different components of work that need to be undertaken and job design is the process of collecting the results of this analysis together to design the end product – the job to be filled. The terminology used in the job analysis process is confusingly interchangeable in the modern Human Resource environment and it is worth redefining some of the terms for the purpose of clarity.

KEY POINTS

▶ Task
A piece of work which can be identified in terms of its end results or objectives.
▶ Job
A number of tasks which are sufficiently alike to be grouped together and allocated to an individual.
▶ Position
The individual's place in the organisation. Some jobs require only one person to do a particular group of tasks. Other jobs may require a number of positions to be filled.
▶ Job description
A summary description of information relating to a particular job. This may be a very individual job which has just one position or a job which has a number of different positions.
▶ Person specification
A statement derived from the job analysis process and the job description of the characteristics that an individual would need to possess in order to fulfil the requirements of the job. Sometimes this document is referred to as the personnel or job specification.
▶ Occupation
A group of similar jobs.

Job analysis methods

A number of techniques are available to the line manager or the personnel practitioner who is going to undertake the task of job analysis and resultant job design. Whatever type of job analysis methodology is used however, there is a common requirement for information. This will normally be secured from an existing post holder but can come from other sources including the supervisor or manager, other post holders in a peer group, technical experts and documentation external to the organisation which describes the kind of work required (for example a Government Inquiry Report). The information can in turn be collected in a number of different ways including: self reporting (by the existing job holder using some form of time recording method); individual interviews (usually by a trained job analyst with the post-holder or manager); group methods (with the peer group or a collection of post-holders), and observation (a development of the work study school of job analysis).

Once collected a body of data clearly exists from which to analyse the information and to filter it ready for the job design process. Some of the traditional techniques used for analysing job data are listed in the following examples.

1 Standard systems (functional job analysis) a technique filing the data under three categories of Data, People and Things which produces a narrative job description.
2 Position analysis questionnaire, which breaks down the information to even more detail in terms of information input, mental processes, work output, relationships with other persons, job content and other job characteristics.
3 Management position questionnaire, a technique which compares jobs with other jobs to try and expose the differences between them.
4 Critical incident technique. This technique focuses on the recording and analysis of critical incidents that are considered imperative to the successful performance of a task or job and those that are related to failure.
5 Results orientated description. This analysis and description explicitly states the standards expected from the employee and by which their performance in the job will be evaluated.

Whichever method is used, the output will be a collection of information about the characteristics of the job which may then be used in the job design process.

Job design

The purpose of job design is to take the raw material presented by job analysis and turn it into a job description and person specification. A job design is essentially a creative process because it allows the manager or personnel practitioner to take the raw data and to describe it in units of work to be carried out and in that process create different types of job. There is no correct job design methodology; much will depend on the resources of the organisation, the range of tasks to be performed, and the locations they are to be performed in and this will heavily influence the jobs that result from it. Small businesses, for example, will usually compress a large range of tasks into individual jobs given the limits on their resources and the need for a multi-skilled approach by their staff.

Broadly speaking, the larger and more complex the organisation, the more diversity and specialisation that will exist. Whatever organisational style is taken in approaching job design, the content and style of the resultant job descriptions and person specifications will go a long way in determining the successful operation of the recruitment and selection processes that flow from it. Style is of particular importance and it is advisable to describe tasks or duties using active verbs and the present tense, use concise wording avoiding duplication, and distinguish between tasks and areas of responsibility which the post holder will be required to carry out. An example model job description is provided in Figure 5.1.

The job analysis and job design processes are not without their flaws however. First, a successful job description is based on the assumption that the job analysis is thorough enough in describing the range of tasks to be undertaken. This is more important the more technical and specific the tasks that are to be under-

JOB DESCRIPTION:	Personnel Officer (Recruitment)
REPORTS TO:	Personnel Manager
REPORTED TO BY:	Personnel Assistants (X 2)
JOB SUMMARY:	To manage all the organisation's main recruitment functions including job analysis reviews, preparation of job advertisements, representation at job fairs and all the administrative processes in connection with the resulting recruitment activity. To manage and direct the work of two Personnel Assistants in related recruitment tasks.

MAIN DUTIES:

1 To manage and direct all the organisation's main recruitment functions and to supervise staff performing day-to-day tasks in this respect.
2 To liaise with managers and undertake periodic reviews of jobs when they fall vacant to determine when and how a replacement should be found.
3 To identify and prepare all appropriate recruitment advertising tools, including advertisements in local, national and trade press and special campaigns (eg local radio and Internet) as required.
4 To manage all the main administrative tasks associated with responses to advertisements, preparation for short-listing and arrangements for interview and selection as required.
5 To ensure all appropriate procedures are followed to secure the appointment of staff including references, checks and contracts of appointment.
6 Other duties associated with recruitment that may be allocated from time to time.

Figure 5.1 Model outline job description

taken and is less critical when one is looking at more general managerial types of role. Modern organisations are also increasingly finding job descriptions restrictive because they are often used to encourage inflexibility and demarcation lines between staff and skill groups. They are also increasingly less appropriate for top management positions and project roles where individuals need to map their own work territory linked to a set of organisational objectives. Lastly, of course, job descriptions can very quickly become out of date in the dynamic modern organisational environment. But for all these drawbacks, the job description remains the cornerstone of a job design in the modern organisation and has the following benefits:

- It is a relatively simple system for describing the range of work required to be performed by individuals, groups and the organisation as a whole.
- It is a way of holding individuals accountable for the performance of those tasks and for linking any rewards to their performance.
- It allows organisations to clearly define their skill requirements and from this build their recruitment and selection, retention, training and development strategies.

The person specification

One of the major criticisms of personnel management in the 1970s and 80s, was that too much concentration was made on describing the kind of work that was required to be done and not enough attention paid to the critical factors required in defining the human characteristics to perform those tasks.

A model person specification is included in Figure 5.2. Note the welcome emerging tendency for the person specification not just to state the individual characteristics in terms of qualifications, experience and aptitude, but also to focus more on personality traits and how these different characteristics can be described.

	ESSENTIAL	DESIRABLE
PHYSICAL MAKE-UP	Good attendance record Ability to undertake training and duties compatible with the role	
ATTAINMENTS	General educational background	Relevant experience/qualification in health care Demonstrate caring experience (e.g. child/elderly relative)
SPECIAL APTITUDES	Ability to understand and carry out assigned tasks and instructions Effective communication and positive interpersonal skills Recognise own abilities and limitations Motivated and committed to work in health care	Prepare written reports on advice of registered nurse, relating to care of patients or specific occurrences
GENERAL REQUIREMENTS	Demonstrate an understanding of the responsibilities in relation to patient's property and valuables, respecting cultural values Demonstrate an understanding of the importance of cultural and other differences in providing safe and sensitive care to patients Responsible and caring attitude Interest in personal and professional development	General life experience/skills Able to assess priorities and identify patients' needs

Figure 5.2 Specification for healthcare assistant grade "A"

5.5 Recruitment strategy and practice

So, armed with clearly defined job description, person specification, produced as the result of some job analysis and job design processes, the organisation is ready to set in train the recruitment processes. But first, some further questions have to be asked even if a properly designed framework exists for a job and the description of the individual who is needed to fill it. Given the huge growth in the employee costs over the last twenty years, organisations usually use the opportunity of the occurrence of a vacancy to ask some testing questions about how, when and whether the post should be filled:

QUESTIONS

1 Can the work be reorganised amongst other employees or contracted out?
2 Can the work be filled by the use of overtime?
3 Is there scope for technology to replace manual input?
4 Can the job be broken down into different part-time or flexible patterns?

If, at the end of this critical analysis, it is determined there is a vacancy to be filled, then attention must turn to the various methods of recruitment and how these can be combined into an effective recruitment strategy.

Recruitment methods

The answer to three questions will usually help to determine the recruitment method that is best suited to fill the vacancy:

QUESTIONS

1 What is the type of job to be filled – is it managerial, executive, professional, technical, clerical, manually skilled or manually unskilled?.
2 Is it a single post or one of a number that need to be filled together at the same time?
3 How quickly does the post need to be filled and what is the budget available for the recruitment process?

There is a more bewildering array of recruitment methods available to the line or personnel manager of today than ever before. Figure 5.3 below lists the range of recruitment methods used by a sample of one hundred private and public organisations in 1997 for recruitment purposes. All of these methods have benefits and drawbacks as highlighted.

Recruitment advertising

Notwithstanding the growth in use of job search and head hunting as methods of recruitment, recruitment advertising remains far and away the most common way of attracting individuals to vacancies in an organisation. The job advertisement needs to be examined from three main aspects. First, where is the

METHOD	NUMBER OF ORGANISATIONS	PRO'S AND CON'S
Internal advertising	95	• Cheap and quick but limited choice
Advertising local paper	50	• Relatively cost-effective and speedy but limited field to choose from
Advertising national paper	72	• Quite expensive, lengthy, but wide appeal
Advertising trade journals	60	• Expensive, lengthy, but bespoke appeal
Advertising radio, TV	12	• Very expensive, speedy and responsive; wide appeal
Job centres	62	• Cheap and quick but very limited choice
School, college visits	40	• Cheap, longer-term method than can be tailored to job need
Word of mouth, personal recommendation	35	• Cheap and relatively speedy but haphazard
Executive search	15	• Expensive, quite lengthy but a quality tailored choice

Source: Survey via IPD 1998.

Figure 5.3 Range of recruitment methods

advertisement placed and at what audience is it aimed; secondly, what are the features of the advertisement based on this audience; thirdly, through what means is the advertisement placed?

Where to advertise

There are a number of potential avenues for recruitment advertising. The first, which is used by most organisations at sometime or other is the internal advertisement within an organisation. The advantage with this approach is that it is usually cheap requiring internal circulation only, it is likely to be able to attract a suitable candidate quickly without them having to go through the often arduous process of leaving their prior organisation; and it promotes career development within the organisation. The disadvantages, of course, are that the number of applicants are by definition limited and it may not be possible for the organisation to satisfy the person specification from this limited pool. For this reason, many organisations seek to recruit from outside the organisation using a number of different media. The choices open to them are advertising in the local press; advertising in the national press; or advertising in bespoke technical media. In recent years the use of the Internet, TV and local radio can be added to this as other forms of media available to the progressive employer.

Equally, the time-honoured tradition of placing a vacancy notice outside the shop or factory premises where vacancies existed is now used much less as patterns of employment have moved away from the immediate vicinity of the local community. The decision of where and how to place the advertisement will of course depend on the individual the organisation is trying to attract and the resources they have available to them. So if it is unskilled work and the advertising budget is limited an advertisement in the local press may well suffice, depending on the local employment market situation. If the position is professional or requires a particular skill set, then generally speaking the more the advertising budget and the more specialist the media it is placed in. It may well be possible to recruit a teacher through a national newspaper or through the teaching press, but a speech or language therapist may require some very specialist advertising indeed. Nonetheless, once a decision is made about where and how to advertise the organisation will need to turn its attention to the composition of the recruitment advert itself.

Recruitment advert

Compare some advertising copy for say a personnel manager post in the public sector twenty years ago to one today, and the difference will be startling. The flat, rather anodyne presentation of twenty years ago: "local Authority seeks high calibre personnel manager to manage and lead a busy Personnel Team . . ." is much more likely now to carry punch in the message and be presented in colour with a banner headline to attract an interested applicant of the right calibre. So, much more typically, one might find the job listed in a box in full colour under the heading "looking for the ultimate career challenge in personnel management? Then look no further". The job is much the same, but clearly the presentation of it and the market it is trying to reach is quite different.

The components in this modern advertisement, no matter how dynamically presented, will still include the following key information:

KEY POINTS

> ► Name and brief details about a recruiting organisation. This will say something about what the organisation does, its profile and its aims, even if in a few words.
> ► The job title and a brief synopsis of the duties. This does not call for a job description but will need to say something about the range and scope of work that the job will undertake. Job titles can have very different meanings in different settings so some explanation is required.
> ► Brief synopsis of the person specification. The key requirements of the person specification will need to be summarised to make sure that those responding to the advert can satisfy them. Also it will need to list formal qualifications, experience, and other special aptitudes required for the vacancy.
> ► Salary and benefits. Most employers now give full presentation to the salary and benefits available for the job. The terms of "salary negotiable" or "competitive salary" are still used in certain employment fields but are increasingly

less attractive to candidates. They will also want to know something about the hours of work, location, pension and other benefits available.

▶ Application arrangements. Finally, the interested applicant will need to know how they can obtain a job description, person specification or other employment documentation, described more fully below, and will be given a contact telephone number, e-mail address, website, or postal address to which inquiries can be directed.

Methods of advertising

Having determined where the organisation is going to advertise and what the nature of the advertising copy will be, there are essentially two choices open to the advertising organisation. First, organise the advertising process on an in-house basis or secondly, contract out to a specialist recruitment agency. The first is an attractive option if the organisation either recruits very infrequently and mainly uses local markets where the need for an attractive advertising copy is less, or has high quality resources in-house to run essentially an in-house recruitment advertising agency. Increasingly, however, small to medium-sized organisations contract the service out given the specialist nature of the activity and the discounted rate which advertising agencies can get in national and trade media for advertising space. Such agencies also usually have the facilities to design and produce high-quality advertisements at short notice and arrange for their appropriate insertion in the chosen media. Nowadays this also extends to the design of website pages, and even the preparation of television and radio commercials where the budget will allow.

Recruitment documentation

As referred to above, attention will also need to be given in the recruitment process to what goes in to documentation sent out in response to an inquiry for a job vacancy. Much again will depend on the nature of the job, the resources of the organisation, and the market they are aiming at. Organisations have quite different traditions and standards in this respect and there are widely differing practices. So, a small engineering firm looking to recruit a receptionist locally may place their advertisement in a local newspaper and simply send out a brief job description and person specification in response to a vacancy inquiry. A large multinational company, on the other hand, seeking to recruit a top executive will probably put together a highly professional, expensive recruitment brochure, designed specifically for the job in question, that will include job description, person specification, details of salary and benefits, information about the organisation, perhaps a copy of their business plan and a whole range of ancillary information to help inform and attract a high-calibre candidate. Each organisation will also have its own design for eliciting a job application. Some ask for *curriculum vitaes* (CV.), whilst others ask for the completion of an application form.

Generally speaking, there used to be a divide between public and private sectors with the former looking for the completion of an application form and the latter preferring the CV. Today the distinctions are much more blurred, and the most senior positions sometimes call for both. The advantage of the application form is that it allows the recruiting organisation to dictate the nature of the information provided by asking the candidate to fill in answers to questions. The CV, of course, is very much in the hands of the applying individual who can tailor their own information and put the best presentation on it. Whichever form the recruiting organisation uses, it is also likely to ask the applying candidate to supply other information such as an occupational health declaration, names of references, or referees who may be approached, and sometimes a birth certificate or other personal information about the employee depending on the nature of the job being filled.

5.6 Selection techniques

In this section we will examine what the recruiting organisation does with the completed application forms or CVs it collects in response to recruitment advertising, executive search or whichever other form of recruitment method it utilises. There are a number of clear stages in the selection process that constitute a good practice approach, and these can be summarised as short-listing, tests and exercises, presentations, the selection interview, recording the outcomes, making a decision, and securing the appointment. We will examine each of these stages in turn.

Short-listing

Short-listing is a key activity in the recruitment and selection process, not the least that it is the first stage at which decisions are made about the suitability of individuals and has implications for the final appointment decision and equal opportunities. Because it is a stage of the process that may be open to a challenge (that is there may be a complaint from a candidate that they have been discriminated against in a decision to exclude them from the final short-list), there are clear principles to be adopted.

KEY POINTS

> ▶ All or as many as possible of the final *interview panel* should be involved in the short-listing process. They should use only the completed application forms or CVs as a basis for short-listing.
> ▶ They should short list only against the *essential and desirable criteria* included within the person specification.
> ▶ The decisions relating to the short-listing process should be *recorded* in some way.

It is essential that this stage of the process remains objective, and does not rely on extraneous information. So the sole considerations are that the individual meets the person specification and that the number of applicants is whittled down to a reasonable and manageable number to produce a short-list for final selection. What this reasonable number is will depend on the number of jobs available, the resources of the organisation, and the importance of the position. Typically, a final short-list of five or six candidates is a desirable number from which to make the final selection decision for each vacant post. So, for example, a company looking to recruit half a dozen trainee sales representatives may look to make this selection from a short-list of twenty-five or thirty candidates. At the other end of the spectrum, there may occasionally only be two or three candidates who meet the person specification or indeed none at all.

In these circumstances the organisation will have to make a decision about whether it proceeds to the next stage of the recruitment process or aborts it because the choice available to it is not sufficient. It is important to remember here that having agreed a person specification, the organisation should stick to it because it is a disclosable document to a court or a tribunal in the event of a challenge. So, if the organisation says certain criteria are essential, then all short-listed candidates will be expected to meet these in full. Equally, desirable criteria are just that and do not have to be met in full by each candidate unless there is a huge over-subscription for the post.

Tests and exercises

Having made a decision on the composition of the short-list, the organisation will then have to determine the composition of the final selection stage. One consideration that finds favour with many organisations now is the inclusion in the final selection stage of some form of testing and practical exercises against which to assess candidates. The most common form of tests in use in selection practice today are psychometric tests which are usually operated under licence by a major supplier such as Savil and Holdsworth or Pricewaterhouse Coopers, and are designed to test personality, managerial competencies, numerical ability, or indeed any other skill requirement of the job in question. These tests have been benchmarked and evaluated by use in organisations over a number of years and are generally regarded as reputable.

However, some of them have attracted criticism for not favouring the interests of candidates from ethnic minority backgrounds because they require an often sophisticated use of an application of the English language. However, many of the leading brands are aware of this criticism and design their tests accordingly. The result of the test will be a score which can be compared to the performance of candidates both in the trawl in question, or by comparison with candidates generally for jobs of that type in the recruitment market as a whole. The results will be a useful addition to, but not a determinant of the outcome of the selection process.

Whilst such psychometric tests are often used for senior professional managerial positions, other kinds of application may warrant the use of some other form of test of competence or ability. Traditionally this has taken the form of, for example, a typing test for a word processor operator, or sometimes the use of a role play exercise for those who use interactive or communication skills in their work (for example receptionist). Much will depend on the nature of the skill required and how easily it can be practised or tested in a simulated environment.

So it may be easier to test the application of some form of craft or practical skill than the more nebulous people-related skills that many occupations require in service industries today. Whatever approach is adopted, the recruiting organisation will have to decide how to organise the test, whether to run it alongside the final recruitment interview and what weight to attach to the results. Passing such a test with flying colours does not necessarily mean the individual is the best candidate for the job, and received wisdom suggests that the results of such tests should be used as one factor only in deciding on the final appointment.

Presentations

Alongside the use of tests and exercises, the presentation is often used in the final selection interview to test the mental ability of the applying candidates. Presentations are often used in recruiting for jobs where the communication and presentation skill of the individual is a key part of the work involved. So for a training officer or a sales manager it will be quite reasonable to ask them to come to the interview prepared to give a ten-minute presentation on a relevant topic area. The use of such presentation techniques is usually used to assess three skill areas:

1. The ability of the candidate to *analyse* information and present it coherently to a diverse group of people (the selection panel)
2. The ability of the individual to collect information and present it in an *accessible form* (either by the use of an overhead projector, slides, or even some computer application)
3. The *communication and presentation* skills of the individual in the clarity of their presentation and the coherence of their representation of it.

When deciding whether or not to use such a presentation technique, the selection panel must first decide what they are looking to judge from it and how they will assess it. So, for example, if all the above factors are going to be assessed, the panel will need to agree some rating scale to compare the differing presentations of the candidates. It will not be enough simply that one produces high-quality slides whilst another does not as the assessment is looking for a more all-round performance.

The selection interview

Whether or not any ancillary tests or exercises are used, the selection interview remains the tried and tested way most organisations undertake their final selection processes. The selection interview, of course, is not a perfect tool in itself. It has inherent weaknesses in that it is subjective, it is judging people in an artificial situation and is making snapshot judgements about often long-term career development and about presentation given in a very short period of time. Nonetheless, it remains the best recruitment tool available and is universally used as is the short-listing process. The approach to the conduct of the selection interview is one of the key stages of the recruitment and selection process and requires a methodical approach:

The composition of the selection panel

Organisations adopt very different approaches to the composition of their selection panels. Good practice suggests this should always include the line manager for the position in question, a personnel representative or advisor, and in some cases an external assessor or professional advisor depending on the nature of the post in question. Of equal importance may be the gender and racial mix of the panel depending on the mix of the candidates being interviewed. A mix of genders is always preferable where there are candidates of both genders, and a similar approach should be adopted to matters of ethnic origin where at all possible. This is not political correctness, but rather trying to ensure a sound equal opportunities approach and to help the candidates for the job feel as much at ease as possible. Many good employers now also insist that those who sit on selection panels have undergone training in recruitment and selection practices and have the necessary skills to undertake this important task. After all, they reason, they are making very important investment decisions on behalf of the organisation and so should possess the necessary competence to do so.

The format for the interview

Again much will depend on the nature of the organisation and the job in question. If the interview is part of a much more sophisticated assessment centre approach, which includes psychometric tests, presentations, a visit to the workplace, informal meetings or even a lunch with colleagues, as well as the final interview itself, then the format of the interview will be dictated partly by these other events. It may be, for example, that the panel will wish to have the result of any tests or exercises undertaken in front of them when they conduct the interview. Generally speaking, the panel should elect a chairman (not necessarily the most senior person and often the immediate line manager for the post in question) to organise the panel and to provide the introductions. A typical good practice approach for a selection panel would be as follows:

The panel's procedure

The *panel meet* before the final interviews and discuss the range of questions they would like to ask based on the person specification and the applications in front of them.

KEY POINTS

▶ Each panel member will agree the *appropriate questions* they will ask and will ask the same questions of each candidate
▶ The chairman of the panel will provide the *introduction* to each panel member and explain their role, and explain what the *composition* and length of the interview will be. Each panel member should then ask their questions in turn capturing the *answers* in note form
▶ Each candidate should be given the opportunity to ask one or more *questions* of the panel

▶ Once the candidate has left the interview the panel should record their *assessment* of him or her using an agreed pro forma (see example interview assessment grid at Figure 5.4).

This recording aspect of the selection interview is very important. It has a number of benefits if performed properly. First, once the panel reach their final decision it allows an accurate record of the reasons for that decision to be played back to the candidates telling them why they have been successful or unsuccessful in this case. This feedback should normally be handled by the chair of the panel or one other nominated member, but not different people as this will lead to inconsistencies in the feedback process. The other advantage of having clear records of the interview is in the event of any challenge against a decision made on equal opportunities grounds. So, if a woman complains of sex discrimination following the appointment of a male candidate, the panel will be able to clearly show why they chose the male candidate and why he was the preferred candidate in this case. Without accurate records, this will be difficult to substantiate and almost impossible for the members of the panel to have accurate recall of, some months after the event.

CANDIDATE'S NAME:. _____	
JOB TITLE: _____	
INTERVIEWER'S NAME: _____	
DATE OF INTERVIEW: _____	

ASSESSMENT SCALE:
1 = Poor candidate 2 = Below acceptable standard 3 = Fair, borderline
4 = Good candidate, appointable 5 = Exceptional candidate, appointable

EDUCATION AND QUALIFICATIONS	1 2 3 4 5
WORK EXPERIENCE AND TRACK RECORD	1 2 3 4 5
PERSONALITY AND STYLE	1 2 3 4 5
ATTITUDE AND MOTIVATION	1 2 3 4 5
HEALTH	1 2 3 4 5
Notes:	
Suitable for appointment:	YES/NO
Signed: _____	Date: _____

Figure 5.4   Model interview assessment grid

Once a decision is made, of course, this can then be communicated to the successful candidate and once an initial verbal offer has been made effectively a contract of employment begins to be formed (see Chapter 3). At this point the offer is normally put in writing by the personnel or HR department giving details of pay and terms and the terms and conditions of employment that will apply. Unsuccessful candidates should also receive letters explaining why they were not appointed to follow up the verbal rejection that comes from the chair of the panel or other nominated panel member.

The appointment

So, with the final selection decision made which is the culmination of the recruitment advertising, application, short-listing, testing, presentation, and interviewing process, all that remains for the employment organisation to do is secure the services of the individual it has offered the position to. Assuming matters of salary and terms and conditions can be successfully negotiated and secured, there is the matter of checks and references to pursue. These have become increasingly important aspects of the recruitment and selection process, particularly in occupations where individuals work with vulnerable or at-risk groups. It is for this reason that exemptions were made to the *Rehabilitation of Offenders Act 1974* which means that those who have been found guilty of crimes who seek to work with the vulnerable do not enjoy the same provisions regarding spent convictions as other offenders do when applying for mainstream positions.

So, for example, social workers employed to work with children, teachers, or those who work with the elderly or the mentally ill are required to have a police check undertaken about them which will disclose any previous convictions. Refusal of employment on these grounds will be a legal reason provided the nature of the occupation justifies it, and provided the nature of the offence is serious. For the same reason, failure by an applicant to disclose such a criminal conviction for one of these "reserved" occupations will also be a reason to make them ineligible for appointment. The failure of organisations in education and social care to undertake such checks in recent years has often been found to be at the root of major inquiries into abuse in child care and led to the establishment of such national inquiries into recruitment and selection practices as the *Warner Inquiry* into the appointment and selection of staff working in children's homes (1993). Specialist advice and reference to the codes of practice produced by these inquiries should be sought by those personnel practitioners working in these specialist fields.

References are an important addition to the information available to the employing organisation in deciding whether or not to confirm an offer of appointment. The verbal offer of appointment following interview is normally made subject to satisfactory references, health checks and sometimes police checks, and careful account should be taken of these references in determining whether or not to offer a post. Those providing references are required to be honest and accurate in doing so under the law, and ambiguous or nebulous wording in references supplied by previous employers should be followed up in writing or on the telephone if doubts remained, or discussed with the individual themselves. Remember that at the stage it is provided the reference is a confidential document provided by the referee, but once it becomes part of the employee's personal file it may well be disclosable to the employee (see Chapter 14 for reference to recent case law in this area). However, this is very much a case of "buyer beware". If a previous employer tells you that the person to whom you are considering offering the job was sacked for dishonesty or fraud, then, unless the applicant can show that this was wholly unjustified, they are best avoided.

Similarly, the occupational health check or screening that is undertaken prior to employment is an important part of the information available before the offer is confirmed. Much again will depend on the practice used by the employing organisation (see Chapter 12 for more details), but this screening process should basically say whether or not the individual is fit to undertake the work required of them. This does not mean they have to be in perfect health, and indeed the employment of those with disabilities is to be encouraged providing they can perform the work required. The Occupational Health Advisor or Physician should be able to advise on this and may require a copy of the job description or person specification to help them make this judgement, and they may undertake a full medical or more detailed examination where they have doubts. Nonetheless, as with the reference their advice should be considered as part of the final appointment decision-making process.

A summary of the recruitment and selection process in overview terms is provided in Figure 5.5.

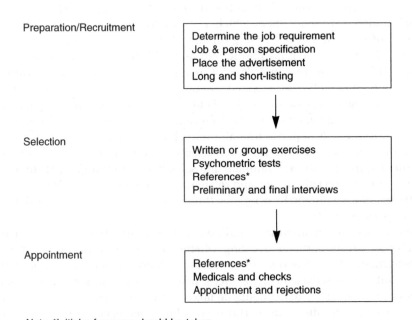

Note: *Initial references should be taken up prior to interview and followed up upon appointment.

Figure 5.5 Overview of recruitment and selection process

5.7 Retention

Although as an HRM topic area, the issue of retention could be as easily discussed under the heading of training and development, or employee relations, it is traditionally appended to recruitment and selection because research has shown that success in retaining staff begins with the recruitment and selection processes. Many organisations fail to realise that the processes they pursue in recruiting and selecting staff are often the best public relations they can buy for their organisation and company. So, the organisation that shows interest, provides accurate and timely information and is caring towards the prospective or new employee is much more likely to retain their services in the future. Retention studies are varied and complex, and warrant a detailed examination beyond the scope of this book. For the purposes of this work, however, we will look at four key components to successful retention: induction; terms and conditions of employment; training and development; and communication and support facilities.

Induction

A large proportion of new starters resign in the first few weeks of their employment; the reasons are many and varied but are usually because it is difficult for them to settle into the new organisation with its different ways of working and inevitably strange environment. Organisations therefore do all they can to try and militate against this tendency in the first few weeks of appointment by investing in induction training programmes. Research shows that the greater the investment in employees at this stage, the less the likelihood of a retention problem. The construction of the induction training programme will depend very much on the environment and culture of the organisation the new recruit is joining. So, for example, a newly recruited prison officer will have the focus of their induction work, security and associated procedures because clearly this is an important aspect of a prison officer's work. Conversely, the induction for a retail check-out operator will focus very much on till procedure and customer service. The typical components of a standard induction programme which can run for hours, days or even weeks is as follows:

- The organisation, its history, development, management and activity
- Personnel policies
- Terms of conditions of employment
- Employee benefits and services
- Physical facilities in the workplace
- An outline of the different jobs and work entailed in the organisation
- Health and safety measures
- Social interaction with other employees
- Physical orientation to the workplace

Many organisations invest enormous resources in their induction programmes and they usually pay benefits. Indeed secondary, tertiary or follow-up induction programmes are used by many organisations to ensure all the information they wish to impart is properly disclosed to employees over a period of time and the individual has the opportunity to properly assimilate into the new working environment.

Terms and conditions of employment

As is dealt with in more detail in Chapter 6 the pay and benefits package offered by an organisation will often go a long way in determining its success in recruitment and retention. Pay is clearly an important factor in itself although less important than many employers think, as many retention studies show. Often, the important consideration in terms of remuneration is the "felt fairness" of the remuneration package on offer when individuals compare their pay with that of colleagues and comparable pay groups. However, the natural human tendency in the workplace is for self-development and employees will often look at the other terms and conditions of employment as key factors in successful retention. So it may often be some of the less obvious fringe benefits that make the difference between an individual staying with an organisation or not. Employees who are tied into good pension schemes later in their careers are much more likely to stick with an organisation than not because of the risk of disruption to their retirement benefits caused by leaving the organisation and the pension scheme. Similarly, individuals who accrue generous leave entitlements linked to their length of service are much more likely to stay than not. What individuals are often looking for in the pay and benefits package, however, is some reflection of their value and worth to the organisation and this goes beyond the remunerative value of their pay and conditions package.

Training and career development

Once established at work with a supportive set of terms and conditions most employees will be interested in advancing and developing their careers. Few talented and successful individuals want to stand still and most want to feel that they are learning and progressing in the workplace. The organisations that invest in the training and development of their staff, particularly those that operate to *Investors in People standards*, are therefore much more likely to succeed in retaining their staff than those that do not. First, the organisation is more likely to produce the skills it requires and therefore has less need to look to the open recruitment market, and secondly the individuals are likely to have scope for personal growth and development whilst remaining within the organisation. Assuming this investment in training and development can be linked to these individuals' own personal career progression, then the ideal marriage will have been found. Of course there is a risk that the more an organisation invests in the employee's personal development, the more at risk it is to losing them to the vagaries of the employment marketplace. Whilst this is undeniably true, the nurturing and development of the individual in terms of training investment is clearly a strong factor of success in staff retention (see Chapter 9).

Communication and employee support

As we explore this "softer" retention territory, studies of the subject will show that the organisation that invests heavily in communicating with and supporting individual employees again is likely to fare much better than those that do not. Communication is an explicit part of the *Investors in People* framework and it is an important facet of employee development because employees who feel they are well communicated with and have the opportunity readily to contribute their views and feedback are much more likely to identify with the organisation's goals and direction and to be better motivated than those who do not. Indeed, good and strong communications have a mercurial attraction for most organisational analysts. Studies of successful organisations that do repeatedly well in the recruitment and retention stakes consistently show those that have good communication frameworks and networks to be amongst the leading organisations. Similarly, a common symptom of a failing organisation that suffers from poor employee motivation and morale and does less well in terms of recruitment and retention is a high level of poor communications.

There are a number of forms for communication to take:

KEY POINTS

- ▶ Written communication in the form of in-house journals, magazines and briefing
- ▶ Team briefing, the cascade system for briefing from the top down to the bottom of the organisation
- ▶ Staff appraisal and personal development planning on a cyclical and systematic basis
- ▶ Staff forums and consultation linked to representation by trade unions in the workplace
- ▶ Staff development groups and employee networks which build on the top–down communication basis.

The organisation that communicates well both vertically and horizontally, also usually has as a feature of its employment practices good employee support networks and facilities. The reputation an organisation has as a "good and caring employer" is often determined by the way it supports employees when they are sick, experience personal problems, or have difficulty in coping with the demands of the job. So investment in employee welfare schemes, counselling and even sports and social facilities are much more likely to help retain and motivate staff than not. Some of these concepts are explored in more detail at Chapter 13.

So, in summary, employee retention is an equally important aspect of HRM activity as is recruitment and selection. There is little point in an organisation performing successfully in the recruitment markets if it is unable to retain its best calibre staff because it is analogous to "filling the bath with the plug left out". Good retention practice therefore goes hand-in-hand with good recruitment and selection in an organisation and is part of a thread that runs through good and successful employers all the way from the time employees join the organisation, through their induction, training, development, career progression and support.

5.8 Problem areas

QUESTION:
We are having difficulty in filling a key financial management position within my company, and I have suggested using an Executive Search Organisation for this purpose. However, the HR director is opposed to it on the grounds that it is not equal opportunity friendly. Nonetheless our attempts to recruit using recruitment advertising in the past have failed and we desperately need to fill this job. What are the arguments for and against the use of executive search?

ANSWER:
It is true that some organisations are loathe to use executive search or head hunters to fill certain positions because processes do not always invite applications on an open basis to stand the tests of true equal opportunities policies. Nonetheless if an organisation has attempted to fill a job by open recruitment and has strong equal opportunities policies, it is not necessarily incompatible to use executive search or head-hunting methods to fill the job. After all, the argument will be that the organisation has attempted to use open recruitment methods and its overriding responsibility is to fill the key position. You may wish to explore some other alternatives including secondments or job placements with another organisation with whom a reciprocal arrangement can be made, or indeed it may be possible to test the employment market by using other recruitment methods rather than national or trade press. The Internet is increasingly used as a recruitment tool and local radio has also been successfully used by a number of organisations to supplement the more traditional methods.

Good executive search consultants also do not use underhand methods to identify suitable candidates. Broadly, they are going to be searching the same areas that would be tested through the normal advertising media, but rather taking an individual approach to identify potentially suitable candidates and encourage their application for a job. Indeed it is this personal approach that often makes the difference compared to the open recruitment method. Of course, the organisation that always uses executive search to fill its key positions is much more open to accusations about breaches of equal opportunities policies than those that do not and this should provide some reassurance to your director on this issue.

QUESTION:
Our organisation seems to have such a poor track record in recruiting to key appointments. Although it invests heavily in recruitment advertising, it just does not seem to make good quality decisions at the final interview stage and very often has to unpick appointments in the first weeks of an individual starting. The managing director has asked me to have a look at where we are going wrong. Would you provide me with a few clues?

ANSWER:

The logical starting point is to undertake an audit of recruitment and selection methods in the organisation using the advice in this chapter as a template for your study. Many organisations are very successful in identifying the technical competences they require for individuals to perform jobs successfully, but choose people who are ill-suited to work in the organisation either because their personality is not right for the team they are joining or because they are not likely to fit in with the organisational culture. This does not mean that the organisation needs to recruit "clones" to fit in with the company ethos, but there is a particular kind of individual who will work in some environments and not in others. There is an increasing focus on personality traits and what is referred to as "emotional intelligence" in determining whether or not an individual has the right characteristics to succeed in an organisation. Psychometric tests, and particularly the use of personality tests, can go some way to help determine whether individuals have what it takes to succeed in a particular environment.

Although there are some notable examples of individuals succeeding in quite different sectors from the ones they have previously worked in, generally speaking people find it difficult to adjust to the different cultures and environments and if an organisation is looking for quick results this can lead to frustration in the early weeks of an appointment. Many commercial and private sector managers struggle in the public sector, and vice versa, for this reason. It is not about the skill sets for the job, which are often very common, but more about culture and style and ways of working. Your organisation may want to try concentrating more on these cultural issues by getting candidates for jobs to undertake informal workplace visits and "meet and greet" events so that you can see them interacting with people in the workplace. Although this is, to a degree, still a false situation, you are much more likely to gain a fuller picture of their personality and style in this setting than in a formal interview. Conversely, of course, you may find that it is the technical requirements where the problems lie, and this may suggest a strengthening of job specifications, short-listing and interview procedures to help the identification of the right person for the job.

QUESTION:

The managing director of my company is a great believer in the "hiring and firing" principle of staff recruitment and retention. She says she would rather spend money identifying the right person from the marketplace and getting a year's good work out of them than trying to invest in the long term, because, she says, in the end employee's performance always falls away after a number of years. Isn't there some truth in this approach?

ANSWER:

There may well be some validity to what your managing director says depending on the nature of the market and the business you operate in. There is no doubt that in high profit/high turnover industries, such as the investment markets in the City of London, this approach is often used because the injection of new blood regularly and high-pressure jobs that create burn-out beg a constant throughput of new ideas and new people. But most organisations need some stability to aid their planning and investment decisions and want to hang on to their best people. If this is the requirement then a hiring and firing approach is likely to be very wasteful and expensive because no sooner have you identified the right talent than they themselves will be head hunted or lost to a competitor organisation. It is interesting to note here that some of the most successful multinational companies in the world, notably Microsoft and Virgin, succeed on the principle of quality recruitment and retention practices and have many long-serving employees. It is this retention of knowledge and skills that allows them to enjoy business success year in and year out rather than constantly having to concentrate their energies on identifying new talent, although some new blood is obviously an important part of the equation for them.

5.9 Activity

Design a recruitment advertisement for a secretarial position within your organisation. Assume that this post is going to be quite difficult to fill in a competitive market, and produce advertising copy that accentuates the benefits of working for your organisation, the terms and conditions on offer, and identifies the calibre of individual you are looking for. For the purposes of being creative, you can assume that the advertising budget is unlimited at this stage.

5.10 Checklist

- ▶ Recruitment and retention constitute some of the most traditional aspects of Personnel activity.
- ▶ Retention is of equal importance and is considered alongside recruitment and selection issues.
- ▶ There is an extensive legal framework underpinning this area of activity including the *Equal Pay, Discrimination* and *Rehabilitation of Offenders Acts.*
- ▶ The starting point for filling a vacancy is the issue of what is the job to be filled. Job design and job analysis techniques are also explored.
- ▶ A model job description and person specification are provided and are the foundation of the recruitment and selection process.
- ▶ In terms of recruitment strategy a range of recruitment methods are explained.
- ▶ Recruitment advertising is a common aspect and the process, from design to response, is explored.
- ▶ The various stages of the selection process are described from a good practice perspective.
- ▶ Procedural aspects connected with securing a safe appointment at the end of the process are examined.
- ▶ Evidence shows that major themes for retention are induction, terms and conditions of employment, training and career development, and communication.

⚞ 6 Pay and benefits

6.1 Introduction

As the complexity of HRM has grown over the last twenty-five years, with increasingly more complex demands placed by employers on employees in terms of what they expect in work and effort, so too have the demands of employees grown in terms of flexibility in the pay and benefits they receive. As outlined in Chapter 3, the receipt of appropriate remuneration and benefits has always been one of the common law duties placed on the employer by way of consideration for the work that employees undertake encapsulated in the contract of employment. For as long as the employment relationship is recorded to have existed in history, the labourer has always received recompense for his/her endeavours by way of pay and/or benefits in kind. In the feudal system of 700 years ago, the labourers of the day were tied to their work (normally agricultural or craft in nature) and in return would receive some share of the spoils of the land by way of food, basic accommodation and even some rights to land.

The Industrial Revolution of the eighteenth century started to put in place the employment relationship as we know it today, with large numbers of the workers engaged by companies to undertake labour or contracted hours of work (although often excessive and abused by the employers) in return for pay in the form of wages. As the skills required of the new industrial markets grew, so the need for employers to become more and more competitive in what they paid their employees, and in some of the associated benefits they afforded them, increased similarly. So, by the beginning of the nineteenth century, it was no longer enough to recompense the skilled artisan by paying a daily or weekly wage. Progressive employers realised that if they invested in the training and education of their employees, provided facilities for meals and hygiene, and even, in the most sophisticated examples, extended facilities for wives and children they were more likely to recruit and retain the services of the most skilled employees if their services were at a premium in the labour markets of the day.

In this chapter we will examine some of the present-day relationships between employers and employees in HRM terms and the impact that pay and benefits have on the modern employment relationship. As we stand in the middle of the information, technology and electronic commerce revolution and similar massive upheavals to labour markets, the way employers seek to reward employees through pay and benefits are also changing enormously. The accent today is providing competitive remuneration packages with new innovative methods of providing benefits to staff that will make the difference in terms of the recruitment and retention package. Indeed, much has changed from the days when the maxim "a fair day's pay for a fair day's work" described the received wisdom about the pay and benefits package that the good employer should use. In modern labour markets, the supply and demand of appropriate skills are much more likely to regulate the basis for determination of pay and benefits that exist for particular occupations in particular industries at a given time. Of course, these supply and demand factors in the labour market are underpinned by broader economic factors that will dictate the organisation's ability to pay their labour, and the relative supply of the skills that they need in their workforce.

6.2 Legal framework

In this section we will examine some of the legislative developments over the last thirty years, which underpin the way that pay and benefits have developed in the modern contract of employment. The legislation is largely directed at regulating equity and fairness; seeking to establish minimum rates of pay; regulating the way that certain benefits are afforded to employees and, on rare occasions, have even sought to regulate increases in salary levels, particularly in the public sector.

Employment Rights Act 1996

The rate of pay, the intervals at which payment is made and provision for bonus commission, overtime, holidays, sick pay and other terms and conditions of employment, must be included in the written particulars of the contract of employment given by the employer to the employee, the provisions for which are prescribed in this legislation. Further details of contractual provisions can be found in Chapter 3.

Wages Act 1986

This legislation previously regulated the deductions which may be made from employee's pay and made special provision for employees in retail employment. The *Wages Act* itself superseded the *Truck Act 1831*, which placed restrictions on the way in which the payment of wages to manual and other workers may be made, largely being required in cash. The wages that replace these provisions and the method of payment are now determined by the contract of employment. The *Wages Act* provisions which were consolidated into the *Employment Rights Act 1996*, state that no deduction from a worker's wages may be made unless either:

- it is required or permitted by *statutory* or *contractual provision*; or
- the worker has given his or her prior *written consent* to the deduction.

The law also provides some useful definitions about what is not included within the definition of a "wage":

- *loans* or advances of salary
- payments in respect of *expenses* for travel or subsistence
- payments by way of *pensions*
- *redundancy* payments
- *gratuities* or other allowances

The Equal Pay Act 1970

The provisions of this legislation seek to guarantee equal pay for work of equal value so as to avoid discrimination between individuals on grounds of gender where issues of pay are concerned.

The National Minimum Wage Act 1998

This important legislation received Royal Assent on 31 July 1998, and provided the first ever universal legislation covering minimum wages in the UK. Previously, the only enforceable legal agreements relating to minimum pay other than those included in individual contracts of employment related to payments guaranteed by the Low Pay Commission for servicing categories of retail and agricultural workers. The new law is overseen by the Low Pay Commission, who will periodically uprate the national minimum wage provisions subject to government endorsement. The main provision of the Act, which applies to all workers over 18 years of age is as follows:

- with effect from April 1999 the national minimum wage is £3.60 per hour (16- and 17-year-olds and any person engaged on a formal apprenticeship are excluded from the right to this minimum wage)
- a lower rate (called the development rate) is payable to 18 to 21-year-olds and workers starting a new job with a new employer and receiving accredited training. The development rate is £3.00 per hour from April 1999 and £3.20 per hour from June 2000.

The Working Time Regulations 1998

One of the most common misconceptions in UK Employment Law prior to the adoption of the working time regulations was that there was a minimum statutory entitlement to paid holiday for employees in the UK; there was not!

Other than decreeing which days should be regarded as statutory and bank holidays, and other than prescriptions for annual leave included in contracts of employment, the law previously made no stipulation about holiday entitlement, and even bank holidays were not statutorily required to be holidays for employees unless their employer agreed so. The adoption of the working time regulations, which have been adopted under an overriding health and safety directive, is that workers have a statutory right to paid holiday for the first time. All qualifying workers will be entitled to at least three weeks' annual leave in each leave year, rising to four weeks from November 1999.

The Employment Protection Act 1975

This Act created for the first time new statutory rights for women employees, including paid maternity leave and the right for paid time off for ante-natal care. They were updated in the *Employment Protection (Consolidation Act) 1978*, the *Employment Act 1980*, further extended by the *Trade Union Reform and Employment Rights Act 1993*, and are now finally consolidated into the *Employment Rights Act 1996*. The following provisions apply:

- paid time off to receive *ante-natal care*
- fourteen weeks' *maternity leave*
- *protection from dismissal* by reason of pregnancy or child birth
- *maternity pay*
- *return to work* after maternity leave

These provisions are expanded in section 6.7, Maternity Rights and Benefits, below.

Income Tax Regulations 1993

Updated annually, these regulations were consolidated in the *Trade Union Reform and Employment Rights Act 1993* and described the main provisions relating to Pay As You Earn (PAYE) and other statutory systems for deducting Income Tax from employees' pay. Under the PAYE arrangements, the employer effectively acts as a tax collector for the Inland Revenue. In addition, the PAYE system collects national insurance contributions from both the employee and the employer. Employers are provided with a schedule of deductions (known as form P11) for each employee known to be earning amounts above the PAYE threshold which are regulated annually in the Chancellor of the Exchequer's budget. The Inland Revenue will supply details of coding and tax allowances for individual employees that will determine the appropriate amount of tax to be deducted for each employee.

The code will vary according to the individual circumstances of the employee and, for example, for the tax year 2000/2001 will provide an allowance for a single or married person of £4,300 a year, below which no income tax is payable. The regulations also provide for employers to provide employees with certificates of earnings when they transfer from one employment to another, or at the end of each tax year. Form P45, shows the details of accumulative pay and tax paid to date upon leaving the last employment and the employee's tax code. This document is normally needed to pass on to a new employer or upon request to the Inland Revenue. Similarly, each employer must give to each employee in employment on 5 April each year a Form P60 which shows the total taxable pay and net tax deducted, and the tax code used in the previous tax year. It will also include details of national insurance contributions. Under the new Inland Revenue self-assessment scheme, employers now have to provide employees with a copy of Form P11.D, which relates to all expenses payments and other benefits which attract tax, by 6 July. Finally, the regulations also spell out the provisions for payroll giving schemes whereby employees can authorise their employers to deduct up to £1,200 in any tax year from their earnings before tax to pass on to nominated charities (the so-called Pay As You Give arrangements).

Statutory Maternity Pay and Statutory Sick Pay Regulations 1996

These regulations, which again are subject to periodic updating, govern the main rules relating to the payment of Statutory Sick Pay (SSP) and Statutory Maternity Pay (SMP) to eligible employees.

The main provisions for statutory sick pay are as follows:

- The essential requirements for qualification are that an employee must have *4 or more* consecutive days of sickness during which he or she is too ill to be capable of doing work;
- *notify* his or her absence to the employer;
- *supply evidence* of incapacity (self certificate for periods of 4 to 7 days and a doctor's certificate for all periods in excess of 7 days) to become entitled to payment of statutory sick pay.

SSP is not payable for the first 3 qualifying days of sickness (known as the period for incapacity for work) but is payable from the fourth qualifying day onwards until a maximum period of entitlement, currently 28 weeks in any period of entitlement. Of course, many employers have more generous sick pay arrangements as provided for within the contract of employment. Any contractual remuneration paid to an employee for a day of sickness has to be offset against SSP, with employers now responsible for the main administration on behalf of the government.

The entitlement to statutory maternity pay depends on the satisfaction of four main conditions.

1. An employee must have been *continuously employed* by her employer for at least 26 weeks ending with the week immediately preceding the fourteenth week before the expected week of confinement.
2. She must have *ceased to work* for the employer wholly or partly because of pregnancy or confinement.
3. Her *normal weekly earnings* for the period of 8 weeks ending with the week immediately preceding the fourteenth week before the expected week of confinement must not be less than the lower limit for the payment of national insurance contributions (£64 per week in 1999/2000)
4. She must have become pregnant and be confined before reaching the start of the *eleventh week* before the expected week of confinement.

SMP is payable in respect of each week during the maternity pay period which is a period of *18 consecutive* weeks. In general when it starts depends upon when the employee gives notice and stops work. However, the first week of the period cannot be earlier than the eleventh week before the expected week of confinement and not later than the week immediately following the week of confinement. Therefore a female employee may continue to work until the actual date of confinement and still retain her entitlement to 18 weeks of SMP.

6.3 Pay and pay systems

Within the contract of employment, details determining how pay is arrived at for the employment involved, when pay is made, and how changes in pay will be negotiated or determined, will be included. However, whatever the arrangements, the contract for payment will need to meet a number of objectives to satisfy both the employee and employer. Clearly, both parties come with different perspectives, the employer usually wishing to secure the best work and services they can for the least outlay, and the employees naturally wishing to maximise their income through employment. These objectives can be summarised as follows:

Employee objectives:

Purchasing power

The absolute amount of earnings will largely determine the standard of living of the employee with most employees' aim being to maximise their income and so enhance their purchasing power. Modern experience suggests that incomes never keep pace with personal expectations as the desire for betterment is also a universal motivator. Inflation and the cost of living is also likely to erode purchasing power and for this reason pay needs at least to attempt to keep pace with changes in the retail price index.

Felt fair

The notion of a "fair day's pay for a fair day's work" is an old adage, but still underpins the feeling of felt fairness in employment. Most complaints about pay in the workplace are not about the absolute level of pay that individuals receive, but about the pay they receive relative to that of colleagues who they may subjectively judge may be making more or less of a contribution. Such dissatisfaction, of course, can lead to wider de-motivation in the job and is usually symptomatic of broader employment-related problems.

Rights

A feeling that employees have a right to a share of profits particularly affects employees who worked in the private sector. This has been particularly enhanced in recent years with the growth in employee share schemes, profit- and performance-related pay that explicitly tie the profitability and success of the organisation to the employer's growth in income.

Relativities

As referred to above, the relativities between individual and pay groups is a never-ending source of negotiation and sometimes conflict in industrial relations and pay negotiating terms. This was particularly so in the 1970s when the growth in international oil prices and the huge increases in inflation eroded incomes quickly and led to constantly escalating demands for salary and wage increases to keep pace. In the 1990s, with relatively low inflation and a more stable economy, competition for pay increases lessened, although it is still a regular feature of tension and friction in the public sector where the issue of low pay for nurses, local authority manual workers, teachers and other essential but generally not well-paid groups is an annual feature in the economic and political life of the country.

Composition

As well as the total remuneration package, employees are concerned to know how their pay is made up. Broadly speaking, the higher the basic pay percentage of total remuneration, the more satisfied the individual is with their lot. However, incentive bonus, overtime and performance-related payments can provide important additional features in remuneration terms and have long been used by employers to improve productivity output and the employee contribution.

Employer objectives:

Prestige

The good employer, will wish to believe that it "pays well." Indeed, it is unthinkable for the leading edge, highly competitive employer to be paying anything other than amongst the highest rates of pay in its sector or occupational group. Until twenty years ago, and the huge changes in the public sector brought about by the Thatcher Conservative Government, this was almost wholly the domain of the private sector. However, during the 1980s and 1990s, many differentials have also emerged in the way public sector organisations pay their staff and here it is possible to differentiate between those who pay well and those who do not.

Competition

The employer's position in the pay market will depend much upon its resources, profitability, and need to improve its competitiveness. In all walks of life, the leading organisations would generally be those who are the most profitable and therefore can offer the best remuneration packages. In this situation success breeds success so that, for example, in soccer's English Premier League it is no coincidence that Manchester United are the most successful team over the past decade, are almost the most profitable, and are also the best payers, attracting many of the highest calibre footballers accordingly.

Control

Control of the pay bill will equally be important no matter how profitable and affluent the employer. Successful organisations have pay policies to meet their needs and resources, and "cut their cloth accordingly". Organisations who pay over the odds on a recurring basis are likely to hit financial trouble unless they can generate commensurate increases in income or profits.

Motivation and productivity

Pay does not necessarily guarantee improved motivation, output or productivity. Depending upon the sector and the occupation, pay, whilst clearly important, will not always be the number one determinant that motivates or attracts an employee. This is clearly so in many vocational occupations such as nursing, social work, teaching, or even politics where the rewards are rarely commensurate with the contribution an individual makes to society. Measuring output and productivity is also notoriously difficult in jobs that do not involve manufacturing or the creation of a clear end product.

So, for example, the debate currently raging in the UK about the introduction of performance-related pay for teachers focuses largely on how teachers' performance can be assessed. Is it linked to the exam results of pupils? Or on the number of pupils taught and the volume of work undertaken? Or more qualitative measures about teaching methods and outcomes? It is a complex and difficult area and the debate will doubtless continue for sometime.

Cost

As employees are concerned with maximising their purchasing power, so employers are interested in minimising costs relevant to the marketplace. For this reason, employers often invest heavily in salary surveys, or job evaluation schemes, to make sure that their pay strategies and policies keep up with those of their competitors and the relevant market but ensure that they secure the best value for the minimum outlay.

Pay components

Figure 6.1 shows the different components of pay from which the pay of most employees can be identified. The main elements are as follows:

KEY POINTS

- ▶ Basic pay is the minimum pay otherwise known as the standard rate included in the remuneration package. Whilst it may be added to it is only reduced in the most unusual of circumstances.
- ▶ Plussages or premia payments are often added to basic pay to recognise specific working conditions or requirements. For example, some Local Authority manual workers seek payments to compensate for working in very dirty or unhygienic conditions.
- ▶ Premia, however, are more commonly used to describe payment for staff who work shift or unsocial hours rather than performing additional work. Although this can be a feature of the basic rate of pay, it is more normally an addition making the premia a variable payment.

PROFIT/PERFORMANCE-RELATED	• linked to individual, team or company performance
INCENTIVE PAYMENTS	• for productivity or output • individual, team or whole organisation reward
OVERTIME PAYMENTS	• shift patterns • extra hours • rates for weekends, evenings, nights and bank holidays
PLUSSAGE/PREMIA	• unsocial hours • unsocial conditions • market "element"
BASIC PAY	• irreducible • % or total of pay • the "core" element

Figure 6.1 Components of the pay package

▶ Overtime, payment for hours worked in excess of the contracted hours, often attracts an enhanced rate of pay known as overtime pay or overtime hours worked. In some occupations, overtime is a contractual condition as it is known up front that employees will be required to work over and above their normal contracted hours from time to time to meet the job requirements. So, for example, in the police service contracted overtime is the norm. Enhanced pay is usually attached to overtime working.

▶ Profit sharing, performance-related pay and profit-related pay are forms of additional payment and are usually linked to the output of the organisation or personal performance or productivity. They are usually assessed at the end of a financial year when it is possible to look back on the individual's contribution or the organisation's overall performance or profitability and assess payments accordingly. These schemes range from the very modest performance-related pay schemes in operation in the public sector, where additional payments in the range of 2–6 per cent might be paid in addition to the normal basic pay dependent on an employee's contribution; or profit sharing and profit-related payments which can be in excess of the amount of basic pay in highly profitable results-orientated industries such as information technology, or the capital investment markets in the City of London. Some of these payments can be very lucrative and exceed one million pounds a year for some high earning individuals.

▶ Incentive or bonus. An incentive or bonus payment is usually linked to output productivity or performance. Incentives, usually linked to productivity, stipulate that pay will increase by a certain amount dependent on results. A bonus may depend on the overall performance of the organisation or the company and may be paid at the end of the year dependent on profitability.

Pay or salary policy

All organisations, no matter how small or large, will be faced with the issue of determining what their wage or salary policy will be at any given time. A number of factors will help influence how this policy is arrived at.

The economic environment

The macroeconomic environment will go a long way to determining what an organisation pays at a particular time, because its fortunes are bound to be influenced by macroeconomic factors to one degree or another. So whether an organisation is a private company enjoying a time of expansion in boom, or a public sector organisation dependent on the state of public finances, the salary policy will in part be dependent on this backcloth. Generally speaking, when the economic cycle is in an upward turn, labour markets expand, unemployment reduces and there is pressure on maximising remuneration with some skills becoming scarce. In these circumstances organisations will openly compete with one another by trying to maximise remuneration. At times of economic downturn, some organisations will prove more robust than others and be better placed to sustain their previously higher levels of salary. In the most extreme cases, those who cannot will suffer major downturn, redundancy and may even go out of business.

Labour supply and demand

Linked to the macroeconomic picture, much will depend on the relative supply and demand for labour in the particular sector the organisation is employing. So, for example, in the mid 1980s there was a huge boom in the growth of Information Technology industries and individuals with relevant good skills could command high premia in a time of economic expansion. Conversely, with the economic downturn at the beginning of the 1990s, many who had made their fortunes in banking and investment industries in the 1980s suddenly found themselves out of work and their previously sought-after skills no longer needed with an excess of supply over demand.

National agreements

Notwithstanding the influence of the economy and national labour markets, many organisations will be restricted in their ability to pay and have some determination of salary policy through agreements they make with their staff or trade unions in the form of national agreements. This is particularly so in very large manufacturing, private sector and public sector organisations who are employing tens of thousands of employees in particular job categories and need to ensure that they have national wage structures to support the recruitment and retention of staff.

However, even in the large national salary structures there is room for some local determination and manoeuvre.

So for example, in local government in the 1980s there was a move away from the national terms and conditions of employment and salary structures which restricted local authorities from being flexible in pay policy. Local authorities were given the freedom to opt out of these structures and many negotiated their own local scales. Interestingly, however, the late 1990s have been characterised by a return to national structures with many of those organisations who formerly opted out from a national framework returning to it because it provided certainty within their ability to pay.

Government policy

From time to time the government directly intervenes to ensure rates of pay for various occupations, usually in terms of low pay. The wages councils which operated in the 1970s and 1980s ensured minimum standards of pay for various occupational groups and particular those low paid in the retail and agricultural sectors. The advent of the *National Minimum Wage Act* ensures minimum standards of pay for all adult workers in the UK economy which no employer can legally opt out from. From time to time the government have also intervened to cap wage levels, particularly in the public sector through legislation but also in the private sector by pressure and exhortation. This was particularly so in the inflationary years of the mid 1970s, when earnings levels were rigorously controlled in an attempt to reduce wage inflation.

Market comparisons

Some private sector organisations determine the whole of their salary strategies by reference to the pay that their competitors make and adjust accordingly. Generally speaking, those operating in highly competitive volatile markets use salary research and data to inform annual adjustments to their pay policy and thus ensure they remain competitive. The danger with this "leap frogging" approach is that it in itself can become inflationary and means that organisations lose sight of properly structured salary policies as they become wholly driven by the market with its peaks and troughs.

Salary structures

Once an organisation has determined the basis for its salary policy, the next issue requiring attention will be the grading or salary structure within the organisation. As with many aspects of HRM, approaches to salary structures go in cycles. The main approaches can be summarised as follows:

Occupational groupings

The Institute of Personnel and Development (IPD) provide some helpful classification of occupational groupings that normally describe the main headings for salary structure in a typical organisation. They will include *senior and middle managers* (Directors, Heads of Departments and their immediate subordinates), *junior or middle managers* (those who are reporting to the Senior Managers and have front-line supervisory responsibility), *technical and specialist staff* (personnel who have professional or technical skills who may often be in a single-occupation post); and *administrative support and ancillary staff* (those providing the main support functions supporting the rest of the workforce).

Of course, the more complex the organisation the more multidisciplinary and specialist the workforce tends to become. So, for example, in a typical NHS Trust one will find senior managers, junior and middle managers, administrative support staff, ancillary and manual staff, and highly specialist professional groups including doctors, psychologists, occupational therapists and so on. These group headings are a useful way into the salary structure descriptions in each organisation, not the least because each group is often bound by its own set of salary parameters.

Salary grades and steps

The traditional salary structure in an organisation will create a number of grades or salary steps, which will often be overlapping, that describe the different occupational groupings and how individuals can move between them. Figure 6.2 describes a typical salary structure for a small to medium-sized NHS Trust showing the different occupational groups, and some of the salary structures that will exist within them. A number of factors will go to determine the size of the salary ranges and the differentials between them.

Sticking with the personnel profession as an example, the salary will need to have regard to career progression and differentiate between the different levels of responsibility in the organisation. The personnel assistant, normally the most junior position, will need a range of salary points to reflect experience and qualifications, but also will need to provide a differential to the pay offered to the next rung on the ladder, normally the personnel officer. The larger the organisation the greater the range and disparity of salaries that will exist between top and bottom.

The problem with *incremental* progression is simply that it rewarded no more than remaining in post and performing satisfactorily. So in a grade of say 5 incremental points, with an individual joining the organisation appointed at the bottom point, he/she would simply need to stay in post for 5 years to progress to the top of the grade. Performance- and competence-related progression would depend on some system of appraisal or performance management being in place to judge how the individual is doing and to reward them appropriately against set criteria which evaluate performance and/or competence. Performance-related progression led the way from the early 1980s to the mid 1990s and allowed individuals to progress through grades very quickly dependent on the nature of their performance. However, feelings that *performance-related pay* did not judge the whole contribution of the individual fairly and of itself became standardised led to the accent on competence-related pay in many organisations in the late 1990s. The spirit behind competence-related pay is that the individual's overall contribution in terms of their skills, aptitudes and abilities are judged and salary progression rated accordingly. Indeed in some organisations the progression is explicitly tied to the obtaining of qualifications be they professional or vocational. So, in the HRM example, the personnel assistant could not progress to the top of

£	Managers	Doctors	Nurses	PAMs	Ancillary
100,000					
90,000	CEO	Consultants			
80,000	CEO	Consultants			
70,000	Executives	Consultants			
60,000	Executives	Consultants / Senior Registrars			
50,000	Executives	Consultants / Senior Registrars	Nurse Consultants		
40,000	Heads of Dept.	Senior Registrars / Juniors	Nurse Consultants		
35,000	Heads of Dept.	Senior Registrars / Juniors	Nurse Consultants		
30,000	Heads of Dept.	Juniors	Nurse Consultants		
29,000			Nurse Consultants		
28,000			I, H, G, Grades		
27,000			I, H, G, Grades		
26,000			I, H, G, Grades	OTs	
25,000			I, H, G, Grades	F, E, D, C, Grades / OTs	
24,000			I, H, G, Grades	F, E, D, C, Grades / OTs	
23,000			I, H, G, Grades	F, E, D, C, Grades / Rehab	
22,000			I, H, G, Grades	F, E, D, C, Grades / Rehab	
21,000				F, E, D, C, Grades / C, B, A, Grades / Rehab / Craftsmen	
20,000				C, B, A, Grades / Craftsmen / Maintenance	
19,000				C, B, A, Grades / Craftsmen / Maintenance	
18,000				C, B, A, Grades / Craftsmen / Maintenance	
17,000				C, B, A, Grades / Craftsmen / Maintenance	
16,000				Maintenance	
15,000					Domestic Supervisors
14,000					Domestic Supervisors
13,000					Domestic Supervisors
12,000					Domestic Supervisors
11,000					
10,000					

Figure 6.2 Salary structure: NHS Trust

the grade until he or she has completed the professional training or competence requirements for the whole job.

Spot salaries

Disenchantment with incremental grading systems led to the growth in use of the spot salary system in many organisations in the 1980s. Based on the organisation's salary policy, a number of spot salaries were determined for different jobs which took account of their relative weight and importance (often determined by job evaluation), market comparatives or judgements around the individual's worth. The advantage for this approach is that it led to a much more tailored remuneration package that could reflect organisational or individual needs. The downside of spot salaries, however, is that it became much more difficult to describe a coherent salary structure and policy because in any occupational grouping a number of individuals could be paid quite differently according to their "spot". None of these structural solutions are, of course, mutually exclusive, and it is possible to have a grouping of spot salaries in something akin to a grading or incremental structure. This is the compromise that many organisations who went down the spot salary route sought in trying to establish clear structures.

Job evaluation

Job evaluation has been the cornerstone of determining salary structures within organisations and in some cases the driving salary policy by linkages to salary market surveys for over forty years in the UK. Indeed job evaluation is a major HRM topic by itself and can only be covered in overview terms for the purposes of this book. Job evaluation is a methodology for ranking the relative worth or weight of jobs in an organisation dependent on their content. Drawing its origins from the work study related school of job analysis (see Chapter 5, Job Design), job evaluation has frequently been referred to as a scientific and objective method for determining these relativities. However, whichever job evaluation methodology is used the data collected by it and the judgements made through it are still performed by humans, and are therefore necessarily to a degree subjective; there is no such thing therefore as a wholly scientific job evaluation method. Nonetheless, job evaluation methods go some way to removing the subjectivity that would otherwise go to determining how jobs differ from each other, and which should attract different remuneration accordingly.

Because the product of a job evaluation is usually a job value or score, it is relatively straightforward to group the results together to create some kind of rational job and pay structure. So, for example, if the chosen job evaluation methodology uses points scores, it is possible for an organisation to compare two quite different jobs and their resultant scores and make a judgement about their relative worth. So, if a laboratory technician scores 400 job evaluation points, and an administrative officer the same, the company can determine that they are both worth the same salary in salary structure terms. Similarly, universal job evaluation methodologies that are widely used by many organisations (for example, the Hay Methodology), can be used to compare jobs across organisations or even sectors. That does not mean to say that the salary attached to them will be the same because of factors influencing the organisation's salary policy and its position in its own particular market. It will be possible to say, however, that a 400 point value job is of the same weight as that in another organisation regardless of organisational circumstances.

Job evaluation is normally carried out by a trained job analyst. Using some of the job description and job design techniques described in more detail in Chapter 5 a trained analyst can be used to assemble a database of job evaluations to help inform the job hierarchy in the organisation and so assist any creation of a salary structure and salary policy.

6.4 Holidays

Next to pay, one of the biggest factors which helps determine the attractiveness of a job package will be the holiday or annual leave entitlement that accompanies it. Twenty-five years ago the talk in personnel management circles was about how information technology would so revolutionise the world of work that the fully automated office, with people working largely from home, and a reduction in the working week to four or even three days was just around the corner. Twenty-five years later in the middle of the information technology revolution, the paperless office is indeed a reality and the ability for many types of worker to operate from home exists. However, the reduction in hours in the working week has not matched the expectations of the personnel gurus of the mid 1970s. The reasons are many and complex, and whilst we no doubt enjoy much better-quality leisure time than that of our parents' or grandparents' generations, the pressures contained in the working week, and the excessive hours worked by many, particularly in the UK, mean that the holiday entitlement becomes all the more precious.

Although the inception of the working time directive introduced for the first time a minimum statutory holiday entitlement for adult workers in the UK, holiday entitlements have long been established as an essential part of the employment contract for most major employers in the UK. Indeed by comparison with some of their European, Japanese or American counterparts, major UK organisations have always been regarded as generous in terms of making provision for annual leave. Other than ensuring compliance with statutory minimum requirements, most employers rely on market comparisons to determine what constitutes a reasonable holiday allowance in the contract of employment.

Allowances and entitlements

Typical allowances in the UK range from the statutory minimum of 20 days rising to a maximum in most organisations of between 30 and 35 days. There are, of course, some notable exceptions, particularly in the teaching profession where paid holidays in the range of 12 to 14 weeks are not uncommon. However, most teachers will argue that they have to work during a large proportion of this time to prepare for the next term's educational programme, and these arrangements therefore have to be regarded as exceptional. There are essentially three ways of determining policy about holiday arrangements:

1. linked to *grade or seniority* in an organisation, with the most junior staff starting with the lowest level, and the highest allocation only obtainable in the most senior position at the top of the organisational tree. There is a perversity in this logic, because very often the people at the top of the organisation have the greatest pressures on them and are least able to take advantage of their full leave allowance.
2. *universally applied* on the basis that everybody who makes a contribution to the organisation needs to have a reasonable facility for taking holidays and annual leave. So, some more progressive companies make the same leave

allocation, say a norm of 25 or 27 days to all employees regardless of rank or seniority.

3. tied to *length of service* and there is perhaps a clearer logic to understand here. Instead of grade or salary being the determinant, the annual leave allocation will be dependent on how long an individual stays with an organisation. This encourages retention, with the highest allocation going to individuals who have been in post for say more than 10 years. However, the downside of this cumulative approach is that it then becomes much harder for such individuals to move to other organisations.

Other leave issues

Once an organisation has determined its approach to the allocation of annual leave, and attended to the administrative functions of recording and monitoring allowances, there are one or two other ancillary issues to deal with. The first, is the attitude to *statutory public and bank holidays*. Much here, of course, would depend on the nature of the business, with, for example, those working in the catering and retail industries often being required to work on bank holidays and being rewarded through enhanced pay and/or time off in lieu. It should be noted that notwithstanding the introduction of the working time directive minimum holiday entitlements, public and bank holidays are not statutory holidays for everyone, and it is up to the employer to stipulate in the contract of employment how these arrangements will work. Indeed, in those sectors where working on bank holidays is the norm, the compensatory arrangements for staff will often be a major issue for negotiation and bargaining in the workplace with staff associations and trade unions.

The second issue will be the determination of what to do for those staff who for one reason or another are *unable to take their full leave* allowance. Most organisations have parameters in place to regulate to some degree when and how staff can take their holidays. These will not normally be enshrined in the contract of employment but will constitute custom and practice or local arrangements that are implied. So, for example, some organisations stipulate that part of the holiday must be taken at times convenient to the business (for example at Christmas or the summer when the business effectively closes down, such as in parts of the manufacturing or car industry). Others will stipulate that leave cannot be taken at certain times of the year or when other members of staff are absent, or a multiplicity of other arrangements depending on the organisational circumstances. These will be legal arrangements provided they have been discussed and agreed with staff or staff representatives, are described properly in the contract of employment and do not in any way breach the minimum requirements of the working time directive.

6.5 Pension arrangements

The principal legislation governing pension schemes is the *Pension Schemes Act 1993* together with the *Pensions Act 1995*. It is not possible here to explore the law on pensions or the practical implications of developing and administering pension schemes in great detail as it is a major subject in its own right. However, the provision of an occupational pension is a major part of the pay and benefits package and an essential piece in the HRM jigsaw, so an overview can be provided. There are three major considerations here: first, the range of pension schemes available; secondly, the different types of occupational pension scheme in existence; and lastly, some of the current issues being debated about pension provision in the UK.

Types of pension scheme

There are essentially four types of pension scheme which can be summarised as follows:

State schemes

The state runs two schemes, a *basic pension* arrangement and *SERPS* (State Earnings Related Pension Scheme). Every individual in work in the UK is obliged to contribute the standard amount for the basic scheme which provides an old-age pension upon retirement for men and women. For those employees who earn over a certain amount, known as the lower earnings limit, the percentage of salary earned between this limit and the higher salary level, known as the upper earnings limit, is also payable. Both these payments are deducted from salaries as part of the national insurance contribution. SERPS, established in 1975, is designed as a fallback for employees who do not benefit from occupational pensions. Organisational pension schemes which meet prescribed minimum standards may apply to be contracted out of SERPS. Contracting out is the normal practice for larger organisations, not least because both employer and employee then pay lower rates for the national insurance contribution. So, the minimum position for any employee who has been engaged in work for a significant period of time is that they will have the state pension scheme to fall back on, and in the absence of an occupational or personal pension, some entitlement to SERPS.

Occupational pension schemes

Occupational Pension Schemes come in many forms. They are normally funded by *contributions* from the employee (at the standard contribution rate of about 6 per cent per salary per annum) and a similar contribution from the employer. Some larger organisations (previously with Civil Service, and some major private companies) provide *non-contributory* pension schemes for employees which is a major perk. The way these different schemes are organised in terms of contribution and the benefits they pay is discussed later in this section but whatever arrangements are in place, the pension scheme must provide equity of access for both men and women, meet the state guaranteed minimum pension requirements, and make appropriate arrangements for employees who die in service and for widows, widowers or dependants.

Personal pensions

Personal pensions came into their own in the 1980s when the then Conservative Government opened up a large part of the pensions market. Employees without access to an occupational pension scheme, or who already were in one were encouraged to join in on the personal pensions band wagon and take out an arrangement with one of the leading life companies in operation at that time. Tax relief incentives were offered by the government to encourage and fuel this growth and there was a massive explosion in numbers of staff opting for this arrangement in the last half of the 1980s and the first half of the 1990s.

Some of these arrangements fell into disrepute, however, when it became apparent that many of the provisions of these personal pensions would not pay out the level of benefits anticipated because the investments made either in stocks and shares or in other capital markets did not reach expectation. The misselling of personal pensions became a national scandal and led to a government inquiry, with companies who were found guilty of mis-selling having to pay compensation on a massive scale in the second half of the 1990s.

Personal pensions continue to this day, but have the major disadvantage that the employer does not normally make any contribution, and the investment stands and falls on what the individual pays in and the success of those investments over the years.

Occupational scheme arrangements

Accepting, therefore, that occupational schemes are those that attract most credibility and support in the workplace today, it is worth examining the different arrangements for contributing to and benefits arising from them.

Average salary schemes

Average salary schemes take into account both *length of service* and the *salary* that the employee has earned in each of those years. The critical figure is the average of all the yearly salaries that the employee has earned during their employment. They are usually calculated on $\frac{1}{60}$th or $\frac{1}{80}$th of what the employee has earned. If there was little inflation and the employee had only made modest progression within the organisation, the average salary would be close to the final salary of the employee and therefore may produce a pension that was realistic. So, for an employee working 40 years with one organisation on an 80th scheme, and an average annual salary of £30,000 per year, the maximum pension entitlement upon retirement would be $\frac{40}{80}$th $\times$ £30,000 = an annual pension of £15,000 per year. In addition, a lump sum will be payable upon retirement normally equivalent to three times that of the annual pension and using the worked example above, equivalent to £45,000 as a retirement lump sum.

Final salary scheme

A final salary scheme, as the name suggests, takes into account the *employee's final salary* as well as the length of time that he or she has contributed to the pension fund. For each year of contribution the employee earns the right to receive a specified proportion of their final salary as a pension. Again, schemes are normally calculated on the basis of $1/60$th or $1/80$th. This means for each year of contribution the employee is entitled to receive the relevant proportion of their final year's salary and a £50,000 per annum employee with a maximum service of 40 years, in an 80th scheme the resultant pension would be £25,000 per annum with a lump sum again of the order of three times this amount.

Money purchase schemes

Money purchase schemes are organised in a different way from the schemes above as there are no guarantees about the final level of pension. Both the employer and employee contribute to these schemes in much the same way as to other types of occupational scheme by paying a percentage of current salary. The pension benefits from the scheme are entirely dependent on the money that has been contributed and the way it has been invested. If the investments have been very profitable and there has been little inflation then the final pension may turn out to be very advantageous.

Money purchase schemes produce a lump sum available upon retirement and this is used to buy the appropriate pension. However, in years of very high inflation this type of scheme has severe drawbacks and this accounted for their decline in popularity in the 1970s. Money purchase schemes however, are seen as flexible and more easily transferable between employers as the value of the pension is easily identifiable and portable at any point in employment.

Problems and challenges

There is a considerable debate raging in the UK economy at present about the *adequacy* of the current state occupational and personal pension arrangements to provide for individuals in retirement. The concerns have been based on a diminishing proportion of the UK population being in full employment and in turn the population working for less years than previous generations did and therefore reducing the scope for contributing to pension arrangements for retirement. Indeed, it is not unusual for employees to take early retirement in their 50s, particularly at times of economic recession when organisations are looking to cut back and seek volunteers for voluntary redundancy and early retirement. Most occupational pension schemes commence contributions at age 18, so at a normal rate of contribution an employee retiring at the age of 52 will be 6 years short of their full contribution. In these circumstances there are only two possible solutions to ensure a full pension entitlement. First, either the employee has to contribute more as a proportion of their salary whilst they are in employment, sometimes known as additional voluntary contributions; or, secondly, the employer needs to make a greater contribution or ensure that their investments realise better benefits. Indeed, the debate has extended from occupational schemes to state provision, with a considerable body of opinion now arguing that the state provision should be enhanced either through an increased national insurance contribution or by insisting that individuals take out certain types of personal or occupational schemes to top up the state provision.

The second problem area relates to *portability*. Whilst occupational schemes still have enormous advantages, one of the problems with average and final salary schemes is their portability between employers, particularly where the new organisation offers a different entitlement to the previous organisation. Previously, employees sought a solution when changing employers by obtaining a refund of pension contributions which they could then invest in the new employer's fund. However, as this in turn has harmful impacts on the overall pension arrangements, many occupational schemes now have strict rules about time limits during which refunds may be sought and in any event the value of the transferring investment may be diluted by constantly seeking refunds and changing employers.

Part of the response to these problems is the creation of *flexible pension* arrangements as part of the total benefits package offered by an organisation. This will offer employees a range of occupational pension arrangements from a minimum legal provision to enhanced provision with employee and employer contributions geared accordingly. The employee who opts for the maximum pension may not be able to make use of other organisational benefits as it is essentially a menu approach. This encourages responsible and older employees to invest more for their retirement. Human nature being what it is, however, many people do not start thinking of pension arrangements until they are well into their 40s. So there is an equal danger that the flexible menu approach to pension purchase plans will still fail to make proper universal provision. A summary of the types of pension scheme available is given in Figure 6.3.

6.6 Sickness and sick pay

One of the most skilful balancing acts the HR practitioner will have to perform will be in relation to the area of managing sickness absence and the payments arising therefrom. A good employer must provide adequate sick pay and access to sickness absence when employees are genuinely ill and help them return to work as soon as possible. However, there is clearly equal scope for abuse and employers need to balance their welfare and support responsibilities with proper control mechanisms to ensure a healthy workplace. The role of the Personnel or Human Resources Department in managing sickness absence can be summarised as follows:

Advisory

The Personnel Office has a very clear advisory role for both employees and managers in managing sickness absence. Given that the source of information about sickness absence will often be a computerised Personnel Information System (see Chapter 7), the Personnel Department will often be best placed to advise man-

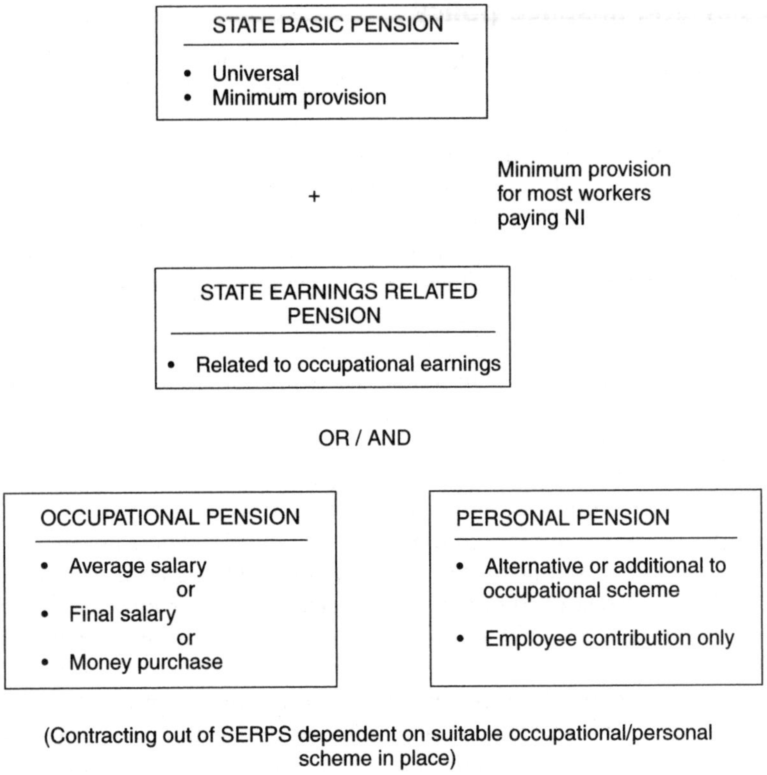

```
┌─────────────────────────────────┐
│  STATE BASIC PENSION            │
│  ────────────────               │
│  • Universal                    │
│  • Minimum provision            │
└─────────────────────────────────┘

                                    Minimum provision
              +                     for most workers
                                    paying NI

┌─────────────────────────────────┐
│  STATE EARNINGS RELATED         │
│         PENSION                 │
│  ────────────────────────       │
│  • Related to occupational earnings │
└─────────────────────────────────┘

              OR / AND

┌──────────────────────────┐     ┌──────────────────────────────┐
│ OCCUPATIONAL PENSION     │     │ PERSONAL PENSION             │
│ ─────────────────────    │     │ ──────────────────           │
│ • Average salary         │     │ • Alternative or additional to │
│        or                │     │   occupational scheme        │
│ • Final salary           │     │                              │
│        or                │     │ • Employee contribution only │
│ • Money purchase         │     │                              │
└──────────────────────────┘     └──────────────────────────────┘
```

(Contracting out of SERPS dependent on suitable occupational/personal scheme in place)

Figure 6.3   Types of pension scheme

agers on patterns of sickness absence and what to do about employees who are often sick. This will often include a referral to the Occupational Health Service and will involve the manager in seeing the individual upon return to work to try and ascertain the reasons for absence and what can be done to support the employee in the future.

Monitoring

The Personnel or HR Function will also have a role in monitoring sickness absence to ensure the delicate balance between welfare and control is maintained. This is particularly so when there is long-term sickness absence from the workplace that may involve serious illness or injury. It is important that individuals who are off sick for such protracted periods have proper arrangements for keeping in touch with the workplace and ensuring that the Occupational Health Service or Advisor can provide frequent commentary on their ability to work. This may include regular visits to the home of the individual to make sure they are receiving appropriate communication from the workplace and that their long-term absence is not allowed to go unnoticed.

Sick pay and absence policy

Organisations need to have a sickness absence policy to describe the *procedures for reporting* sickness absence, the arrangements for submitting self certification and medical practitioner certificates as appropriate, the role of occupational health in monitoring and dealing with referrals of sickness absence, and the interface between sickness absence and disciplinary procedures. The latter will need particularly careful handling. The policy will also need to describe carefully the interface between statutory sick pay and the occupational sick pay scheme. Different organisations adopt different approaches to the development of these policies and the way that they monitor sickness absence.

Some organisations are very rigorous about *monitoring and controlling* sickness absence because the loss of individuals, even for a day, can be critical for their service. So, for example, a small retail business will severely miss an individual who is away for a day which may lead to curtailing opening hours with a necessary reduction in the turnover and profits. Large employers are generally better placed to absorb sickness absence, but again will want to ensure that they have proper processes in place to monitor and control sickness absence.

There are no hard and fast rules about what constitutes *good practice* in this area. So long as it relates to organisational circumstances, and can be demonstrated to be fair and reasonable, it may be appropriate to automatically refer any individual who has more than a certain number of days of short-term sickness absence to the Occupational Health Service for an opinion or to conduct interviews with them to try and ensure there is no abuse. Equally many organisations take a rather more relaxed attitude and take the view that creating thresholds of itself produces a feeling amongst staff that they have a certain minimum entitlement to sickness absence in a particular year.

Whatever systems are in place, they need to be clearly *communicated* to employees as part of the ancillary information in the contract of employment and the sickness absence policy needs to describe arrangements for monitoring and control and referral as appropriate. Most employers link sickness entitlements to length of service. So, typically, an employee in his/her first year of service may be entitled to 1 month's full pay and 1 month's half pay in an occupational sick pay scheme. Typically this will rise by yearly instalments to a maximum of 6 months' full pay and 6 months' half pay after 6 years' continuous service. Again these entitlements need to be spelt out in the contract of employment and need to ensure that they prescribe the minimum requirements for statutory sick pay described at the beginning of this chapter.

6.7 Maternity rights and benefits

As with sick pay, there is an interface in the workplace between the minimum statutory entitlements to maternity leave and pay and those an employer may choose to provide as part of their occupational arrangements described in the contract of employment. The provisions of both can be summarised as follows:

Ante-natal care

An employee who is pregnant and who has on the advice of her medical practitioner or midwife made an appointment to attend an ante-natal appointment has the right not to be refused time off during her working hours to enable her to attend the appointment and to receive pay accordingly. Employers who consistently fail to meet this obligation will be in breach of the *Employment Rights Act* and will be open to legal challenge. There is no minimum qualifying period of employment to entitlement for ante-natal appointments and it is open to any female employee who is pregnant.

Protection from discrimination

It is automatically unfair to dismiss a female employee for any reason connected with her pregnancy or indeed to discriminate on grounds that are directly connected with it (which may lead to a claim under *the Sex Discrimination Act*, see Chapter 8). So it would be automatically unfair to dismiss a woman at the end of her period of maternity leave where the employer finds out she is pregnant and does not want to absorb the costs of related illness. Similarly a woman must not be selected for redundancy on grounds of pregnancy. As with the right to ante-natal care, there is no qualifying period for this entitlement and it is a protection that applies from the first day of employment for the female employee.

Maternity pay

As outlined above, there are also entitlements to statutory maternity pay for all women in employment. To qualify for statutory maternity pay, a woman must have been in employment for at least 26 weeks ending with the week immediately preceding the fourteenth week of the expected week of confinement. The provisions for pay are those outlined in 6.2 above. Additionally, many employers provide more than the statutory scheme and have a contractual right to maternity pay included within the contract of employment. Typical occupational schemes provide for up to 18 weeks of pay as per the state's scheme, with periods of full and half-pay included in the entitlement. A typical arrangement will include 6 weeks' full pay and 12 weeks' half pay, the latter being repayable by any female employee who does not return to work after her period of maternity leave. Whatever the occupational arrangement, the statutory minimum entitlement (SMP) must be observed.

Maternity leave and return to work

Any employee who is absent from work at any time during her maternity leave period is entitled to protection of the terms and conditions of employment which would otherwise have applied to her, such as holiday and sick pay entitlements. In order to qualify for these benefits the female employee must notify her employer of the date on which she intends to begin her absence on maternity leave, which must be no earlier than the eleventh week of confinement, and do so not less than 21 days before this date.

If the employee intends to return to work earlier than the end of her maternity leave period, which can normally be for a period of up to 40 weeks, including paid and unpaid leave, she must give her employee not less than 7 days' notice. The right to return to work is afforded to any employee who has been continuously employed for at least 2 years at the beginning of the eleventh week before the expected week of confinement. She has the right to return to work at any time during the period beginning at the end of her maternity leave period and ending 29 weeks after the beginning of the week in which the childbirth occurs, producing the maximum entitlement to 40 weeks' leave. It is her right to return to the job in which the employee was previously employed or an equivalent job on terms and conditions no less favourable than would have applied if she had not been absent at any time since her maternity leave began.

There is no right to return to work on a part-time basis or on terms more profitable than those previously enjoyed before the pregnancy. At the end of the maternity leave period, the employee may postpone her return by a period of up to 4 weeks providing she can produce a medical certificate saying she is unfit for return to work. The employer may similarly postpone the return for a period of up to 4 weeks to make suitable arrangements for her return provided there are good reasons to do so. If an employer fails to provide a job on equivalent terms to which she left, the employer will have been regarded as automatically dismissing the employee under the unfair dismissal legislation. The only exceptions to these provisions are very small organisations who employ five or less employees, or in ones where the organisational circumstances change so drastically that it is not reasonably practicable for the organisation to reabsorb the employee back into the work place (that is where there has been a major contraction in employment leading to redundancies, although this is not a fair reason for redundancy in itself).

6.8 Other benefits

With increasing competition for scarce skills in the marketplace, many employers are looking to develop innovative benefits packages to recruit and retain key staff. Some examples of the other benefits offered by employers seeking advantage include:

EXAMPLE

1 Private health care insurance
  for the employee and their family at discounted rates or funded wholly by the employer.
2 Discount purchase schemes
  for use in major retail and leisure outlets.
3 Social and sports facilities:
  covered in more detail in Chapter 13.

4 Provision of company, lease or car allowances
   to aid the performance of business travel or as a straightforward "perk" (some tax liabilities apply).
5 Travel and subsistence allowances
   provided to reimburse employees' travel costs, sometimes with a "profit element" (NB in which case this will usually attract an income tax liability).
6 Relocation packages
   providing temporary housing for the relocating employee, financial assistance with the cost of moving house (legal fees and so on), or assisted house purchase schemes (NB financial assistance in excess of £8,000 per relocation is taxable).
7 Provision of clothing, uniforms and equipment
   to assist the employee in performing their duties efficiently and safely (again, some tax liabilities may apply).

6.9 Problem areas

QUESTION:
I think that the concept of restructuring is often a tool for managers to play around with from time to time without producing any real additional benefits to the individual or the organisation as a whole. We have consultants in the office at the moment reviewing our salary structure for the third time in a decade. What is the point in this kind of exercise?

ANSWER:
Your scepticism is understandable given the way some organisations never seem to be able to settle on the correct salary structure. The answer probably lies in the fact that there is no correct structure, only a set of arrangements to meet the organisation's needs at a particular time. Much, of course, will depend on the type of organisation you work for and the sector you operate in. If your company is in a highly volatile market, then it is understandable that the company are constantly needing to review and amend their salary structures to deal with issues of recruitment and retention. The acid test here will be whether the new salary structure works, regardless of the upheavals it may bring to the people that work for the organisation. More importantly, however, are the tests of fairness, relativities and motivation produced by the salary structure.

It is a fact of life that everybody moans about pay and pay structures in the organisation they work for; there is no such thing as an employee who believes their pay package is absolutely right! But the true test is how your organisation fares in recruiting and retaining and in dealing with feelings of unfairness or even grievances related to pay structure. You are right to say that you can play around with structures forever, but the real test lies in organisational effectiveness.

QUESTION:
The salary structure in my company used to be wholly market driven, but we found ourselves caught in the spiral of constantly trying to play catch-up with our competitors. We have decided to take a fresh look, therefore, and are thinking of using one of the leading job evaluation methodologies in the marketplace. I hear con-

flicting reports about how good these are. Some say they provide a genuinely scientific and objective tool for ranking jobs, others that they are just as subjective as me and my personnel manager sitting down and thinking up a range of salaries for our different job types.

ANSWER:

There is a difference posed by the question you ask, between determining a salary policy and salary structure for your organisation. A salary policy will say something about where the organisation wants to be in the overall marketplace, and its policy for getting there, and maintaining its salary position. Most organisations of one sort or another do this by reference to the pay market for their sector or the occupations they employ, be they in the public or private sectors. The introduction of a job evaluation methodology will do much to help you produce a rational salary structure within your organisation and this can be linked to salary policy by reference to the marketplace and salary surveys. There is no such thing as a wholly scientific or objective method of job evaluation, because at the end of the day any scheme will have to be applied by human beings who must to some degree be subjective in their judgements about jobs.

However, there is no doubt that some of the leading schemes, such as the Hay Job Evaluation Scheme, go a long way to removing subjectivity because of the way the methodology is assembled and some quality assurance checks built into the process. The advantage with such well-used schemes as Hay is that because of their wide use throughout both public and private sector organisations it is possible to cross reference jobs of similar weight or point scores and make comparisons between them. So when a Hay Job Analyst talks about a "typical 434 points job", they will immediately recognise something about the size and complexity of the job in question. There could, therefore, be some very real benefits for your organisation in employing this kind of methodology and it is worthy of exploration.

QUESTION:

A female secretary who was recently absent on maternity leave has come back to work and is proving to be a real nuisance. Since she returned three months ago, she has either been absent sick, taking her accrued annual leave, or asking for time off to sort out childcare arrangements. It has reached the point where the managing director has told me to get rid of her by whatever legal means I can. Are there ways that I can tackle her absence given that she has just returned from maternity leave?

ANSWER:

The simple answer is 'yes you can', provided that the reasons for dealing with her dismissal are genuine ones related to attendance or performance and not because of her recent maternity-related absence. Remember that any maternity-related dismissal is automatically unfair, no matter what the reasons for it. It is a fact of modern employment practice that women are entitled to maternity pay and leave, a right of return to work, the right to accrued annual leave and access to various family friendly policies to enable them to accommodate childcare. This is built into both UK law and recent EU directives.

The key question to ask is whether her absence would have been a problem compared to an employee who had not just had a maternity-related absence. Is she taking more time off than is reasonable in comparison to these other employees? If the answer is 'no', and the real reason relates to her maternity and its associated absences, then there is no legal route you can follow to dismiss her. If, however, you can establish that there is a pattern of absence that cannot be properly substantiated and is not properly authorised by the taking of annual leave or genuine sickness, then you can take action. The procedure to follow will be that outlined in Chapter 4 in dealing with a dismissal.

6.10 Activity

Describe the main features you would expect to find in a model sickness absence policy for your organisation. Remember that the policy needs to strike a balance between the welfare and health of employees and the need to properly control and regulate absence from work. Ensure that any reference to an occupational health service the organisation uses is clearly spelt out in your outline policy.

6.11 Checklist

▶ The provision of pay and benefits as part of the contractual relationship between employee and employer has grown in complexity as working relationships have developed over the last three hundred years.

▶ The legal framework covering pay and benefits has increased significantly in the past few years with the inception of the *National Minimum Wage Act*, and the *Working Time Regulations*. Other legislative requirements cover methods of pay, equal pay, maternity leave, sick pay and regulations covering PAYE.

▶ Employees and employers have different objectives to pursue in securing pay.

▶ Employees are concerned mostly with purchasing power, fairness and relativities. Employers are more concerned with prestige, control and competitiveness.

▶ There are a number of different components in the pay package including basic, premia, overtime and performance-related pay.

▶ The pay or salary policy of the organisation will be determined by the economic environment, supply and demand for labour, and market comparisons.

▶ Salary structures revolve around the different occupational groupings and salary grades and steps that organisations wish to reflect.

▶ Job evaluation is often used to drive salary structure and salary policy in organisations.

▶ Next to pay, the holiday or annual leave entitlement is a major benefit within the total remuneration package. There is now a national minimum provision for the first time ever in the UK.

▶ The different types of pension scheme available are explored including state schemes, occupational schemes, and personal pensions.

- ▶ Occupational schemes are examined in some detail including average salary, final salary and money purchase schemes.
- ▶ Entitlements to sick pay and maternity pay schemes are explored in this chapter.
- ▶ Some examples of other benefits that are provided by some employers are given.

☒ 7 Personnel information systems and workforce planning

7.1 Introduction

The post-war image of the personnel clerk sitting at a desk looking at record cards and personnel files to sort and sift data about employees contrasts vividly with the modern management of workforce data. In the information technology age, an increasing amount of workforce data is held in computer storage with sophisticated software packages available to store, retrieve, analyse, filter and present the information contained within it. The marketplace is full of personnel information systems that will store and retrieve data quickly and efficiently and provide most of the statistical requirements of the modern Human Resource manager. This section deals with the growth and development of employee information, and looks at some of the uses to which it can be put, most notably workforce planning.

Workforce planning has suffered more than most aspects of Human Resource management in that it is seen as being in fashion on almost a cyclical basis. In the 1960s, it was the cornerstone of good personnel management technique with the concept being that organisations could develop workforce plans and strategies to define their recruitment and development needs for the next five to ten years. The massive upheaval in patterns of UK and world employment in the 1970s and 1980s (often created by information technology itself) produced much more complex, volatile and competitive labour markets and suddenly the concept of workforce planning (known then as manpower planning) became passé. However, the development of strategic HRM as a fundamental arm of business and organisational strategy over the past decade together with the emergence of sophisticated workforce planning technology and modelling techniques have once again brought this branch of HRM back into vogue. Although the employment trends and markets it attempts to describe are now much more complex, the need for organisations to take at least a medium-term view about their workforce needs and trends is becoming more imperative as employee costs continue to grow.

The other important aspect relating to employment data is less to do with proactive strategies and more to do with being able to support and defend good employment practice. In an increasingly litigious age, it is very important for a good employer to be able to produce records and data to support employment practice. So be it that information relating to the ethnicity of job applicants in relation to an equal opportunities claim (see Chapter 8), or risk assessment information concerned with good health and safety practice (Chapter 12), or modelling future recruitment needs based on turnover and employment patterns (Chapter 5), employee information is the life blood of the modern Personnel Department. Although the paperless Personnel Office is now a reality in a few organisations, the ability of modern personnel information systems and software to manipulate, analyse and present data makes this a very valuable tool in modern HRM.

7.2 Legal framework

The legal framework governing the collection, storage and use of data about employees is similar to that which affects employee support and welfare (dealt with in Chapter 13). Legislation governs the rights employees have to be able to inspect and ensure the accuracy of the data stored about them, the responsibilities employers have, and how they collect and use this information.

The *Data Protection Act 1984* (updated by the *Data Protection Act 1998*)

Under the 1984 Act, any information about an employee stored on a computer must comply with the Act's provisions and protects the confidentiality of the data stored (it must not be disclosed to third parties without the employee's authorisation) and the rights of individuals to inspect, check and monitor the information stored about them on a regular basis. The 1998 Act goes further and extends the law on data protection to cover paper files as well as computer records. The key principles of the data protection legislation can be summarised as follows and provide that personal data shall be:

- *processed* fairly and lawfully.
- *obtained* only for specified and lawful purposes and shall not be processed in any manner incompatible with those purposes.
- *adequate, relevant* and not excessive in relation to the purposes for which it is processed.
- *accurate* and where necessary kept up to date.
- *kept* for no longer than is necessary.
- treated as *confidential.*

The *Access to Medical Records Act 1988* (and *Access to Health Records Act 1990*)

These acts are particularly relevant to occupational health-related issues and will often come into play in the handling of disciplinary or capability issues in the workplace (see Chapter 10). The 1988 Act gives an individual employee right of access to medical reports relating to them which are supplied by a medical practitioner or occupational health advisor for employment purposes.

By the same token an employer may not apply for a copy of such a report without the employee's consent. The 1990 Act tightened up loopholes in the 1988 legislation and extended its scope including the right for inaccurate records to be corrected and the broadening of the definition of who constituted a general practitioner or health professional.

The *Trade Union Reform and Employment Rights Act 1993*

This piece of legislation is particularly relevant to the collection and storage of employee data, because it draws together information enshrined in earlier legislation (the *Employment Protection Consolidation Act 1978* and the *Contracts of Employment Act 1970*) about what should be included in contracts of employment. More details of this legislation are provided at Chapter 3, but it is relevant here because if the contract is the underpinning document for the employment relationship between employee and employer, it follows that the kinds of information that employers should keep relating to employees should be concerned with items defined by the contract. Although the employee's personal file should naturally contain information about pay, conditions of employment, references, any information relating to sickness absence, any record of disciplinary warnings or actions, and other relevant employment-related data it should not normally stray into areas of the employee's private life unless they specifically have disclosed it and bought it into the employment relationship.

7.3 Categories of employee data

All organisations need to keep at least basic records about the individuals they employ. These normally exist in the form of a personal file held manually and may be supplemented with additional information for payroll purposes. Generally speaking, the larger and more complex the organisation, the more sophisticated its personnel records will be, and the more information about employees under different categories will be stored. For categorisation purposes data can be grouped under a number of headings as follows:

Contractual information

Derived from the contract of employment itself, this information will be held either in manual and/or computerised form and relate to:

- Grade, pay scale or *salary* information
- Information drawn from the employee's application form about previous occupations and *career history*
- Details of *qualifications* and training the individual has undertaken
- *Contact information* including home address, telephone numbers and details of next of kin

- *Equal opportunities* information concerning gender, age and ethnicity
- Information relating to *other terms and conditions* of employment including pension arrangements, annual leave, company car (where provided), relocation, or other employee benefits.

Confidential information

Although this information may in part also be drawn from the contract of employment, it will also include other data which is sensitive and needs to be treated separately and confidentially. It will include:

- Copies of any *references* obtained from previous employers at the time of appointment
- Information relating to *employment screening* or any occupational health referrals undergone by the employee whilst in employment
- Information relating to any *disciplinary* action taken against the employee (note: this must be current and relevant – see Chapter 8)
- Details of any *grievances* the employee may have made or any referrals they have sought under the organisation's whistleblowing policy
- Any material relating to *health and safety* in the workplace affecting the individual employee
- Material on matters of a *personal* nature which the employee has brought into the employment relationship or is otherwise relevant to it

Performance management information

The next category data concerns information that will be collected during the employment process to help the individual's performance at work and may legitimately be used for appraisal and performance management purposes where this is included as part of the contractual arrangements.

- Details of the employee's *sickness* and attendance record (or this may be kept under the confidential section where there are particular issues at play)
- Information relating to job *performance* progress
- Records of any previous *appraisals* undertaken on the employee's performance (although these may be kept in a separate system)
- Records of any particular *achievement* or meritorious performance by the individual concerned

Training and development

Organisations usually operate a separate employee information system concerned with the training and development of their staff. This again can be accessed either in manual and/or computerised form and will typically include information relating to:

- Principal *qualifications* and academic achievements of the employee (as recorded in the contractual section above)

- Record of any *training courses* undertaken before the employee commenced the current employment
- A record of any *training* undertaken during the current employment
- Record of any *special qualifications*, records of attendance, competence awards obtained by the employee
- Details of any recorded *training needs* or a personal development plan agreed as part of the appraisal or performance management system (again this may be recorded separately)

Employee support and welfare

Finally, employers may keep information relating to information concerned with employee support and welfare where this becomes part of the employment relationship. An example here would be a separate recording system used by a confidential employee counselling service where the information has disclosed highly confidential information to a staff counsellor or advisor. This must be kept quite separately from the employee's main personnel file and information held about them on a central computerised personnel information system. However, such records are often maintained to keep track of individual counselling or welfare services provided for the individual, and these may become relevant and have a legitimacy if there is a particular problem or indeed a dispute to resolve at a later stage in the employment relationship. Further information on the kinds of transaction that can take place under this heading are dealt with in Chapter 13. Although there are many categories of employee data which an employer may legitimately keep that will help inform and protect the employment relationship, we next need to turn our attention to how this data is collected, stored, retrieved and used as part of the modern HRM approach. Much, of course, will depend on the number and type of systems the employer uses to track and retain the information.

7.4 Types of personnel information system

Given the array of employee data that can exist, it is clearly a very important consideration for employers to decide how they are going to collect and store information about their staff. The following describes the types of personnel information systems that may be found in the modern organisation:

Manual personnel files

The manual personnel record is alive and well in all but the most sophisticated of modern organisations. Despite the growth in the use and sophistication of computerised systems (see below) manual data still has a huge number of uses in the workplace. A manual personnel file would typically be held centrally by the Personnel Department and will record one or more of the categories of data described above. It has stood the test of time as the cornerstone of employment records because:

- It is *inexpensive*
- It is *easy to access* for practitioners
- It provides a *simple* way of storing information that the employee supplies in written form
- It is easily *transferable* to the manual files

Good practice in the operation and storage of the modern personnel file suggests the keeping of data in separate sections within the main file itself.

Typically, information about the contract of employment would be kept in the open part of a personnel file and other confidential performance management and personal material would be kept in separate sections. Data relating to training and development would not normally be stored in the central file and information of a highly personal nature relating to employee support and welfare should not be kept in the central file on any account. The need to keep accurate and up-to-date manual records becomes all the more important given the rights bestowed on employees by the *Data Protection Act 1998*. As this now requires data stored manually to be accurate, up-to-date and relevant and not disclosed to other parties without permission or good reason and then to be open to inspection by the employee, it is crucial that the personal file complies with these requirements.

It is poor employment practice to store information about an employee on the file that is not known to the individual and which does not meet the requirements of the *Data Protection Act*. So, a manager who wishes to make a note on the employee's personal file about something which he/she are unhappy about in the employment relationship will be in clear breach of these requirements. Any such action would have to be disclosed and recorded as part of agreed disciplinary, appraisal or performance management systems.

Payroll systems

The management of the organisation's payroll is often not part of the function of Human Resources. In most organisations, the payroll is run by the finance department or is outsourced and managed externally to the organisation as a whole. However, the input to the payroll system is usually derived from personnel data, and there is, therefore, an obvious and clear link between the two. In all but the smallest of organisations, payroll systems are now sophisticated and heavily computerised. They employ advanced techniques for calculating salaries and allowances and other benefits and updating and uprating these automatically to be sure that the correct pay reaches the correct employee at the right time. The payroll system may also be linked directly to other information systems that collect information about employee working times and patterns and will include the recording of overtime, shift working or other arrangements that will affect and influence pay.

Although there are still many types of stand-alone payroll systems, increasingly these are linked or integrated with personnel information systems. In this "personnel driving payroll" system there is a direct computer linkage between personnel data, with one triggering a change or response in the other. So, as a personnel assistant amends details about an employee's pay from a personnel perspective, there is an automatic and reciprocal calculation in the payroll system to ensure this is reflected in terms of salary. It is not generally good practice to have payroll systems that drive personnel data. The reasons for this are largely to do with defining the main source of data and confidentiality.

Given that most of the information that drives pay is derived from the activities of the Human Resource Department, the primary source should normally be the personnel input into the system. This should ensure accuracy, protect confidentiality and ensure the correct flow of information in the organisation. Once this data becomes "owned" by payroll (and this is particularly so where payroll is run external to the organisation) there is a danger that the integrity and accuracy of the data will be lost.

Computerised personnel information systems

There is now a bewildering array of personnel information systems on the market that are capable of storing and manipulating contractual, confidential, performance management, training and development and employee support and welfare data, in stand-alone, integrated, or networked systems. For the purposes of this book, it is important to understand some of the differences between these types of computerised information system.

Despite the retained advantages of the manual personnel record, computerisation has come into its own in the area of personnel data, storage and retrieval as it can be seen to "add value", gives speed and accuracy of information, and extends the applications to which it may be put. There follows a summary of the benefits of an accurate and reliable computerised personnel information system.

Reviews of personnel data

Because the decision to set up a computerised personnel information system requires the original input of data, this can often mark a review of the data that is held by individuals and will lead to a sifting of information to ensure what is left is accurate and relevant. Manual personnel files are notoriously abused and used to store extraneous information that does not really belong there. The audit of the employee information that the creation of a personnel information system requires can of itself be a very useful checking exercise.

Possible uses of information

As will be discussed later in this chapter, the great constraint in terms of manual records is the one-dimensional use of data that can be produced from it. Whilst it may be a reliable way of eliciting information about, for example, sickness absence, it is difficult to integrate information about sickness absence with attendance records, shift patterns and other performance management data. New forms of information generate new ideas and generally speaking will allow the organisation to be much more innovative in its use of employee data. This in turn should lead to better decision making and use of human resources within the organisation.

Corporate business planning and development

Use of a computerised personnel information system can give the Human Resources Department the information and opportunity it needs to play a greater part in the corporate business planning and decision-making processes. The aggregation of individual employee information, the analysis of trends, and the application of workforce planning techniques are much more strategic than operational human resource planning tools. If the organisation's Human Resources manager can come to a meeting armed with a clear picture about wastage rates, he/she is much more likely to be able to influence the organisation's strategic human resource planning processes.

Better services to managers

There is no doubt that one of the great benefits of modern computerised and HR systems is the flexible and efficient service it allows the Human Resource Department to provide to line managers through providing information about absence, turnover or individual employee data. Improved quality and quantity of information that can be provided will also allow the Human Resources Department to monitor activities more effectively, thus providing better guidance and advice for line managers in turn.

Information requests

As referred to in the introduction to this chapter, it is becoming increasingly important for organisations to be able to respond to requests or demands for information to provide data about both the quality and quantity of their HR processes. So be it, a trade union wanting information about recruitment practices, or a complaint from an individual about unfair treatment in relation to a redundancy, computerised personnel information systems are much more likely to be able to provide the information required quickly and accurately.

Types of system

So, the advantages of using the computerised Personnel Information System (PIS) rehearsed, what type of system might the modern Personnel Department acquire for use? There follows a summary of the main types of computerised personnel information system currently on the market.

Comprehensive PIS

A comprehensive PIS is one which attempts to cover all or most areas of employee information listed above and is usually designed by or for and operated within the Human Resources Department. It may be a stand-alone or integrated system (see below) that will have as its primary aim the requirement to draw and manipulate employee data for use by the Human Resources Department and in turn by line managers themselves. Because of advances in computer software, Personnel Information Systems can now be purchased for as little as £15,000 including the costs of both hardware and software installation. It does escalate, of course, dependent on the number of users of the system, how many different points of access there are and whether the system is networked or integrated with other systems over one or more sites.

Expert systems

A whole new generation of personnel computerised tools are now becoming available. These are known as expert or knowledge-based systems. An expert system has a built-in knowledge base that contains judgmental and qualitative knowledge and can be used interactively. Initially, the application of such systems in personnel was limited and related to information applications such as that of job analysis and job evaluation. However, bespoke systems like these are becoming increasingly well-used for training and development purposes. So, for example, data can be fed in relating to an employee's training needs and the output from the software about the most appropriate or preferred training courses or learning methods for the individual. These intelligent systems are becoming more sophisticated and are increasingly being applied to the whole spectrum of HR activity.

Computerised tools

These are systems or applications that cover one or a very small number of HR tasks and are not intended for expansion into a comprehensive system. They are not like expert systems in that they do not have the information to provide judgmental or qualitative knowledge, but rather are used for bespoke purposes such as accident recording or training information. The growth in sophistication and reduction in price of software packages means that these applications are becoming less used and being replaced by comprehensive or expert systems.

Human resource networks

In the 1980s, there was huge growth in the use of Human Resource networks that provided information rather like that available via teletext. Given the growth in the use of the Internet, these resource networks have been absorbed as part of the data that can be provided by the modern Internet infrastructure. The type of information that can now be obtained of an HR nature that exists on "the net" includes salary survey information and updates on employment legislation.

Integrated systems

As referred to above, many modern personnel information systems are now integrated with payroll or other management information systems to form an integrated service. The advantages of an integrated payroll and personnel system include: the lack of duplication of records; consistency of data for common use and application; and reduction in costs of use and storage. Many of the computerised software packages and systems currently on the market are of an integrated nature and are ideal for the small to medium-sized organisation that is seeking a computerised personnel information system "off the shelf".

1 Prepare a business case	*Try to identify costs/benefits*
This is an important document which will help you clarify what you are trying to achieve. It will also help you to enlist support from your organisation, including the budget holders who need to give approval to the purchase of the new system! Before you choose your system you need to decide why you are really doing this. What are your drivers for change? What do you aim to achieve? How will you judge whether your aims have been successful?	The following questions will help you to clarify what you want: ▶ What are the reasons for change? ▶ What can you put into this (money/time/people)? ▶ What do you want out of it? Too many organisations end up being dissatisfied with their system because it does not produce the outputs they need. ▶ What will happen if you don't do anything?
2 Decide what you want	*Also bear in mind*
You really only have three options in choosing a system – do you pick a package off the shelf, get one written for you, or customise a commercially available product? ▶ Draw up a detailed specification describing exactly what the system must contain, what it must be able to do and how it will do it. This approach attempts to match the system to the organisation and its existing practices and procedures. ▶ Produce an outline specification only, and match the organisation to the system. This approach is appropriate for organisations that are prepared to adapt their procedures to the system.	▶ Whether it needs to integrate with other systems or with your intranet, and how. ▶ How you will get information into the system. ▶ What outputs you require from the system and how easy it should be to write inquiries and reports. ▶ IT requirements – must the system conform to your organisation's IT standards or strategy? ▶ How many people will use the system, and in what ways? ▶ The user-friendliness of the system.
3 Evaluate the market	*What criteria can you use to help you narrow the choice?*
Draw up a structured process whereby you can document any decisions made and weight factors according to their importance. Make sure that all stakeholders are represented in the decision-making team. *How can you find out what is available?* ▶ Go to specialist exhibitions ▶ Ask experts/colleagues/professional networks ▶ Read articles and news reports	▶ Budget – not only for purchasing the system, but also for implementing and running it ▶ Kit ▶ Supplier reputation ▶ Timescales ▶ Ability to integrate with other systems ▶ Ease of input ▶ Quality of outputs

4 Check costs	What is covered by the stated costs?
	▶ A single, multi- or unlimited user licence
	▶ Training and documentation
	▶ Support for implementation
	▶ Help with tailoring or customising
	▶ Integration with other business systems
	▶ Upgrades and annual maintenance
	▶ How much additional budget is available for hardware. IT communications, implementing the system, training users, providing a help desk?
5 See the system in action	
Such demonstrations are a useful starting point, but make sure that you also see the system in action in a real-life situation. Your supplier should be able to give you a list of reference sites, where you will be	able to talk to system-users. Some suppliers will let you use the system in your organisation for a trial period before you make your final decision.
6 Sign the contract	
The final part of choosing your system will entail some detailed contract negotiation – until this is over you cannot be quite sure you have actually got what you want.	Responsibilities on both sides should be laid down and understood. You'll need expert help for this stage, to avoid later arguments.

Figure 7.1   A model specification for a computerised HR system

Whatever the type of system the organisation chooses to procure is likely to depend on a number and range of employees, the different types of conditions of service on which they are employed, number of locations in which the organisation operates and its financial and information system resources. Whatever the resultant decision about a computerised system purchase, the key to success is in matching the organisation's information needs with the system requirement or specification. A model specification for a modern computerised personnel information system is provided at Figure 7.1. This outlines the kinds of information features and modelling requirements that will be needed for a medium-sized organisation employing between one and two thousand employees, operating from one site but with a number of different categories of employee and types of terms and conditions of employment.

7.5 Data applications

Whichever type of computer system and manual back-up system is used, the most critical element is determining what comes out of it and how this meets the organisation's needs. Part of the process of designing the specification for the system outlined above will be determining the kinds of application that the system will be used for. Some typical computerised PIS data applications can be summarised as follows:

Listing reports

As the name suggests these reports contain lists of information grouped together by category of employee, or by age, job title, length of service or any other kind of employee category. They are factual data lists and merely exist to provide a summary of information under the category and to replace that that would otherwise have to be drawn manually from a manual record system.

Statistical reports

These summarise information on a more analytical basis, for example comparing the total sickness levels for a department on a quarter-by-quarter or year-by-year basis and comparing these to the organisational trends as a whole. Statistical reports will be provided normally in matrix form and can also be converted into graphs, pie, bar and other forms of charts for easy visual representation. A typical statistical analysis of absence trends is shown at Figure 7.2.

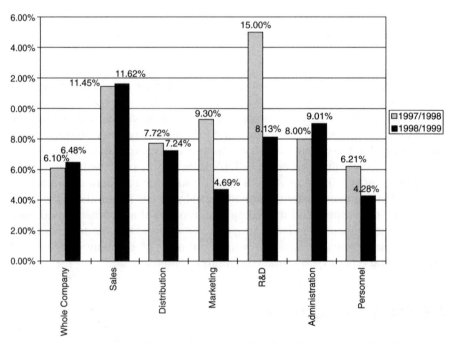

Figure 7.2 Statistical analysis of absence trends: chart showing annual sickness for 1997/98 1998/99 – Zantec Ltd

Ad hoc reports

Ad hoc reports are sometimes called random reports and are a facility usually produced from a random report generator within the computerised system. The difference between an ad hoc report and a standard statistical report is that the standard reports have to be built into the computerised software and therefore have to be defined as the system is being developed. The ad hoc report facility enables previously unthought of reports to be defined and requested at any time. They of course depend on the data existing in some form but may provide for a unique combination of events to be produced together. These will often be required when there is a need to respond to a particular information request (for example in response to a claim about breach of equal opportunities in a recruitment and selection process where information about equal opportunities monitoring, and recruitment and selection trends is needed to be drawn together into the statistical analysis).

Modelling

Modelling is a form of simulation which answers the question "what if"? Modelling can be very helpful when trying to work out the likely impact of a decision relating to the workforce. So, for example, such a modelling technique might be used to predict the likely increase in the organisation's total pay bill by predicting the outcome or effect of different levels of pay award for different groups of staff. Another typical application will be in trying to design shift patterns to predict the total available amount of work hours available and matching to staff availability.

Automatic letter production

This facility is usually linked to a word processing package and provides the HR Department with the opportunity to create standard or automatic letters such as contracts of employment, letters regarding pay increases, or other forms of contractual variation. They save a huge amount of administrative burden and the manual production of tailored information.

Diarising

Diarising facilities exist in most software packages and allow the user to ask the computer to give a reminder once a certain time period has elapsed. This is particularly helpful in conjunction with absence-recording procedures, probationary employees, and the monitoring of grievance and disciplinary procedures where there are prescribed time periods.

The implication of all these data applications, of course, is that the modern human resource manager has to become much more computer and data literate than his or her predecessor of twenty-five or thirty years ago. It is no longer enough for the modern practitioner to be aware of the types of data that exist and the uses to which they can be put. Increasingly, today's practitioner needs to be able to understand the inter-relationship between some of the different data sets described here and some of the increasingly sophisticated modelling applications. Of course, once we begin to tread the road of sophisticated statistical applications, we start to enter the arena of modern workforce planning which is the ultimate destination of ad hoc reporting, modelling of "what if" scenarios.

7.6 Workforce planning

Although workforce planning existed as a branch of HRM long before the invention of the modern computerised HR information system, it has really come into its own as an aspect of organisational resource utilisation and planning given the assistance the computerised systems and software packages can give. This is not just because computers are much more accurate in computing employee data and predicting employment trends. It is also because they have the facility for integrating and linking different groups of data, combining these and producing an integrated analysis. Workforce planning is a sophisticated and important arm of HRM in its own right and there are a number of excellent texts available to provide detailed reference for the interested reader (see Selected reading list). However, for the purpose of this book it is important to have an understanding of what workforce planning is, the context it operates in, the sum of the workforce planning activities that can be undertaken and some of the different methods that are used in these activities.

The first consideration therefore is to provide a meaningful definition of modern workforce planning. Much of this definition will be derived from the nature of the organisation in which it is used and the description of its core business activity and reference back to this and the kind of HRM activity the organisation needs and undertakes is thus a useful starting point. So strategic HRM is much more likely to need a sophisticated set of workforce planning requirements than an operational or control and welfare model will. Once the organisation and HRM context is properly defined the following is a useful definition which sums up the essence of workforce planning activities:

> Workforce planning aims to maintain and improve the ability of the organisation to achieve its corporate objectives, through the development of strategies designed to enhance the contribution of the workforce at all times in the foreseeable future. (Steiner 1971)

In practical terms what this means is:

- to ensure that the organisation employs the *right number* of people with the right skills and abilities at the right time;
- to ensure that this workforce is utilised *effectively and efficiently*;
- and to improve human resources by *providing development* and satisfying the need for employee development and skill enhancement.

Of course, planning the workforce of tomorrow is not like planning the organisation's revenue budget for the next year. The nature of the human resources is different and the context for workforce planning recognises some key principles.

KEY POINTS

- ▶ that organisations need people with *different skills* to operate *in different places* at *different times*
- ▶ both a surplus and deficit in the required level of human resources are *wasteful* or potentially damaging for the organisation
- ▶ the human resource needs to be *nurtured and cared* for in a way that other resources do not
- ▶ human resources are *dynamic and unpredictable*
- ▶ *external factors* including the local and national economy, labour markets and government policy will have an impact on the environment in which workforce planning operates.

Manpower planning activities

So much then for the theory and context for workforce planning activities that can be carried out to ensure that future workforce requirements can be accurately predicted and put in practice. The main planning activities which are used as practical applications focus on:

- Forecasts of future demand for human resources
- Consideration of changes in the way the workforce will be utilised and the effect this has on demand
- Analysis of the current workforce supply
- Forecasts of the internal workforce supply that will be created as a result of the organisation's current policies
- Forecasts of external workforce supply relating to factors such as local and national economic indicators
- Reconciliation of forecasts and feedback on them
- Resultant decisions and workforce plans.

Some of these activities have a rather technical component, and it is possible to enter some sophisticated statistical territory using them. In essence though, the concept of workforce planning is simple if the following questions are considered:

QUESTIONS

1 What kind of workforce does the organisation currently employ?
2 What kind of workforce will it require to employ tomorrow based on what is known about the organisation's development and business plans?
3 What is going to happen to the existing workforce based on current tends?
4 What kind of workforce supply exists in the marketplace based on what we know about macro- and microeconomic indicators?
5 How can the organisation hope to obtain and procure the services of the workforce it requires to bridge the gap for the future?

Workforce planning methods

In this section we will consider how some of the workforce planning techniques described above can be used to produce the necessary forecasts required and these are most easily described under the various activity headings listed above.

Methods for forecasting the demand for human resources

There are two main types of workforce planning method under this heading, objective and subjective. Objective methods depend on the use of statistical information to predict what would happen in future. Some of these use historical information, such as looking at past trends in the workforce to predict what will happen. So, typically, it will look at organisational activity over the previous years to try and work out what will be needed in the next five and will look at the growth in business activity and its relation to what has happened historically. Such analysis will not necessarily predict what happens in the future and this is particularly so with the radical changes in information technology and modern working methods that we are currently experiencing. A more subjective method, therefore, will be to look at managerial opinion or judgement to try and make an assessment of what is needed, referring to the objective statistical information but not relying on it wholly. So, if in a production organisation an increase in output of X required an increase in workforce of Y this may be tempered by the judgement of the production manager who knows that improved technology and equipment means he/she can reduce this forecast by 10 per cent, based on his/her own workplace intelligence.

Methods for changing workforce utilisation

The emphasis on workforce utilisation varies considerably depending on the nature of the organisation and the type of work to be performed. There are a vast range of factors which may change the way that the workforce is utilised, including some notable examples.

EXAMPLE

1   The introduction of new materials or equipment
2   Changes in the way work is organised
3   Organisational growth and development
4   The introduction of productivity, incentive bonus or incentive share schemes
5   Introduction of staff flexibility and ways of working.

The important issue is to consider these changes in utilisation (either actual or predicted) and bring them into the workforce planning equation. So, for example, the computerisation of the whole or part of workforce activity will have an enormous impact on the demand for the workforce of the future and the way it will be utilised.

Forecasting internal workforce supply

This is the most common workforce planning method in that it relies on manipulating data about the current workforce and trends that can be drawn from it. Some of the key workforce analysis techniques include:

Turnover index

This is sometimes called the wastage rate and looks at the number of staff who leave in a given period compared to the total number of staff employed who could have left. The equation is:

$$\frac{\text{Leavers in year}}{\substack{\text{Average number of staff in post during} \\ \text{the year by 100\% or turnover rate}}} = \text{the \% wastage}$$

Stability index

This index is based on a number of staff who could have stayed throughout the same period. Usually staff with a year's service are expressed as a percentage of staff in post one year ago, namely:

$$\frac{\text{no of staff with one year's service at a particular date}}{\text{no of staff employed exactly one year before} \times 100} = \text{the \% stability rate}$$

Methods for forecasting external workforce supply

Analysis of internal workforce trends and supply can only tell us so much about the workforce of tomorrow; we also need to compare this to information about the external supply and this will depend on a number of factors.

EXAMPLE

1　The planned closures and opening of other workplaces in the area within the same industry or sector.
2　Housing or infrastructure developments.
3　Local unemployment levels.
4　Previous experience of skills that are difficult or easy to recruit in the area relevant to the occupation concerned.
5　Output from the local education system.
6　Facilities for government training schemes or special development initiatives.

What this analysis will produce ultimately is some description of the local, national or in some cases international economic context for the workforce. So, for example, if a company is concerned with employing staff in the car industry, we will know that we are dealing with a multinational workforce that is influenced by international macroeconomic policies affecting both the production of cars, the techniques for producing them and individual government policies that will affect the demand for and use of motor vehicles. A topical example will be national demand for nurses in the NHS in the UK. Because it takes a number of years to train a qualified nurse, it is possible to work out how many are currently in training and the kinds of national investment decision that will affect the throughput of this national training system in the years to come. This information can then be successfully related to the information produced from the internal workforce supply analysis referred to above to try to predict the likely numbers of nursing staff required for the future against those that are likely to exist in reality.

These demand and supply forecasts, therefore, need to be compared and decisions made to produce a resultant workforce plan. The product is likely to be a plan that looks at some key factors:

KEY POINTS

- ► Workforce supply related to the timing and approach to recruitment, transfer, redeployment or redundancy
- ► Workforce utilisation looking at the way that the workforce will be used in the future that will have an impact on working patterns and employment policies
- ► Training and development plans that will look at how the organisation needs to train and develop its staff to meet its future skill requirements
- ► Other personnel plans that will look at salary, appraisal, working conditions and industrial relations policies that all have an impact on both the quantity and quality of working life within the organisation.

7.7 Problem areas

QUESTION:

A new employee has approached me, the HR manager for the company, to ask if he can see a copy of the reference that was written about him by his previous employer which now sits on his personal file. Although the reference is largely good, it is critical in one or two areas and I am concerned about breaching confidentiality of the previous employer by sharing it with the employee. What should I do?

ANSWER:

The overriding duty of confidentiality in the case of personal data is to the individual about whom the data is held or written. Under the provisions of the Data Protection Act 1998, individuals have rights to see information that is held about them in manual records as well as computerised records as previously provided by the Data Protection Act 1984. Your employee, therefore, has every right to see a copy of the reference that is written about her/him. To protect the integrity of the employer who provided the reference, it is good practice to seek their permission first, and there should no problems so long as what they have provided is in good faith and is accurate and honest.

QUESTION:

We are short of space in the office in which my company is located and I am wondering about getting rid of some of the manual personnel files we hold on our 800 employees. We have a very effective and reliable computerised HR Information

System and I am wondering if I am required to hold the data in manual form about them?

ANSWER:

Although there are some examples of "paperless" human resource offices, there are very few who would entrust the whole of their personnel information to a computerised system. If for any reason the system should crash, the organisation would be left very vulnerable without any written records whatsoever. Space clearly is an issue for some companies and organisations, but the key is holding essential information only in manual or written form. The guidance provided above in this chapter gives an indication of the kinds of data that might be stored and extraneous information should be culled as part of an audit either taken upon the creation of a computerised Personnel Information System or at a periodical updating for the purposes of the Data Protection Act.

To assist in this many organisations undertake audits once a year and send staff a pro-forma to check accuracy and filter out extraneous material. The other compelling reason for retaining a manual or written record is that so much of the information given to you by the employee will be in that form and should therefore be retained manually. Examples are copies of educational certificates, birth certificates, health declarations and the originating application form. Although it may be possible to convert much of this data into a computerised record, the original manual record should be kept for legal and good practice purposes.

QUESTION:

I have seen a computerised HR Information System in operation at a partner company and am very impressed by it. Although our business is completely different from theirs I can see it has a ready application for us. The representatives have been round to display their software and I am tempted to buy it off the shelf. Should I carry out a thorough investigation?

ANSWER:

The key issue in purchasing a good computerised HR Information System is not so much about shopping around (although looking at comparative systems and comparing specifications and prices will be of value) but about ensuring that the organisation produces its own specification to meet its employee information needs. Only when you have undertaken this exercise will you be able properly to specify the system you wish to purchase. Many small organisations buy high-powered and sophisticated systems that have a capacity they will never need to use because they only need basic record-keeping and data manipulation.

Equally, the opposite is true with large complex organisations having systems that are unable to provide them with the statistical and ad hoc reports they need properly to analyse the workforce, establish trends and undertake workforce planning. So the key is in defining the organisational or user specification and the example provided in this chapter is a guide to how this might be prepared. Many modern computerised HR Information Software packages are relatively inexpensive, and will run on most computer systems. There is plenty to choose from and most can meet the basic data requirements of all but the most demanding organisation.

QUESTION:

I am somewhat of a sceptic when it comes to workforce planning, or as we used to know it, manpower planning. I work for a large government agency now and all our attempts to undertake workforce planning in the past came to nothing because the needs of the organisation or the government of the day changed radically and our predictions were then quickly out of date. What is the point of spending time and effort compiling a detailed workforce plan?

ANSWER:

You are absolutely right to assert that much of the effort that has gone into workforce planning in the past has been wasted and this can go some way to explaining why this branch of HRM has been devalued in recent years. However, workforce planning is now coming back into its own aided by the modelling of facilities available on computerised HR Information System software. The key is in tying these statistical workforce projections to the environment in which the organisation operates. Although it may not be possible to predict all the external factors that will have a bearing on the way your organisation works, a medium-term view can usually be taken, even in government agencies where the influences of politics can be so volatile. Governments publish expenditure plans for the medium term and it is possible to elicit a short- to medium-term view for most aspects of government service. Indeed, workforce planning is usually harder in volatile commercial markets where huge changes in product definition, the skills required and the subsequent labour markets may arise in quite short spaces of time. This is particularly true in the information technology industries and in what is now known as "E Commerce" using the Internet.

However, the author would contend that it is better to have a plan even if it does become out of date than not to know the general direction of travel. This will tell you for example whether you need a large or small number of a particular occupational group based on your own internal workforce trends, including turnover and recruitment patterns, what you understand about your organisational business development and the external marketplace. Perhaps one of the reasons why workforce or manpower planning failed in the past was because it simply failed to tie itself properly to the corporate business planning processes. That is why it is important to strategic HRM that workforce planning is integrated as a proper resource planning tool linked to financial and business objectives.

7.8 Activity

Your managing director/chief executive has asked you to produce an urgent report on the storage and use of personal data within your organisation. Produce a report listing the various categories of information you currently hold about employees, breaking these down into appropriate categories. Based on your analysis advise the managing director/chief executive on the best type of system(s) for your company dependent on size, location, complexity and financial resources. The managing director/chief executive has asked you to ensure that whatever proposal you come up with is compliant with the *Data Protection Act 1998*; you will need to reassure him/her of this in your planned arrangements.

7.9 Checklist

- ▶ The collection, storage and filtering of personnel information has been revolutionised by the introduction of computerised HR Information Systems.
- ▶ Most organisations continue to run manual and computerised systems side-by-side – there are benefits to both.
- ▶ The *Data Protection Acts* place responsibilities on employers to ensure the accuracy and relevance of both computerised and manual data stored about employees.
- ▶ Employee data falls into different categories: contractual data; confidential data; performance management information; training and development records; and information relating to employee support and welfare.
- ▶ There are a range of Personnel Information Systems available: manual personnel files; payroll systems; and computerised systems.
- ▶ There are, in turn, a range of computerised systems available; and each perform different tasks.
- ▶ Some typical applications of these systems include listing reports, statistical reports, ad hoc reports and modelling facilities.
- ▶ Workforce planning is greatly enhanced by the use of a computerised system.
- ▶ Some workforce planning techniques and applications are explored in this chapter.

▪ ⱱ 8 Equal Opportunities

8.1 Introduction

One of the major topics of HRM, which would distinguish the work of today's manager or practitioner from his or her predecessor of thirty or forty years ago, is the often emotive and complex subject of equal opportunities. It is a topic that inspires mixed emotions: fear, because through ignorance many are daunted by the prospect of handling issues relating to sex, race, disability, ageism or sexual orientation; antagonism, either because of real prejudice, or because of a reaction to what has become termed "political correctness" in forwarding the cause of equality of opportunity in the workplace; and confusion, because the reality of tackling equal opportunities in a sound HR framework is often confused with the more sensational and misleading headlines. In reality, all that the law and good practice demands is reasonableness and equity in the treatment of employees and prospective employees in employment matters. Of course, this does not mean that the law cannot be confusing. Because precedents set by case law can substantially stretch the boundaries of the original legislation, the main body of equal opportunities legislation is often used by the litigants to test the interpretation of the law and by implication, the views of society as a whole, on matters that were never originally conceived as part of the originating legislation, and still today stand outside statute. The key to understanding and adopting good practice in the management and promotion of equal opportunities rests on four key elements.

KEY POINTS

- ▶ Understand the legal framework
  As we shall discuss in this chapter, the legal framework is the cornerstone of good HR practice and needs to be understood before the more complex practice issues can be considered.
- ▶ Understand the basis of good practice
  Many organisations follow admirable standards in the management and promotion of equality in the workplace, and some of those good practice standards will be focused on in this chapter.
- ▶ Understand the need for sound procedures
  As with most sound HR management, sound procedures encourage and promote good attitudes and sound organisational behaviour and these derive from the good practice and legal framework described above.

► Understand the real issues
Because there is often much hype about equal opportunities-related issues, it
is easy to get drawn into the emotional overkill that is often associated with
debating these issues. The real issues simply boil down to promoting equality
of opportunity for all employees and not discriminating against one group in
favour of another.

8.2 Legal framework

Prior to the 1970s, typical personnel practitioners would have readily understood
what was required of them in terms of the law and equality of opportunity in
the workplace. The legislative framework was very simple: outside the *Disabled
Persons Acts (1944 and 1958)*, which established a quota system for the employment of the disabled (by common consensus a failure as evidenced by the very
low levels of employment of disabled persons in most UK organisations by the
end of the 1980s) and understanding that HR practice with integrity begs that
overt direct discrimination is not to be encouraged, there was little to comprehend. A decade or so later, and the world had changed radically. The explosion
of equal opportunities legislation in the mid 1970s, was enhanced and developed
by case law and further statute in the 1980s, and the updating of disability discrimination in the 1990s is now being accompanied early in the new millennium
by further major developments – particularly concerning race and potentially
affecting age and sexual orientation. There are several key pieces of legislation
relating to equal opportunities.

Sex Discrimination Act 1975 (amended 1986)

This cornerstone piece of legislation introduced legislation that outlawed discrimination on grounds of sex and marital status. Sex discrimination is defined
in the Acts as:

- treating a woman/man less favourably than the opposite gender purely
  because of their sex.
- applying to a man/woman a condition which is applied equally to the opposite sex but which is such that the proportion of one sex that can comply with
  it is by definition in the minority.
- the employer cannot show the condition to be justifiable irrespective of sex; it
  is to a man or woman's detriment because they cannot comply with it.

The legislation goes on to define the differences between *direct* and *indirect*
discrimination. An example of direct discrimination would be specifying in a job
advert that men only need apply for a particular job; an example of indirect discrimination is creating the circumstances whereby an individual of one gender
or marital status is likely to be successful and the other not (for example not
promoting part-time work which is bound to discriminate against women
given that women make up over 80 per cent of the part-time workforce in

the UK). This important distinction applies to all the main equal opportunities legislation.

The *Sex Discrimination Act* (and the *Race Relations Act* that followed it) also makes provision for important exemptions as follows:

- where being of a particular sex (or race) is essential to the performance of the job (ie on the grounds of decency, privacy, personal service provision etc)
- where being of a particular race (or sex) is essential to the needs of the job (eg for reasons of authenticity, a classic example being a Chinese waiter for a Chinese restaurant)
- or the provision of personal services to an ethnic group.
- taking positive action to encourage greater representation of minority groups in the workforce where they are currently under-represented.

These exemptions are collectively referred to as *genuine occupational qualifications* and are important provisions which may be used legitimately by employers within the equal opportunities legislative framework.

The *Race Relations Act 1976*

As with the *Sex Discrimination Act*, this outlaws discrimination against employees or job applicants on grounds of race, colour, nationality or ethnic and national origin. As with sex discrimination, discrimination in these terms means:

- treating a person less favourably on racial grounds than other people would be treated:
- applying to a person a requirement or condition which is or would be applied to some other people but which is such that the proportion of one racial group that can comply is in the minority;
- the employer cannot show the condition to be justifiable irrespective of race;
- it is to the detriment of the person because he or she cannot comply with it.

As with sex discrimination, the principles of direct and indirect discrimination apply. In this respect it does not matter whether or not the discrimination that results from an employer's action is intended or not; it is the effect of the actions that counts.

Equal Pay Act 1970 (and 1983 amendment regulations)

This is the legislation that introduced the concept of equal pay for work of equal value and is covered in more detail in Chapter 6.

The *Disability Discrimination Act 1995*

This legislation radically altered the law in relation to disabled employees. The Act introduced a new definition of disabled person and repealed the provisions of the *Disabled Person's Act 1944* relating to the registration of disabled persons and the obligation of employers to have a quota of disabled people in their employment. More importantly, the new legislation has for the first time in the UK made it unlawful to discriminate against disabled persons in employment and other areas in line with the provisions of the *Sex Discrimination and Race Relations Acts*. The *Disability Discrimination Act* provides some important definitions of what constitutes a disabled person. A disabled person for the purpose of the act is likely to have an impairment that affects one or more of the following:

- mobility
- manual dexterity; physical coordination
- continence
- ability to lift, carry, or otherwise move everyday objects
- speech, hearing or eyesight
- memory or ability to concentrate, learn or understand
- perception of the risk of physical danger.

The *Rehabilitation of Offenders Act 1974*

This Act is part of the equality legal framework given the requirements it places on employers in certain circumstances to disregard "spent" convictions for the purposes of considering previous offenders for employment. It is dealt with in more detail in Chapter 5.

The *Trade Union Reform and Employment Rights Act 1993*

This act consolidates and summarises previous provisions relating to trade union membership and rights and makes it unlawful for an employer to either directly or indirectly discriminate against an employee or potential employee on grounds of their trade union membership or because of their role as a recognised trade union representative in the workplace. This legislation also consolidated the provisions of the *Trade Union and Labour Relations Act 1992* which effectively ended the closed shop, the practice whereby it was compulsory for individuals to belong to a trade union if they worked in a particular environment. The right to trade union membership, and/or recognised representation and activity, is fundamentally enshrined in UK employment law and individuals are automatically protected from discrimination on these grounds as originally established by the *Employment Protection Consolidation Act 1978*, which introduced the concept of fair and unfair dismissal. The *Employment Relations Act 1999* also introduces new provisions regarding trade union recognition and representation that support and develop this principle. This is achieved by allowing trade unions automatic rights for representation in the workplace where a certain proportion of the workforce wish it to be so (see Chapter 10).

The *Health and Safety at Work Act 1974* and *Disclosure of Information Act 1999*

These pieces of legislation are not commonly associated with equality of opportunity but they are included in the legal framework because they confer on employees important rights which prohibit employers from discriminating against employees for activities related to them. The *Health and Safety at Work Act* asserts an important statutory right and indeed duty on employees to take responsibility for their health and safety in the workplace and their right to complain and draw attention to major deficiencies which they believe are to the detriment of this. Similarly, the *Disclosure of Information Act* introduces the concept of whistleblowing to the workplace and asserts the right of individual employees to be able to do this without fear of recrimination or punitive action from their employer where they do so. They are therefore part of the discriminatory framework and should be included in the consideration of the equal opportunities issues.

8.3 Codes of practice

Amongst all the employment legislation that affects HRM, the codes of practice issued under the auspices of the *Race Relations, Sex Discrimination* and *Disability Discrimination Acts,* are amongst the most important that exist and their provisions need to be considered by employers when developing their own policies and procedures and creating good practice in the workplace.

KEY POINTS

- ▶ Equal Opportunities Commission code on good practice in employment
- ▶ Commission for Racial Equality code (relating to discrimination on grounds of race and ethnic origin).
- ▶ Code of practice issued by the government on disability discrimination in employment which is to be followed up by a code of practice soon to be issued by the newly established Disability Rights Commission.

Each of these codes unpacks some of the detail of the respective parent legislation and deals with issues relating to recruitment, selection, promotion, transfer, training and development, discipline and grievance in the workplace that are likely to have an impact on individuals. The key provisions of each code are considered as part of the body of good practice described below.

8.4 Good practice

Under this section it is possible to draw together formal guidance that has been issued on good practice in issues relating to race, sex and disability in the form of the various codes of practices, and the development of good employment practices that have been drawn from the main provisions of the legislation. It is worth noting here that there are common traits to the *Sex Discrimination, Race Relations* and *Disability Discrimination Acts* when grouped under a number of headings.

Recruitment and selection

Advertisements must not discriminate on the basis of sex, marital status, race, ethnic origin or disability. This means that job titles need to be gender- or race-sensitive and indicate the acceptability of an individual on objective grounds. Given that the use of the male prerogative still dominates use of the English language, most organisations now adopt an equal opportunities statement within their recruitment advertising to make it clear that even if they are advertising a post as a "chairman" invitations are invited from all parts of the community and will be treated no less favourably on grounds of gender, race or disability. But, the potential to discriminate does not just end with the recruitment advertisement. As we will consider below, the handling of the whole recruitment and selection process is the area in which a claim of breach of equal opportunities legislation is most likely to occur. So each and every aspect have to be considered important components.

KEY POINTS

▶ The process for *short-listing* candidates and the quality of the person specification against which they will be short-listed. It is vitally important that this process considers candidates on their merits against the person specification and for no other reason. Records should be kept of the short-listing process in case of a complaint and so that reasons for non short-listing are readily available.

▶ The *selection process* must be rigorously fair and, if at all possible, the selection panel should be reflective of the mix of candidates being considered by it. There are some important considerations here. First, any ancillary aspects of the process including workplace visits, presentations and other selection techniques should be equally attainable by any competent individual regardless of gender, race or disability. Psychometric tests have come under particular criticism from certain groups because it is felt that they are very culture-insensitive to those from ethnic minority groups, focusing as they do particularly on use and understanding of the English language which can indirectly discriminate against ethnic minority applicants. The use of reputable branded tests is the key to safety in this aspect. Of course when it comes to the selection interview it is not always possible to ensure a completely representative mix on the panel. But common sense needs to prevail. If all the applicants for a key managerial job are female, it is common sense to have at least one female member on the panel. Equally, organisations that operate in multi-ethnic communities with a multi-ethnic workforce should be striving to employ a workforce that is broadly representative and is recruited and selected on the same basis. Again the keeping of records is the key to being able to withstand or respond to any challenge in the process.

▶ The *questions* asked at interview should be drawn from a common list for all candidates and not seek to discriminate in any way. It is still staggering that, after thirty years of equal opportunities legislation, the number of times that women complain about the differential treatment afforded them in interviews compared to their male counterparts is considerable. For example, men with families of young children are rarely asked how the family intends to provide for their care consequent upon a job offer. Invariably, women are asked this question and it is this differential treatment that creates a feeling of discrimination. Either the question should not be asked, the presumption being that the individual has made satisfactory arrangements to be able to undertake the job they apply for, or the question should be asked of all candidates dependent on their personal circumstances. Again, accurate record keeping is very important in this aspect of equal opportunities recruitment and selection.

Promotion, transfer and regrading

Once appointed to a position, the employee is afforded the same rights under the discrimination legislation as prospective employees. Although the recruitment and selection phase of the HRM process is the one most vulnerable to a discrimination claim, equally careful handling must be ensured in dealing with the internal transfer, promotion or regrading of existing employees. The same principles apply here as with the other aspects of discrimination good practice. Affording equality of opportunity is the key as in the recruitment and selection process. Many organisations have now developed their own internal ground rules governing promotion to internal-only advertised vacancies linked to career progression schemes.

The criteria that are used to underpin these rules need to be equal opportunity-friendly so that there is the same access to promotion, transfer or regrading opportunities regardless of gender, race or disability. Throughout the 1990s, when many women were achieving rapid promotion in the public and private sectors alike, the terminology was of women breaking through the "glass ceiling" which had previously been viewed as having inhibited women obtaining the most senior positions in organisations.

Although the majority of senior managers who are members of the British Institute of Management are still male, the proportion of women has trebled in the last decade and the signs are that women will dominate senior management positions in the next decade or so. However, many that have achieved this progression will say that it is in spite of their organisation's HR policies rather than because of them. So the same rules apply to the constitution of internal-only promotion career progression or transfer panels as they do to the recruitment and selection process for external candidates. Regrading has become a thorny issue in recent years. There is a considerable body of evidence that women are still paid considerably less than men for work of equal value despite legislation existing to discourage this, and the evidence shows that men are much more likely to be regraded within their current job than their female counterpart. Subtle, indirect discrimination is indeed still at play and has not yet been fully eradicated in the UK workplace.

Disciplinary, grievance and disputes procedures

The Sex and Race Discrimination Acts and the Codes of Practice issued by the Equal Opportunities Commission and Commission for Racial Equality respectively focus on the right of employees to have equal opportunity under disciplinary grievance and disputes procedures. The principles of equity and fairness again apply here, and consideration is given to the construction of model disciplinary, grievance and disputes procedures in Chapter 10. One of the most common areas of difficulty that organisations struggle with in relation to the handling of disciplinary and grievance matters on gender-related issues is that of maternity leave. This is also considered in more detail in Chapter 6 of this book.

Training and career development

Closely allied to issues of promotion and transfer, the concept here is that individuals should be afforded equity of treatment in terms of access for opportunities to undertake training and career development and the benefits and facilities that accompany them. Two particular considerations are paramount here. First, much of the access to and delivery of training is geared on the notion of the 9 to 5 permanent employee from an English-speaking background. Employers with a diverse workforce having a mix of genders and ethnic minorities need to consider more flexible approaches to ensure that their practice remains fair. So, affording women the opportunity to attend training programmes on a part-time basis or to flex their hours to support their attendance on a full-time basis, and tailoring programmes to reflect the culture and backgrounds of the large bodies of employees from different ethnic minorities will be the hallmarks of good equal opportunity practice in this area.

8.5 Sex discrimination

The Equal Opportunities Commission Code of Practice, published to support the introduction of the *Sex Discrimination Act* in 1975, provides useful guidance for employers to ensure they both stay within the law and promote good practice in the treatment of individuals on grounds of gender or marital status. Apart from covering the procedural issues referred to above in relation to recruitment and selection, promotion, transfer, training, discipline and grievance procedures, there is a body of good practice that will distinguish a genuine equal opportunity in the area of gender and marital status. It is worth bearing in mind that a person complaining of discriminatory treatment under the *Sex Discrimination Act* does not have to have a minimum period of qualifying service to do so. Indeed, whilst the law still requires an individual to present their complaint to a tribunal before the end of a period of three months beginning when the act complained of occurred, in many discrimination cases tribunals will waive this requirement.

Employers therefore proceed in ignorance at their peril in this area. Because most discrimination under the *Sex Discrimination Act* is against women, good employers seek to provide HR policies that encourage the appointment and promotion of women and redress the balance in the workplace. It is no coincidence that the growth of women in senior management positions in the 1990s has been accompanied by a much more flexible attitude to work which usually better suits the women who are most often the carers of young children or elderly relatives. Other positive action that can be described as good practice under this heading includes:

- Provision of *workplace nurseries,* childcare arrangements and other family-friendly policies to encourage the employment of women.
- Bespoke *training programmes* for the promotion of women's careers in the workplace, especially geared at women returners who have been out of work for some time and whose confidence needs bolstering.
- Effective *role modelling* by senior managers in the organisation to encourage other female employees to seek promotion and undertake major career development.

EXAMPLE

> In, *Holmes v. The Home Office* 1984, a key employment tribunal decision, the Home Office were found to have indirectly discriminated against a senior civil servant, Mrs Holmes, by not affording her the opportunity to work more flexibly. The law here relied on the test of a comparator, basically asking the question if the treatment of Mrs Holmes was discriminatory because of the disproportionate effects it had on her as a woman compared to men employed in her Civil Service grade. Her case was upheld, and the Home Office had to find ways of accommodating a more flexible pattern of work for her; the lessons are obvious.

8.6 Race discrimination

The *Macpherson Inquiry* into the death of the black teenager Stephen Lawrence, published in 1999, has had a massive impact on British society and the treatment of racial discrimination by UK institutions. The Macpherson Inquiry found that institutional racism was rife in the Metropolitan Police, and, in its wake, the government started to take major steps to ensure its eradication, not just in the Police but in public services as a whole, to respond to the main findings of the Macpherson Inquiry – insensitive policing, an inherent discriminatory attitude towards young black men, an unrepresentative workforce, and the absence of role models at senior levels in the force – are still mirrored in many aspects of British society. Good employment practice in the sensitive area of race and ethnic origin therefore requires the creation of organisational climates that seek to represent the community from which the workforce is drawn or served. The *Code of Practice* issued by the Commission for Racial Equality to support the introduction of the *Race Relations Act* in 1976 identifies some areas of good practice.

KEY POINTS

1 Positive action to encourage the recruitment of a greater proportion of ethnic minority applicants where they are under-represented in the workforce through targeted recruitment campaigns.

2 Equal opportunities audits and monitoring so that the employer has accurate information on the make-up of both job applicants and the current workforce and can track trends accordingly. Employers beware: it would be extremely difficult to defend a claim of racial discrimination particularly in the recruitment and selection process without some form of ethnic monitoring being in place (either as a stand-alone document or in the form of an equal opportunities questionnaire – see model in Figure 8.1) because they will simply have no information on which to draw to defend their current practices.

3 Positively promote equal opportunity through *employment policies* that make it clear that racial discrimination, and the bullying and harassment that often accompanies it, are disciplinary offences and will be firmly tackled if proven.

4 *Culture-sensitive training*, again either as a stand-alone activity or part of a wider equal opportunities training to try and educate and promote equality of opportunity. This is particularly important in the infancy of a diverse workforce, when staff are recruited from ethnic backgrounds and there is no tradition of multi-ethnic working.

Equal opportunities

We are committed to equality of opportunity in service provision and employment and welcome applications from all sections of the community.

This information will be used solely for monitoring purposes. It will be treated as confidential and will be retained by the Personnel Department. It will not be shown to the selection panel.

1   Post applied for   _____

2   Surname   _____

3   Gender   _____ Male [ ] Female [ ]

4   How would you describe
     your ethnic origin:

Black – Caribbean	[ ]	01
Black – African	[ ]	02
Black – Other	[ ]	03
Indian	[ ]	04
Pakistani	[ ]	05
Bangladeshi	[ ]	06
Chinese	[ ]	07
White	[ ]	10
Other (please specify)	[ ]	08

If you do not wish to disclose the information please tick the box   [ ]

5   We are taking positive steps to encourage the recruitment of people with disabilities. Do you consider yourself to have a disability that you would like to tell us about?

        Yes [ ]
        No [ ]

If you have answered yes to the above question please supply any information which would help us to make an interview or employment more accessible for you:

Figure 8.1   Model equal opportunities questionnaire

In the case of *Singh v. The West Midlands Passenger Transport Executive* 1986 Mr Singh was an applicant for a job of bus driver. He was the only black candidate on a short-list of twenty applicants, and failed to be appointed. Mr Singh brought a claim to an employment tribunal claiming discrimination on grounds of race. Unfortunately for the West Midlands Passenger Transport Executive, they were unable to provide records showing the ethnic origin of the applicants for the job or indeed the proportion of ethnic minority bus drivers working for their organisation. The employment tribunal therefore ordered that this information be collected and this created an important benchmark case encouraging employers to introduce appropriate ethnic monitoring procedures.

One of the major criticisms of both the *Race Relations* and *Sex Discrimination Acts* as currently constituted is that it is notoriously difficult to prove an allegation of indirect race or sex discrimination, particularly when it involves alleged institutional discrimination of the type asserted by the Macpherson Inquiry. For this reason, the Commission for Racial Equality has proposed a number of far-reaching amendments to the *Race Relations Act* and at the time of writing the government is introducing a new Race Relations Act to incorporate some of these amendments. The recommendations include:

- a positive right not to be discriminated against on grounds of race.
- the burden of proof will move from the applicant to the employer.
- there will be new definitions of indirect discrimination.
- there will be enhanced protection against victimisation.
- there will be a requirement for public sector organisations to enforce statutory contract compliance.
- a contractor supplying goods or services will need to demonstrate that they are a genuine equal opportunities employer themselves.
- ethnic monitoring will be compulsory where there are more than 250 employees.
- tribunal time limits for bringing a case will be statutorily extended to a minimum of six months.

The burden on employers is therefore only likely to increase in the sensitive area of equal opportunities management.

8.7 Disability discrimination

For nearly fifty years the rights of disabled persons in employment were protected by the *Disabled Persons Act 1944* and its supplementary legislation of 1958. These acts were largely introduced as a way of getting those injured or maimed in the Second World War back into employment and it is no surprise that by the early 1990s there was a broad consensus that the legislation no longer fitted the needs of modern employment practices. The *Disabled Persons Act 1944* required employers to have a quota of disabled people in their employment but given that most employers failed to meet this quota and gained exemptions provided by the law, and the Act did nothing specifically to outlaw direct or indirect discrimination against the disabled, the legislation widely fell into disrepute. One of the positive aspects of the Act was the introduction in the post-war years of the concept of sheltered employment for those who had severe disabilities and could not work in normal jobs. However, fifty years on these patterns of employment seemed to be patronising and ineffective in integrating the disabled into normal employment.

The Disability Discrimination Act 1995 radically altered the law in relation to disabled employees. The Act introduced a new definition of a disabled person, repealed the provisions of the *Disabled Persons Act 1944* and for the first time in the UK made it unlawful to discriminate against disabled persons in employment and other areas. Under the Act a person has a disability if he or she has a physical or mental impairment that has a substantial and long-term adverse effect on their ability to carry out normal day-to-day activities. Although guidance was issued by the Secretary of State at the time of the implementation of the Act, these definitions have been stretched by case law.

A Code of Practice was issued by the government to accompany the introduction of the new Act and it is important to note here that the indirect discrimination provisions provided under the *Race* and *Sex Discrimination Acts* do not apply with the disability to discrimination. The reason is that the *Sex Discrimination* and *Race Relations Acts* both allow for a test of indirect discrimination by comparing the way an individual is treated on grounds of race or sex with a comparative group (eg for a woman with a man and for a black person with a white person). The *Disability Discrimination Act* is not able to make this comparison because there are clearly substantial differences between an able and disabled person and a comparator must therefore be another disabled individual in employment. This makes the concept of indirect discrimination difficult to uphold and is the reason it is not included in the legislation. In terms of direct discrimination, however, comparisons can be made with able-bodied people (eg if an individual with a disability was dismissed for poor timekeeping, an employment tribunal would be justified in comparing the treatment of this individual with one who did not have a disability).

Under the *Disability Discrimination Act* there is an onus on employers to make adjustments to work of the environment in which an individual works to accommodate the disability of a job applicant or an individual in their employment who becomes disabled during the course of their work. Failure to comply with this duty will amount to discrimination. In an important benchmark case of *Morse v. Wiltshire County Council* – 1999, an employment appeal tribunal gave guidance arising from this case about the duties placed on employers both during employment and in relation to dismissal in making reasonable adjustments to work. There follow examples of the steps which an employer may have to take to comply with this duty.

EXAMPLE

1   Making adjustments to premises.
2   Allocating some of the disabled person's duties to someone else.

3 Transferring the disabled person to fill an existing vacancy.
4 Altering the hours of work.
5 Changing the place of work.
6 Allowing an employee to be absent during working hours for treatment.
7 Special arrangements for training.
8 Modifying equipment.
9 Modifying instruction or reference manuals.
10 Modifying procedures for testing or assessment.
11 Providing a reader or interpreter.
12 Providing supervision.

At first glance this is a major responsibility for employers to contemplate and could work against the interests of disabled people. However, the Act does provide a facility for employers to justify discriminating against disabled people. These grounds will be analogous to the economic, technical and organisational reasons that may justify a variation of contract or indeed lead to a redundancy. So, for example, a small employer of limited resources may simply not be able to make adjustments to premises without so impairing their profitability as to make their concern unviable. Equally, they may not have the range and staffing resources to be able to redeploy an individual who is disabled and for this reason the legislation does not apply to an employer who employs fewer than 20 employees.

As with the *Race* and *Sex Discrimination Acts*, the remedy for any individual who feels they are treated less favourably on grounds of their disability is by making an application to an employment tribunal which has the same powers as in relation to the other discrimination acts. In parallel with the provisions of the other Discrimination Acts the government provided for the establishment of a National Disability Council to advise the government on its overall strategy for disabled people and to issue a *Code of Practice* rather like those issued by the Equal Opportunities Commission and Commission for Racial Equality. However, in a recent development, the government have proposed the replacement of the National Disability Council by the Disability Rights Commission, and legislation has been going through Parliament to establish this body which would have powers parallel to those of the Equal Opportunities Commission and Commission for Racial Equality. There is a plethora of emerging case law that helps interpret and apply the Disability Discrimination legislation but a summary of the tests that tribunals are using to consider the definition of disability will help the employer in establishing whether or not there is a disability issue to deal with in the first place. The grounds are:

- Does the complainant have an impairment which is either mental or physical? If there is doubt as to whether a mental illness falls within the definition it is advisable to ascertain whether the illness is mentioned in the World Health Organisation's International Classification of Diseases.
- Does the impairment have an adverse effect on the complainant's ability to carry out normal day-to-day activities?. The focus of the legislation being on the things the complainant cannot do rather than the things they can.

- Is the adverse effect substantial (ie more than minor or trivial, rather than very large)?
- Is the adverse effect long-term?

Other than in special cases such as progressive conditions the key question is whether the physical or mental impairment is likely to last (or has lasted) for a year or more.

If the above criteria apply to an employee then the duty not to discriminate falls on an employer in line with the provisions outlined above. It is obvious therefore that although disability does not tend to attract the banner headlines of discrimination on grounds of sex or race, the wide scope for interpretation of a disability makes it an extremely difficult territory for an employer and the reference to the Act, the accompanying Code of Practice or specialist advice is advisable given the recent developments in case law.

8.8 Sexual orientation and ageism

These are interesting aspects of discrimination activity in that the current primary legislation on the UK statute book does not specifically cover discrimination against individuals on either grounds. Given the high publicity provided to cases such as *Grant v. South West Trains* 1998, which came before the European Courts of Justice, there is a commonly held public misconception that sexual orientation is covered by the law; it is not.

EXAMPLE

In the *Grant* case, the complainant, Lisa Grant, was employed by South West Trains and lived with her lesbian partner Jill Percy. Ms Grant's contract of employment provided that she would be granted travel concessions, such as fee-free and reduced rates, as were applicable to a person of her grade. Her contract also stated that her spouse and dependants would be granted travel concessions. A spouse was defined to include those who were married or those who had a statutory declaration that they had been in a meaningful relationship which had lasted two years or more.

On 9 January 1995 Lisa Grant applied for a travel concession for her partner with whom she declared she had had such a meaningful relationship for over two years. However, South West Trains refused her application on the grounds that the travel concession scheme only applied to unmarried couples who had a partner of the opposite sex. As Lisa Grant and Jill Percy were a lesbian couple they were therefore ineligible.

Lisa Grant brought employment tribunal proceedings claiming that the travel concession qualified as pay and that she had been discriminated against on the grounds of her sex. The employment tribunal considering the case, having considered a European Court of Justice decision regarding the unlawful treatment of transsexuals, took the initial view that discrimination on grounds of sexual orientation was also unlawful. The matter was referred to the European Court of Justice. However, the European Court of Justice in a benchmark ruling determined that treatment on grounds of sexual orientation did not amount to discrimination on grounds of sex.

The main reason for this is that European law does not regard those who are involved in a stable homosexual relationship as being involved in a relationship which is equivalent to marriage. It therefore has become clear from this ruling that, under the existing law, homosexuals can only complain of sex discrimination if a homosexual male is treated less favourably than a homosexual female or vice versa (that is the comparator group is another homosexual individual).

This is clearly highly contentious territory and has led to complaints from gay and lesbian groups about the overt discrimination that still exists in the European Union and the UK. This is a sensitive area concerning the interaction between employment law and public and legal attitudes. There is no doubt that public attitudes in relation to gay and lesbian relationships are changing. The leading Conservative MP Michael Portillo openly declared in 1999 that he had been engaged in homosexual activities when he was younger but this has not prevented his promotion to the Conservative front bench as Shadow Chancellor of the Exchequer. Such elevation would have been unthinkable even ten years ago and is a measure of changes in public attitudes and opinions towards matters of sexual orientation.

It is reasonable to conclude, therefore, that even though constructs of the current law do not directly outlaw acts of discrimination on grounds of sexual orientation, the reasonable employer would do well not to treat sexual orientation as overt grounds for different treatment of any employee or prospective employee. Although the absence of primary legislation may technically allow a discrimination in these areas, it is inadvisable and hardly at ease with good practice of an open and tolerant employer. In any event, it does seem likely that the next decade will see the introduction of legislation governing sexual orientation in Europe and therefore it is also likely in the UK.

Interestingly, the treatment of transsexuals has a different legal angle to that of sexual orientation.

EXAMPLE

In the case of *P v. S and Cornwall County Council*, the European Court of Justice ruled that the EU's equal treatment directive prohibits the discriminatory treatment of transsexuals. In this case P was employed by Cornwall County Council as a manager of an educational establishment. About a year later P told S, the Principal and Chief Executive of the establishment, that he intended to undergo a sex change operation. P intended to change gender from a man to a woman. At first, S was supportive and tolerant of P and apparently reassured P that his job was not under risk but later changed his attitude. P underwent surgical treatment with a view to gender reassignment and as a result was absent from work on sick leave.

During the period of sickness absence, the governors of the educational establishment took the decision to dismiss *P* and she was given three months' notice of dismissal. *P* brought employment tribunal proceedings claiming she had suffered discrimination on grounds of sex. The European Court of Justice ruled in favour of *P* because "the principle of equal treatment" for men and women is one of the fundamental principles of Community law and the right not to be discriminated against on the grounds of sex is a fundamental human right.

Accordingly the scope of the directive should not be confined to discrimination based on the fact that the person is of one or other sex. The directive is capable of being applied to discrimination arising from the gender reassignment of the person concerned.

In response to this benchmark ruling, the government has recently published a consultation document entitled *Legislation Regarding Discrimination on Grounds of Transsexualism*. It seeks to give guidance to employers and tribunals on the appropriate comparison group for transsexuals and in which circumstances discrimination on grounds of transsexuality may be permissible (for example on grounds of decency and public sensitivities). As with sexual orientation this is another emerging and fast-changing facet of discrimination law. Although transsexuals at the moment are afforded legal protection that is not directly available to gay and lesbian employees, it would not be surprising to see primary legislation linking the two at some point in the future. In the meantime the good practice advocated under the Sex, Race and Disability Discrimination Acts is transferable to these particularly sensitive and difficult areas, and the good employer would be advised to adopt them.

Issues relating to age discrimination have a rather different public profile to those concerning sexual orientation and transsexualism. If public opinion is sharply divided on the former issues, as they relate to sexuality and sensitive areas of personal decision making, there is an emerging body of opinion amongst both the public and professional groups that discrimination on grounds of age should be prohibited by law. The campaign to outlaw discrimination on grounds of age was first highlighted by the Institute of Personnel Development in a public campaign they ran in 1998. This led to the production of a Code of Practice by the IPD and, late in 1999, publication by the government itself offered a Code of Practice concerning age discrimination. Clearly the government does not believe it is yet in the position to promote primary legislation on this issue but rather is trying to encourage good practice by employers by voluntary means and to test its effectiveness.

8.9 Other statutory rights

As outlined at the beginning of this chapter, other statutory rights are afforded to employees which fall under the general banner of discrimination and employers who seek to take action against individuals for asserting these rights are almost certain to fall foul of the law. Two particular rights should be highlighted;

these are the rights of individuals under the *Health and Safety at Work Act* (dealt with in more detail in Chapter 12) and under the *Public Interest Disclosure Act* otherwise known as the Whistleblowers Charter (dealt with in more detail at Chapter 13).

8.10 Problem areas

QUESTION:
My organisation tends to recruit trainee professionals with an age limit of 25 years as a maximum. We do this because our training is long and expensive (it is a legal partnership) and investing in older people is not viable for the organisation. Is this practice legal?

ANSWER:
Strictly speaking the practice your company adopts is within the current bounds of the law provided it does not discriminate unduly against any individual on grounds of sex, race or disability. However, the Code of Practice on age discrimination published by the government in 1999 clearly discourages the practice of age prescriptions in job advertisements and many notable journals and publications are now refusing to accept such advertisements which prescribe age limits. It would be much better, therefore, for your company to remove the age requirement and recruit solely on the basis of merit because the notion of recruiting trainees by virtue of age (based on their powers of learning and potential) is not supported by empirical research and evidence in the employment field.

Many employers have found that the employment of older workers can reap substantial benefits because, whilst it is undeniable that their powers of learning wane with years, there is considerable evidence to show that loyalty and attention to detail and the wisdom that generally accompanies age more than compensate for this. The best advice for your company is to encourage it to withdraw the strict age requirement which will in any event broaden its field of choice. Clearly, if during its selection process the best candidates with the best potential are towards the younger age, then so be it.

QUESTION:
I am very worried by some of the employment practices in my organisation. Although we employ a large number of women none of them ever seem to get promoted to senior managerial positions which are exclusively a male domain. As an aspiring woman manager myself this disheartens me and makes me want to look elsewhere. However, the pay and conditions are good (I work in the retail sector) and I am loath to leave. If I were going to place a constructive proposal before my company what should I say?

ANSWER:
You might try and persuade your company on a number of levels. First, the most subtle approach is to tell it that it is missing out on a vast pool of potential as evidence and

the experience of other organisations show that many women make very good senior managers, at least as good at if not better than their male counterparts. So a straight-forward economic argument may find favour on the grounds that the company need not look outside for its senior management talent but should try and recruit from within by encouraging more women to progress. The company might do this through positive training, in the form of career development for women, through provision of flexible working patterns or childcare facilities, or indeed through some positive action in recruit-ment advertising by encouraging female applicants for senior management positions because of their under-representation (a genuine occupational requirement under the Sex Discrimination Act). If the subtle approach does not work you might try a head-on, albeit more confrontational approach. The argument here would be that it would be quite easy for an unsuccessful internal female applicant for a senior management job to show indirect discrimination on grounds of gender under the Act assuming that she could generally satisfy the person specification. Provided she can do this, the company will find it difficult to resist an application and would be well advised to change its practices. Regrettably, some of the less progressive employers only come round to this point of view once legal action has been taken against them and they are found wanting.

QUESTION:

As a HR manager myself, working in the NHS I am very worried about the impli-cations of the *Disability Discrimination Act*. Many of our staff often incur back injuries during the course of their work and we recently had a case of one making a claim under the *Disability Discrimination Act* saying we had to re-employ them in a clerical position. However, we had no vacancies at that time and it does seem to be unrea-sonable to make these demands on cash starved hospitals. What advice should I give to the hospital's board on this subject?

ANSWER:

The advice you give will depend very much on the resources of the organisation you work for. Given that the NHS is a huge employer of over a million people, it is difficult to argue that the NHS as a whole could not find a way of accommodating the needs of this in-dividual assuming they are genuine. However, what the Disability Discrimination Act *requires in common with the other discrimination legislation is for an employer to show it has acted reasonably. If, for example, the member of staff in question lives locally with no transport and the number of positions you have on that site that do not require manual handling or lifting are few, you may well be able legally to resist their claims under the Act. It would clearly not be reasonable to expect you to pay this person to do nothing for a long period as a supernumerary employee, but a tribunal considering a claim would look at the patterns of your employment and your ability to make reasonable adjust-ments to the work of the individual concerned.*

So the advice you should provide to the hospital board should be to establish a policy relating to disability which has due regard to your organisational resources and exam-ines the scope for redeployment, the possibility of making temporary adjustments to duties, the support you will give to individuals through, for example, occupational health and physiotherapy services, and the attempts you will make to redeploy wider than your hospital in the NHS as a whole. If you can demonstrate these things you are unlikely to be found wanting under the Act.

Scope

- What the policy covers
- Legal requirements (sex, race, disability, equal pay, rehabilitation of offenders)
- Good practice (organisations optional policy on gender, ageism etc)
- Monitoring (Who monitors the policy and law)
- Training (What is provided and by whom)

Gender/Sex

- Recruitment and selection measures
- Encouraging careers for women
- Family friendly issues
- Training and monitoring activities

Race

- Workforce composition activities
- Positive action to promote a workforce representative of the community
- Race awareness training
- Dealing with bullying and harassment (links to disciplinary procedure)

Disability

- Special recruitment measures
- Advice for disabled employees (support and training)
- Complying with the DDA (organisational policy)

Other

- Policy on ageism
- Organisational policy on sexual orientation
- Organisational policy on those with mental health problems
- Training and support measures

Figure 8.2   Equal opportunities policy framework

8.11 Activity

What would a model equal opportunities policy for your organisation look like? Clearly it will need to accord with the main provisions of the *Sex, Race* and *Disability Discrimination Acts* and the emerging guidance in case law on sexual orientation and ageism. A model framework is provided at Figure 8.2. Use this to draw up a policy for your organisation that reflects your resources and circumstances. If your organisation already has an equal opportunities policy compare and contrast it to this to see if there are any gaps. If it does not already, think about drawing one up and recommending it to your senior manager for urgent adoption.

8.12 Checklist

- ▶ Equal opportunities is one of the most complex and sensitive areas of Human Resource Management with which to deal.
- ▶ Although most of the legislation dates from the 1970s including the *Equal Pay Act*, the *Sex Discrimination Act* and the *Race Relations Act*, there have been developments in the last decade concerning disability discrimination and emerging guidance on sexual orientation and ageism.
- ▶ The *Sex* and *Discrimination Acts* include the concepts of direct and indirect discrimination. The *Disability Discrimination Act* only operates on the principle of direct discrimination.
- ▶ Each of the main pieces of statute are accompanied by a code of practice issued by the Equal Opportunities Commission (for sex discrimination), the Commission for Racial Equality (concerning the *Race Relations Act*), and statutory guidance that is likely to be embodied in a code to be issued by the newly constituted Disability Rights Commission (under the *Disability Discrimination Act*).
- ▶ Common threads run through the main legislation concerning the right of individuals not to be discriminated, in relation to recruitment and selection; promotion, transfers and regrading; training and career development; disciplinary, grievance and disputes procedures; and termination arrangements.
- ▶ Good practice for employers includes the development of model policies and procedures; training; the adoption of open and fair recruitment, selection, promotion and training opportunities; and the undertaking of equal opportunities audits and monitoring to test their practices.
- ▶ Although legislation does not yet exist directly affecting sexual orientation and ageism, there is a body of emerging case law which needs to be noted. The government has issued codes of practice concerning age discrimination and transsexuals.
- ▶ The starting point for good practice in this arena is a model equal opportunities policy, an example of which is provided.

⛃ **9** Training and development

9.1 Introduction

This chapter deals with issues relating to the training and development of employees, including appraisals and performance management. In the panoply of HRM issues, it is often seen as being at the "soft" end of the subject. In reality, however, the investment an organisation makes in its employees is very often the hallmark of quality and success and makes the difference between organisations who succeed and those who do not. Particularly in time of an upturn in the economic cycle, when the economy is expanding and recruiting and retaining staff in a competitive market is of the highest priority, investing in training and development can make the difference in terms of organisational competitiveness. Increasingly over the last twenty-five years organisations have realised that to develop employees with the right skills to meet changing organisational needs, and to invest in their learning so as to retain their employment, requires sound training and development strategies. By and large this is an area of HRM that is refreshingly free of legal constraints, although a few pieces of legislation have an indirect application as outlined below, but it is an area in which good practice is essential.

One of the major criticisms of the UK economy over the last twenty years is the lack of investment in training and development at school-leaving age and in vocational and tertiary forms of education. Education has been a priority for both Conservative and Labour governments over the last decade, as they seek to transform the learning culture in the UK to make us more like our European partners, because this clearly is the key to harnessing the skills and knowledge necessary for the UK economy to succeed in the future. Add to this the advent of the "knowledge" economy brought about by the increase in the use of information technology and the learning process becomes all the more important to organisations who wish to be leaders in their field. Despite this wisdom being generally understood, many organisations suffer from poor investment in training and development, either because they do not give it enough priority (the training budget is always an easy target when there is a need to cut expenditure), or because they do not have proper strategies and systems in place to properly focus and target the investment that they make. This chapter therefore deals with developing good practice as the key to sound investment decisions.

9.2 Legal framework

Although there is little that is mandatory in the sphere of training and development, there are some implied duties for employers that can be drawn from some aspects of primary legislation. These include:

The *Employment Rights Act 1996*

The contractual requirements of this legislation, in requiring all employees to receive a written statement of terms and conditions within two months of commencing employment means for organisations where there is a major job training requirement it is important to spell out in the contract of employment what the training prerequisites are. This will be particularly so when the post in question has a trainee status and the employee is joining the organisation specifically to undergo further training that will lead to progression in due course. So a contract of employment for a nurse may include some agreement about their post-registration training that will be a contractual feature of their engagement. Similarly, an HGV lorry driver engaged by a haulage firm may have as a condition of their employment a requirement to maintain their licence and undergo updating training as required and that failure to achieve this successfully may lead to termination of the contract of employment.

Such contractual provisions are legal providing they do not breach equal opportunities legislation (that is they do not have an occupational requirement that discriminates on grounds of sex, race or disability) and they can be reasonably complied with. Some employers have fallen foul of the law in the past in trying to tie employees to staying with an organisation for a period of time in return for the company or organisation investing in their training and development. Such "loyalty" clauses may be included but are open to challenge in the courts, because they are often viewed as unreasonably restricting the freedom of movement of labour which is enshrined in the EU Treaty of Rome. Legal advice should be taken on the drafting of such clauses.

Sex Discrimination and Race Relations Acts 1975/76

As highlighted in Chapter 8 of this book, both these Acts outlaw direct and indirect discrimination and cover recruitment, selection, disciplinary grievance and training and development issues. In the context of training and development it is therefore important that employers seek neither to directly or indirectly discriminate against an individual in terms of access to training and development opportunities on grounds of sex or race, and by implication disability under the *Disability Discrimination Act 1995*. It is thus important to construct training and development policies and strategies that have equality of access for employees providing they meet objective criteria, and are not linked to issues of race, gender or disability. So, for example, organisations need to be careful that if they say that a criterion for secondment to a particular training course is dependent on full-time employment, this does not create a requirement which cannot be equally met by both men and women in their organisation.

Conversely, training and development strategies may be constructed under the banner of "positive action" as legitimate ways of helping address imbalances in the workforce under the provisions of the *Sex* and *Race Discrimination Acts*. Thus it may be perfectly legal to develop a fast-track management development programme for black employees, provided the organisation can demonstrate that there is a genuine occupational requirement to do so (see Chapter 8 for more details). There is an interesting tension here in terms of discrimination on grounds of age. Many organisations still have age barriers in training and development policies because they consider it is not worth the investment to send many older employees on expensive training programmes. Whilst ageism is currently not protected by statutory legislation the government's code of practice on ageism clearly encourages organisations to select on merit and not use age as a barrier or discriminatory factor.

The *Health and Safety at Work Act 1974*

This is one piece of legislation that stipulates a mandatory requirement to provide training for staff in health and safety issues. Employers are also encouraged to provide training in matters such as first aid, health and safety awareness and risk management for the generality of their employees to make sure that mandatory and statutory requirements for managing health and safety in the workplace can be complied with. Much here, of course, will depend on the nature of the organisation and the employment being engaged in. So, for example, an employee in a chemical engineering plant will probably be required to have significant training in managing hazards, the control of substances hazardous to health, risk management and other health and safety facets as part of their normal working life; clearly the requirements for a clerk in an office or a bank will be less but will be expected to cover minimum requirements related to the office environment.

9.3 Training cycle

Given the complexity and range of training and development needs in most organisations, it is useful to have as a starting point a model by which training and development strategies and investment can be managed, regardless of the organisational setting. Figure 9.1 attached outlines a model training process which proposes a rational basis on which to manage what is known as a cycle of training activity. The concept behind this model is that there is a continuous cycle of activity which organisations need to engage in to develop and deliver proper training and development strategies, that is repeated on an annual basis. The various components in the cycle can be described as follows:

Identification of training needs

Identifying training needs is a key stage in the training cycle, designed to answer the question "what actually *is* the training that is required". To achieve

Figure 9.1 Outline training process

this successfully a number of preliminary pieces of information must first be gathered.

QUESTIONS

1 What are the *organisation's goals* and business strategy?
2 What *tasks* must be completed for the organisation to achieve these goals?
3 What *behaviours* are necessary for each job-holder to complete his or her tasks?
4 What *deficiencies* if any do job-holders have in the knowledge, skills or attitudes required to deliver these behaviours?

The answers to these questions will in turn help determine the knowledge, skills and attitudes required that in turn determine the training needs involved. It is also important to consider the different levels in an organisation at which training needs should be determined because their needs are quite different.

Organisational level

At a macro level, organisations will need to determine what kinds of training they require to meet their business strategy and goals. This will be linked to the overall equation of the supply of relevant skills in the marketplace and the nature of the business the organisation operates in.

Departmental level

Different departments in organisations may well have differing needs depending on the skills they utilise, and the profile of the employees they have. So, in a large manufacturing organisation, production and assembly are likely to have very different needs from distribution and supply.

Individual/job level

At this level we are focusing on what the individual needs to address any gap in knowledge, skills, and behaviour that are required to fulfil the job successfully. Training needs here can usually be determined by reference to individual job appraisals, dealt with later in this chapter.

Thus the information that may be required to adequately assess organisational training needs includes the organisation's overall business or development strategy; a more local or departmental business plan or set of objectives; individual job descriptions; and material gleaned from performance appraisal on individual post holders. In training jargon, the first two components are often referred to as "top down" training needs and the latter "bottom up" training needs. Indeed, large organisations may well describe their training and development plans and strategies in this way, denoting the separation between organisational, departmental and individual needs.

Develop a training strategy and plan

Once an identification of training needs has been assembled at organisational, departmental or individual level, the organisation will need to determine how it plans to address those needs. This is often referred to as a training strategy or, on a more tactical level, a training plan. A typical training strategy/plan will outline the main components of training and development the organisation needs, and how these will be resourced. It will stop short of specifying exactly who the training is for, how it will be delivered and when they will access it (dealt with below under Training Programme), but it will give an overview of what the organisation's needs are and how they are going to be addressed with reference to budget and workforce requirements. A model training plan is outlined at Figure 9.2.

The training programme

If the training and development strategy or plan provides an overview of how the organisation intends to address its training needs, the programme will fill in the detail. It will talk about the different kinds of training and learning solutions the organisation can offer (full-time courses, short courses, on the job training, self-teaching computer packages, vocational or NVQs or coaching) and where and how these will be delivered. Training programmes may be prepared for individuals, departments or the organisation as a whole and may run over different time spans running from days, weeks, months or even years. A model training programme for health and safety training is described at Figure 9.3.

Delivery of training and learning solutions

The practical implementation of the strategy/plan and programme will be the delivery of the training and learning solutions described by them. Flexibility and choice are the key words in successful training delivery. Given that access to training and learning solutions is an expensive investment for most organisations, the

Target group	Type of training	How delivered	Frequency
All new staff	Induction: primary secondary	In-house, rotational In-house, by department	Monthly Monthly
All staff	Mandatory: First aid Health & safety Risk management	St John's Ambulance Service In-house, department In-house, corporate	Annually Annually Quarterly
New accountancy trainees	Professional: ACCA conversion programme	Local HE college	Annually
Departmental managers and supervisors	Managerial: First line supervisors DMS	In-house, tutored Coaching & mentoring Local HE college	Three-yearly Ongoing Annually
Secretarial and Support Staff	Vocational: NVQ Level 3 Administration	In-house	Annually

Figure 9.2 Model training plan accountancy firm

key will be to ensure that the right individuals can access the right learning solutions at the right time for the right duration. So, running an outward bound leadership programme for top managers in the Lake District may be an appropriate solution but will only be worth the considerable investment if the right staff can attend at the right time. Non attendance of programmes will increase the unit cost of running the training and will decrease the value of the investment to the organisation. Equally putting the wrong individual on the wrong programme is likely to frustrate the individual and lead to a poor translation into skills and knowledge back into the workplace. Increasingly organisations are investing modular, self-taught, information technology-based training and learning solutions. These are much more flexible, cheaper and allow individuals to tailor their requirements to meet their needs. Some of the different types of training delivery are explored later in this chapter.

Evaluate training outcomes

To be sure that the organisation's training and development strategy is properly secured in a realistic programme and the solutions described in this programme are properly delivered to the right people in the right quantity, organisations need to evaluate the delivery of their training and development solutions. There are a number of purposes for training evaluation including:

KEY POINTS

▶ the *monitoring* of the quality of training with a view to improvements for the future; providing feedback to the trainer about the trainee methods used;
▶ to *appraise* the overall effectiveness of the investment in training;
▶ to assist *development* of new kinds of training solution for the future.

Health and Safety for Managers
Venue: The Training Centre
Date: 14 July 2000

09.00	Arrival and introduction	Tutor & group
09.15	The legal framework for health and safely	Tutor
10.00	Case study: The employer's responsibility (group work)	Group + facilitators
10.45	Feedback from group work (plenary session)	Group representatives
11.30	Video case study: When it all goes wrong: The Piper Alpha disaster	
12.15	Discussion of video case study	

LUNCH

14.00	Understanding risk assessment	Tutor
15.00	Group work: developing a health and safety plan	Group + facilitators
16.00	Feedback from group work	Group representatives
16.30	Summary plenary session	All
17.00	Key learning points and further reading	Tutor

CLOSE

Figure 9.3   Model health and safety training programme

Methods of training evaluation vary according to what is to be evaluated but include;

▶ *pro forma* completion by the individual undergoing the training event or activity;

▶ *feedback* and discussion sessions by those who have been involved or who are delivering the training;

▶ *measurement* of work performance and skills comparing those delivered before and after training;

▶ or via a *formal appraisal* scheme (see below).

Whatever method is used to evaluate training outcomes, the results need to be fed back into the training cycle. Only with the feedback this provides can organisations be sure that their training cycle of activity is working properly and that they are making the appropriate decisions about strategy, programmes and methods of delivery. In 1990, the then Conservative Government introduced the concept of *Investors in People* (IIP), a chartermark award for organisations to show that they were investing properly in the training and education, communication and support of their employees. To gain IIP accreditation, organisations will need to demonstrate that they have a rational model in place for identifying training needs, for developing some kind of training strategy or plan, have suitable training programmes in place to underpin these, a variety of training delivery methods to meet organisational and individual needs, and processes and systems for evaluating training outcomes. The training cycle is, therefore, very much a universal framework for managing and investing in training and learning solutions to meet the IIP standard.

9.4 Vocational education and NVQs

In the next three sections we will consider some of the different types of training and learning activity that organisations can engage in. The list is not exhaustive, but summarises the main types of training and learning activity that will be found in most modern organisations. Vocational education and NVQs (National Vocational Qualifications) became a feature of training and education in the 1980s as organisations found that the more traditional forms of off-the-job training, or secondment to full-time professional training, were expensive and difficult to resource by release of employees. In line with developments in primary and secondary education in schools, new ways of learning and of accrediting the learning that individuals were undertaking were developed through the creation of NVQs. The concept behind the creation of NVQs was to create a framework whereby individuals would learn in the workplace, practising the skills and knowledge required for the successful performance of their job, collecting evidence of this and combining this with personal periods of study to show that they had the necessary knowledge and skills to meet the job requirement. There are five main levels of NVQ accreditation as follows:

NVQ Level 1 –   GCSE or GNVQ foundation
NVQ Level 2 –   A-Level or GNVQ intermediate
NVQ Level 3 –   Degrees in academic disciplines
                GNVQ advanced
NVQ Level 4 –   Vocationally orientated degrees
NVQ Level 5 –   Post graduate degrees

9.5 Induction and mandatory training

All organisations need to invest in these types of training and they will take very varied forms dependent on size and resources. Induction training is a way of familiarising new employees into the new organisation and job and can range from one hour to many months depending on the job and the organisation. Mandatory training describes those aspects of training which it is essential for the organisation to carry out for statutory or regulatory reasons. This will include health and safety training and training in other issues essential for the organisation to function properly. Again, the mandatory package may differ from job to job, and from organisation to organisation.

9.6 Management development and professional training

Two of the areas of training and development activity which over the years have attracted a form of cachet are those of management development and professional training. They tend to attract a rather more glamorous image than vocational and more traditional forms of training activity because they are geared by definition to professionals and managers and are usually focused on longer programmes of study leading to professional or managerial forms of qualification. It also follows that they tend to be an expensive investment for the organisation and often the individuals themselves as by definition the organisation is unlikely to make a major investment in individuals who they do not feel are liable to succeed in attaining professional status of one form or another.

Management development

There is a considerable mythology attached to management development which makes it a much broader definition of training and development activity than just about training managers. Management development came about as a major branch of training and development in its own right in the 1960s as the growth in demand for managers who were "professional" grew and organisations found the hit-and-miss process of identifying them, usually by promotion into "dead man's shoes", was no longer satisfactory in the modern competitive world. Although the concept of management training was itself not new in the 1960s, with a wide range of courses available to train the manager of the future, the concept of developing individuals grew. Instead of managers merely being fed information in a course, their managerial capacity and potential was broadened by a wide variety of experiences through which they could acquire skills and knowledge. It is not surprising that the formative years of employee appraisal were focused on the managerial group and it was through this that the concept of individually tailored learning needs grew. As Graves said in 1976: "Managers are better able to develop their own skills if given development opportunities rather than training . . . training should be based on Manager's needs as perceived by the Managers rather than development needs perceived by trainers". So for the first time there was an attempt to combine the formal experience of the managerial training course with the more informal experiences that could be gained through a variety of methods in the workplace. The components of the management development package can therefore be analysed in some detail:

Selection

The selection of the candidate for management development of itself usually attracts a bespoke selection process within the organisation. Managers may be selected by deed of promotion, by external recruitment, or through traineeships where they are specifically groomed to develop managerial skills. The raw material that makes a good manager is itself hard to define because of the multiplicity of factors involved, but in essence managers are usually appointed to be decision makers and it is decision-making skills that organisations usually wish to engender.

The senior manager will normally be a professional from the mainstream of the organisation's core business (for example an accountant or an HR professional) but they may equally be a professional manager or someone who has just trained to take on the managerial role.

Appraisal

As identified above appraisal had at its root a process of identifying managerial skill requirements and indeed in most organisations a form of appraisal will exist for the managerial group of staff even if it is absent elsewhere amongst the workforce. The concept behind appraisal is that in identifying individual needs, the organisation is more likely to successfully tailor the package to the bespoke requirements rather than adopt a broad brush approach. They are also likely to gain ownership of the individual because he or she is intrinsically involved in the process of determining their development needs.

Education and training courses

A training course will usually be a key feature in a formal programme of management development and these in turn can be categorised as follows.

Pre experience courses

These are usually full-time education leading to academic qualification with a management sciences or business studies label and undertaken by younger people as preliminary to a career. The courses provide an education normally based on a study of the academic disciplines of economics, mathematics, psychology, sociology, industrial relations and organisational behaviour, as well as an introduction to the practical area, such as accounting, marketing, personnel and production. The product is usually a graduate with a broad-base understanding of the prerequisites of the management process.

Post experience courses

These usually are full- or part-time education programmes leading to a diploma or masters degree with a management or business label, such as an MBA (Masters in Business Administration) or a DMS (Diploma in Management Studies). They are usually geared for the student who is now in employment (that is an employee) who will be funded and supported in the course of work by the employer wholly or at least in part. There is now little need for individuals to go on full-time secondment to undertake such courses as most of them are available on a modular basis first pioneered by the Open University for degree-level courses. Although the timescale for achieving qualification is longer (up to five or six years compared to two to three for a traditional degree-level course) the same elements can be studied and the result – a degree- or post degree-level qualification – can still be achieved.

In-house training courses

Many large organisations have the added benefit of being able to run their own in-house management training programmes geared at the specific skills which the individual requires to operate in that workplace. Examples would include leadership skills, operating the organisation's disciplinary and grievance procedures, budget management skills and communication processes.

Action learning

The concept behind Action Learning is that management is mostly about judgement and decision making and the conviction that managers need, not education, but the ability to solve these workplace problems. In its infancy in the 1970s, the idea of action learning was shadowing, or job exchange with, another manager to learn "in action" how other individuals in unfamiliar organisations dealt with problem solving. The learning process stemmed from the presentation of an immediate problem followed by acting out the solutions that work and by definition finding those that do not. Such practically orientated approaches have not found great favour with academics who feel this learning by trial and error is a haphazard affair not founded in problem management theory, but action learning has become an integral part of many full-time and part-time management development programmes, with the "sandwich" course concept of periods of academic study interspersed with practical periods of work placement still very much in currency at the end of the 1990s.

Mentoring and coaching

Mentoring and coaching are really extensions of the action learning approach requiring an on-the- job presence to develop skills and knowledge. Coaching is, of course, a term derived from sports education where skills are practised in situations such as on the athletics track or football pitch. The concept is transferred to the traditional workplace and is an extension of the old adage of "sitting by Nellie", the idea being that skills and knowledge are learnt from observing another. Coaching is still very much in vogue today, with student placements being coached, for example, by a chief executive who shadows their work programme and learns how the individual deals with each work situation and transaction in a practical setting. Mentoring is an extension of the coaching concept but is rather more hands-off. The mentor does not have to be in the workplace and indeed is usually an individual outside it with whom the mentee can discuss workplace problems and situations and receive guidance on solutions.

In this sense the relationship between a mentor and a mentee is rather like that between the counsellor and the counselled. The individual will play back work scenarios and the mentor will provide feedback or advice and sometimes just listen and enable the individual to work through the problem for themselves. Within a workplace, mentors can also be used as part of induction training to orientate newcomers in the workplace over a protracted period and ensure the right orientation takes place. Mentoring can be about career enhancement (providing sponsorship, coaching, guidance and support) or a form of psycho social function akin to counselling (role modelling, friendship and workplace counselling). Mentoring is often part of the job package for senior executives who are in high stress, high visibility jobs, providing a release valve for the individual, usually outside the organisation, and a unique problem-solving resource which the manager can refer to on a periodic basis or as and when they have problems.

Professional training

Training for profession, education and practice has been the mainstay of British industrial and service life for the last one hundred years. The concept of professional training as we know it today first emanated from training given to the armed services for those who wished to become officer material. The concept of the dedicated *training school* for the professional officer class, be it in army, navy or airforce, develops the notion of professional training schools and professional qualifications without which the individual would not be deemed fit to practice. The concept was soon translated into a wider industrial, commercial and business setting and now forms the core of the accepted standards for every major profession in the country, from banking through to information technology, from Human Resource Management to accountancy, from estates surveying to medicine.

There are literally thousands of *professional bodies* and institutes who are often self-regulated, but increasingly are influenced by government and set standards which are open to public scrutiny, particularly in the fields of teaching and medicine where such a large body of the public are crucially affected by the service they provide. As the need for the UK economy to compete internationally has increased year-on-year, so have the demands placed on professions which are open to such scrutiny of performance to gain proper accreditation. So, for example, the Human Resource Management professional who passes the examinations set by the Chartered Institute of Personnel and Development, and becomes a member of this professional body, is likely to have undergone a form of training and education and accord to a set of standards that would not be that dissimilar to their counterparts in the United States, Scandinavia or Australasia.

The key issues for organisations in terms of professional training is to what degree the organisation is going to rely on "growing its own" professionals or recruiting from the marketplace. The decision will be influenced by factors such as supply and demand of professionals, the remuneration they can command, and the need for the organisation to train its own professionals in its own individual ways of working. There is usually a mixture of the two at play in most large UK concerns. For example, taking Human Resource Management as a case in point, there is open access to study and become a personnel professional via higher education colleges, universities and business schools using a range of full-time and part-time programmes, that are open to the general public with the right entry qualifications. An organisation that employs a relatively large number of Human Resource professionals may indeed, therefore, choose to recruit individuals coming straight off these training programmes whatever their age. Equally the large concern may also elect to sponsor or directly pay for a number of individuals to undergo training once they have been recruited. So it may recruit from the marketplace for a personnel assistant and then pay for him/her to undergo training by one of the IPD's appropriate levels of training, so that it can develop its own cadre of personnel professionals.

Generally speaking, the higher the costs of professional training, the more likely the organisation is to seek to recruit the skills they require from the *marketplace* than solely rely on developing their own professional staff. It is clearly advantageous to allow the costs of development to be borne either by the individuals themselves or another organisation and to recruit them competitively from the marketplace rather than make the investment themselves. The mix of professionals in a football club is a good example of this balance of strategies at work. An English premier league club will usually have a balance between recruiting from the marketplace (by buying players through the transfer system often at very high fees but knowing they are buying an accomplished professional player) and growing their own by developing young footballers through their own youth and academy approaches so that they develop their professional base for the future. Obviously in most of the commercial and business world, transfer fees do not operate, but the analogy holds true and describes the dilemma most organisations face.

Where organisations themselves are sponsoring and supporting professional training, they will often opt for *part-time* or *modular* approaches to the individual undergoing the professional training programme. This is simply because the costs of release for full-time training are now so high and the organisation has to bear the cost not only of the training fees, but usually of replacing and supporting the individual who is released for the two- or three-year programme. So a modular approach with periods of part-time release for study and periods back in the workplace are much more in favour, with the onus falling more on the individual to study in their spare time. This clearly can put excessive pressure on young aspiring professionals who have the double burden of having to learn the practical skills required of their profession in the workplace whilst undertaking professional study.

Attitudes to so-called professions in the workplace usually go in cycles. In the 1960s, the concept of the "generalist" who was a multi-skilled all-rounder and who could turn a hand to any number of tasks was very much in vogue. This was derived from training in the civil service where the idea of the generalist who can undertake a wide range of tasks was attractive because of the huge variety of work involved in government administration. However, twenty years later the professional was once again in the ascendancy because the growth in complexity as well as variety of work, aided by the growth in information technology, heightened the need for specialist skills founded on the traditional professions. Much of course depends on the state of the labour market and the economy in general. In times of boom and growth, professionals come into their own as there is enough money in the economy and businesses in general to employ a wide range of them depending on the organisation's needs. The more buoyant the organisation the more it can afford to diversify and employ ever-increasingly specialist professionals to undertake dedicated tasks. In times of slump or depression, however, when the economy is contracting, organisations will themselves contract and employ as few specialists as possible and the onus will be on a smaller range of individuals to become generalists. In this scenario organisations are much less likely to employ their own professional staff and instead will buy in expertise as and when needed rather than engage expensive professionals in a dedicated role.

There has been a huge decline in the number of manufacturing, craft and agriculture-based employment over the last twenty-five years as industry has become increasingly automated, and service-based industries have been the growth sector in the UK. The service-based industry is of course focused more on trading in expertise and knowledge, and this industry has itself received huge expansion in recent years with the growth of information technology and the use of the Internet. At the end of the 1990s the UK government was committed to a huge expansion in knowledge-based industries and the concept of "E-commerce" using Internet technology. In this environment, the professional is much more likely to flourish as their specialist skills or intellectual property become the currency in which many organisations trade. So be it a legal firm, a HR advisory service, a tax or accountancy consultancy or a management consultancy, the professionals in these industries are much more in demand and attract higher salaries than the craft or labouring skills required in the more traditional manufacturing industries, which were the backbone of the UK economy up until the mid 1970s.

9.7 Appraisal and performance management

An appraisal is an essential tool in the armoury of Human Resource Management. It has been traditionally associated with appraising the performance of individuals against set objectives to make sure they are making the contribution the organisation requires of them, and in some cases linking this assessment of performance to rewards such as pay. However, increasingly appraisal is seen as a way of systematically developing individuals to make sure their contribution is maximised, they are fulfilled in the job, and have the skills required to develop in the role and to aid retention. Appraisal is used as an interchangeable term with performance assessment, performance evaluation, individual assessment, job appraisal, performance review and a number of other terms all with similar meanings. Organisational appraisal systems are a means to formalising activities for rating the usefulness of a contribution and in this case usually of assessing the financial reward that should accompany it.

Organised and practised well, appraisal can be an invaluable tool in maximising contribution and providing feedback to individuals. Bad appraisals, however, are probably worse than no appraisals at all in that they can create conflict and division and undermine individuals' contributions to the organisation. The aim of formal appraisal systems should therefore be to support and encourage the manager in continually appraising the performance of their staff, and in the more sophisticated systems to encourage individuals to provide full feedback on the organisation and their manager (known as *360° appraisal*). In this section we consider the various stages of appraisal and performance management in the workplace, including the uses to which it is put; the differing roles of appraiser and appraisee; different types of appraisal system; and links between appraisal and performance management and reward systems.

Uses of appraisal

Although the traditional use of appraisal in organisations is to assess past performance, there are a multiplicity of applications that would depend on organisational culture and other systems of performance management that are in place.

Performance objectives

These help improve current performance; to assess training and development needs; to assess increases or new levels of salary; to assess future career development potential; to assist in career planning decisions. As with most aspects of Human Resource activity, organisations select from this menu depending on their circumstances, but it is possible to identify a number of trends.

Management by objectives

In the 1970s appraisal applied in most business and organisational settings and was linked to the notion of "management by objectives". This school of management thinking was based on the notion of setting clear objectives for every individual and department within an organisation which were linked to the organisation's business plan to ensure maximum coordination and efficiency. Indeed this school of thinking underpins most appraisal systems today where objectives are set and the performance against them measured by one system or another. With the accent in the 1980s very much on competitiveness and improving efficiency, appraisal was increasingly linked to pay in both private and public sectors.

Performance-related pay

This usually measured performance on a scale against objectives set and linked pay accordingly. A five-point scale would traditionally have been used, with point 1 being outstanding performance constantly meeting and exceeding all objectives set, whilst at the other extreme at level 5 the individual would be a very poor performer and would normally be referred to the organisation's disciplinary procedures for substandard work.

In the 1990s the linkages to pay had tended to decline (although the introduction of performance-related pay for teachers had been developed as late as 1999). There is an emerging body of evidence that the linkage to pay over a period of time does not improve performance continuously. Clearly this is not true in all industries with the performance bonus still being a large feature of remuneration, particularly in the finance sector, usually linked to the overall performance of the company the individual works in. Performance-related pay has fallen into some decay because of the recognition that the success of individuals usually depends on the wider contribution of the team in which they work. Although the senior manager may have been considered to be an outstanding performer, his or her organisational contribution is likely only to be made possible by the team of people he or she works with. Plus the notion of team rewards and benefits linked to this concept of the whole team contributing is seen as a more equitable way of assessing organisational contribution.

Personal development

In the last half of the 1990s appraisal was seen increasingly as a personal development tool, a way of maximising individual contributions and ensuring the individual has the skills and knowledge required to make that contribution. The notion here is to rely less on a formal annual or bi-annual performance review session, and more on the assessment of performance as a continuous link to an assessment of training and development needs. Indeed, appraisal is still the most common system for the identification of individual training needs in use in the UK today.

Appraisees and appraisers

Who appraises and who is appraised is often the most difficult decision for organi-sations to make when they are introducing or extending appraisal systems. Depending on the span of managerial control, managers may sometimes be asked to appraise too many individuals, which dilutes the quality and value of the process itself. The *appraiser* is usually defined as the immediate manager or supervisor with line management responsibility for the employee who will become the *appraisee*. Received wisdom suggests that the ideal span of control for the appraisal process is between 5 and 9 appraisees per appraiser. This will have implications for the way the appraisal system is organised and the training for both the appraisees and appraisers in the skills of their task is undertaken. What-ever system is used, it is important that training for both the appraisees and appraisers accompanies the introduction of any scheme.

The appraiser needs to know how to structure the interview; how to record information using the pro formas provided; how to ask appropriate questions of the individual, being neither too assertive or too passive; how to practise the art of listening and digesting feedback and information from the appraisee; and how to deal with difficult issues such as poor performance. The appraisee, on the other hand, needs to be able to enter the appraisal interview with confidence and in the spirit of openness; this will require them to practise communication skills that they will not necessarily use in their day-to-day work, to plan and prepare for their appraisal interview, to learn to focus on strengths and weaknesses, suc-cesses and failures, and to focus on personal development needs.

Some more sophisticated appraisal systems depend on *peer* or *group* appraisals. This is where an individual would be appraised on their overall con-tribution and performance by their colleagues rather than their line manager. It requires a degree of organisational and individual maturity to work successfully and not be seen as adversarial, but it has been used successfully in some settings where teamwork is very much the order of the day. To ensure consistency of approach, some other organisations rely on appraisal being undertaken from a central source, often within the Personnel or Human Resource Department. This is particularly true in the retail sector where the personnel function still retains its line management function and will often be involved in carrying out a systematic appraisal of performance of retail assistants.

Very often the appraisal system will require the signing off of the outcome by an independent person, normally the appraiser's own line manager, often referred to as the "grandparent". Their role is usually to try and ensure that the appraisal interview has been conducted objectively, and that no bias has been at play. This is important where there is a feeling that appraisal is used in a negative way and that managers do not have the objectivity to carry out the appraisal without being partisan.

To overcome this kind of problem, many organisations now invest a power of appraisal in the appraisee themselves by undertaking *self-appraisal*. In this sense the subject becomes both appraisee and appraiser, often rating their own performance against some pre-determined scale using objective criteria. This process of self-assessment is an increasingly important component of appraisal schemes because research and evidence shows that individuals are usually very honest in their own self-appraisal and if anything err on the side of understatement rather than talking up their year's performance.

9.8 Problem areas

QUESTION:
The board of directors of my company are thinking about developing a strategy for Investors in People (IIP) accreditation. They have asked me, as their Human Resource Advisor, to prepare a report outlining the potential costs and benefits. Although we have a good tradition in investing in the training of our staff, budgets tend to be devolved to line managers and there is no overall coherent organisational strategy. What kind of issues should I highlight in my report?

ANSWER:
The first consideration you should make in preparing your report is whether or not it is worth the organisation making the investment it will need to gain IIP accreditation. The benefits are clear. First, the employees who currently work for the organisation will know that the organisation has received a significant chartermark which validates more widely the investment it makes in them in training, development, communication and support. Secondly, the chartermark has a cachet in the recruitment market because it clearly goes some way to distinguishing the good employer from one who is not. However, to achieve IIP accreditation is more than just a cosmetic exercise; it requires genuine commitment from the top of the organisation as well as a thorough investment in systems and procedures throughout to be successful. If as you say your organisation is serious about training and development, then this is more an issue about organisation and commitment than resources. The IIP assessors will expect to find evidence throughout the organisation of the existence of a proper cycle of training activity, from the identification

of training needs through to the evaluation of training outcomes. They will also expect the commitment that apparently exists at the top of the organisation to be extended to other managers and for staff to understand their role in the organisation and to know that their training needs are assessed and delivered properly. Thus, whilst the benefits of IIP are undeniable, extensive work will be required to ensure organisational commitment from top to bottom.

QUESTION:

Traditionally, the organisation I work for has invested in a senior management development programme by supporting staff to complete MBA programmes. Increasingly, however, the managing director is concerned about the cost of these programmes and the amount of time off staff require to assist them in their studies. I am about to begin an MBA programme myself and wonder what is the true value to the organisation and myself of this investment?

As with most types of management development and other training, much will depend on what both the organisation and yourself wish to get out of this particular training course, and the quality of the individual programme on which you are about to embark. One of the problems with a broad brush approach to management development training, is that, whilst the organisation ends up with a cadre of managers who have, for example, a DMS or an MBA, they cannot be sure that these programmes are tailored to the organisation's needs or indeed the individual's. For example, some managers are naturally very good communicators and planners, but others have stronger analytical skills. The best investment, therefore, is to identify in detail what these training needs are and define training solutions to address them. The problem with the broad brush programmes is that by definition they have to take a generic approach, although the quality of the finished product is usually good and describes a standard of managerial knowledge and competence that is successfully completed.

Many organisations are now developing their own in-house DMS- or MBA-type programmes on a modular basis where they have a regular ongoing need to train senior managers. The advantage with this approach is that they can relate the studies much more to the work environment, and ensure individual training needs are identified and addressed through the modular programme. Costs both in terms of teaching and time off are also likely to be less through this route.

QUESTION:

I work for a large public sector organisation and we are about to undertake a major review of our appraisal programme which was previously linked to performance-related pay. I have read in many journals and magazines that there is now a turn away from such performance-related pay linkages, but I am equally aware that many organisations are about to set off down this path (for example the teaching profession). What is the current view in the HR profession about pay linkages to appraisal schemes?

ANSWER:

There is no clear consensus about the benefits or otherwise of pay linkages to appraisal. Those for such pay linkages argue that there is an inextricable link between good performance and rewards through extra pay that motivates and encourages the best performers and helps focus clearly on priorities set in the appraisal process. Those who are against say that after a period of time the performance-related pay scheme becomes a norm in itself and employees settle into a normal pattern of working and are no longer motivated by the performance-pay element. They also argue that in many organisations the success of individuals depends on the success of the team they work in and the principle of rewarding the individual is itself wrong. Whatever the merits or de-merits it is undeniable that the number of performance-related pay schemes in existence have decreased over the last five years after a period of sustained growth in the late 1980s and early 1990s. The most commonly quoted reason for this change of practice in these organisations is that highlighted above, that there is a diminishing return from such a performance-related linkage.

However, it is equally undeniable that the strong link to performance in some areas of the private sector, particularly those where there are high benefits available through profit-related pay schemes, continues to attract many supporters. So the jury is very much out. One of the problems in the public sector, particularly in occupations where there is no definite end product as a result of an individual's work, is assessing performance. The common consensus therefore in the HR profession would be that the setting of objectives, the appraisal of those objectives, and their linkage to personal development is worthwhile, and organisations would be wise to adopt or retain such schemes. However, the linkage to pay is very much a consideration for the individual organisation based on their culture, the nature of the service or goods they provide, and the type of work individuals do for them.

9.9 Activity

How would you go about identifying the training needs for managers in your organisation, and constructing a realistic training plan to meet those needs? Describe the processes and steps you would take to undertake this identification and to turn it into a meaningful training and development plan that is relevant to the needs of your organisation and the resources it has.

9.10 Checklist

▶ Training and development is at the "soft" end of HRM issues and is relatively legislation free.
▶ A rational model to managing training – the so-called cycle of training activity – promotes good practice.
▶ This involves the identification of training needs; designing a learning plan; designing a training programme; delivering training solutions; and evaluating outcomes.
▶ NVQs and vocational education are seen as cost-effective and accessible routes to training staff.
▶ All organisations have, as a minimum need, some requirement for induction and mandatory training.

- ▶ There are many different approaches to the design and delivery of managerial and professional training programmes, and these are explained.
- ▶ Appraisal and performance management systems are included in the training and development theme in this section.
- ▶ The Investors in People Chartermark sets a national standard for assessing how well organisations invest in and organise their approach to staff development, training and communications.

M 10 Employee relations

10.1 Introduction

Traditionally the Human Resource function has been concerned with the management of good employee relations within organisations and encompasses the management of discipline, grievance, consultation and negotiating issues including relationships with trade unions. This is, therefore, by definition one of the most difficult tasks of Human Resource Management as the topics include areas of potential conflict that require expert and sensitive handling to ensure productive outcomes. Because these areas of contact between management and employee have the potential to cause conflict in the workplace, it is not surprising that they have been heavily regulated by statute over the years. Indeed, since the beginning of the twentieth century legislation has existed to regulate the activities of trade unions and to harness the power of the employer in the workplace. From the end of the Second World War in 1945 through to the late 1960s, there was a huge growth in the role and power of the trade unions within the United Kingdom, with membership levels reaching an all-time high by the early 1970s.

This era of growth and expansion was characterised by legislation and government policies that gave gradually more and more power to trade unions and therefore the employee in the workplace. The 1970s by contrast were a time of major industrial relations conflict, with tension between employees and employers in major industries characterised by industrial action and strikes on a national scale. This flexing of union power brought an equally strong public reaction and indeed one of the major missions of the Conservative Government elected in 1979 under the stewardship of Margaret Thatcher was to limit the power of the trade unions and "turn back the clock" to restore more power to employers.

The years 1979–1990 are, therefore, largely documented in terms of a reduction in trade union powers and membership, and, not just by coincidence, a slowing down in the growth of employee rights with the balance of power turning back to that of the employer. The last term of the Conservative Government between 1992 and 1997, under Prime Minister John Major, brought a softening of this hardline approach and indeed some key pieces of legislation sought to swing the pendulum back again in favour of the employee because there was an emerging consensus in British society that low wages and "sweat shop" conditions had greatly devalued the UK economy.

The most recent and arguably most interesting phase is that being experienced under the Labour administration elected in 1997. The Blair Government has arguably done more to enhance the power of the individual and trade unions since their heyday of the 1960s and the liberalisation of the workforce, coupled with the adoption of many EU directives, has once again clearly put the employee back in a position of ascendancy. It is not surprising, however, given this rich and varied history of British industrial relations, that the workplace early in the new millennium is a complex place for the Human Resource practitioner. The starting point for understanding current industrial and employee relations practice is therefore to obtain a good grasp of the legislative framework.

10.2 Legal framework

Trade Union and Labour Relations (Consolidation) Act 1992

The present law relating to the power and liabilities of trade unions is governed by this act. It consolidates the provisions of previous legislation including The *Employment Protection Act 1975*, and the *Employment Protection (Consolidation) Act 1978*. These provisions in turn have been updated by the provisions of the *Trade Union Reform and Employment Rights Act 1993* and the *Employment Rights Act 1996*. The summation of all this legislation confers the following rights and restrictions on the powers and activities on trade unions.

* Trade unions have *statutory obligations* to keep accounts and a register of members.
* Trade unions are obliged that all members of their principal executive committees stand for election at least every five years by a process of *secret ballot.*
* Trade unions may collect funds from their members but may not apply them for the furtherance of political causes (the so-called *political levy*).
* Trade unions have a *liability* in law arising out of strikes or industrial action that they and their members participate in
* They are liable as a result of such action linked to the size of their membership up to a limit of £250,000.
* An employee who is a member of a trade union has *rights* not to be refused employment because of their membership of a trade union, cannot be dismissed for membership of or taking part in the activities of the trade union, and has the right to take time off work to take part in trade union activities.

The *Employment Relations Act 1999*

This is a benchmark piece of legislation from the new Labour Government, which confers important new rights for trade union recognition in the workplace. The Act requires employers and organisations to recognise trade unions for collective bargaining and consultation purposes where 40 per cent of the workforce who are balloted wish it to be so. Moreover, the employer must allow such a ballot to be conducted where at least 10 per cent of the eligible workforce wish it to be so.

It therefore follows that in those organisations where there has previously been no or little tradition of trade union activity, and there is a ground swell of support from a significant minority of the workforce, there is now the facility in law for one or more trade unions to be recognised. Indeed, there are strict financial and legal penalties for employers who try to frustrate or prevent this legal recognition process. The same rights also exist under this legislation for those unions who wish to retain their representation in the workplace where an employer is trying to de-recognise them.

The *Employment Rights Act 1996*

This legislation is particularly relevant to the employee relations framework, as it builds on the previous provisions of the *Employment Protection Act 1975* and the *Employment Protection (Consolidation) Act 1978* in updating the rights for employees not to be unfairly dismissed on a range of grounds. These are discussed in more detail in Chapter 4. Where there is trade union recognition in the workplace, a full-time official or local steward will usually become involved in matters of discipline and grievance. Indeed, all the provisions relating to grounds for terminating the contract of employment are relevant in this respect. For the same reasons, the legislation affecting *TUPE* and redundancy protection are relevant as they confer important rights on trade unions to be consulted on behalf of their members when there is a transfer of undertaking or an impending redundancy in the workplace.

The *Works Council Directive*

This EU directive is dealt with in more detail in Chapter 14 but continues the trend established by the *Employment Relations Act* in conferring additional rights on workers to be consulted and have representation in the workplace, this time through the notion of a works council as a consultation process in multinational companies. Although the directive does not of itself confer rights on trade unions but mainly talks about the rights of individual employees in the workplace, given that many organisations organise these rights collectively through trade union representation, the directive is bound to increase the influence of trade unions and staff associations generally. Indeed, much of the thrust of the social chapter EU directives is supportive of the role of trade unions given that they are generally concerned with improving working conditions and the rights of employees to be consulted.

ACAS Codes

Although not formally part of the legislative framework, this is an area of HRM activity where codes of practice issued by ACAS have particular value and are often considered by the courts and employment tribunals in judging employee relations cases before them. Of particular relevance are the codes of practice on:

- time off for trade union duties and activities.
- consultation, bargaining and negotiation.
- disciplinary practice and procedures.
- managing grievances in employment.

The principles in these codes lay the ground for good practice, discussion of which will be developed in this chapter.

10.3 Trade unions and staff associations

Given the many changes to the rights of individuals and trade unions to organise and be represented in the workplace, tackling the issue of trade union and staff association representation can be a daunting prospect for organisations, particularly where they are not used to having such interests at work. In this section, we will therefore concentrate on the handling of individual rights and trade union/staff association rights in the workplace and how these should be dealt with.

Individual rights

Whether or not the organisation recognises trade unions/staff associations for collective bargaining purposes (and it may be required to do so given the provisions of The *Employment Relations Act*) it needs to provide the facility for individuals to belong to a recognised trade union and to undertake legitimate activities within it.

There follows key good practice guidance for allowing individual rights and representation.

KEY POINTS

▶ Make it clear in *employment literature*, staff handbooks or even employment contracts that trade union membership in the workplace is encouraged
▶ *Allow facilities* for individuals to participate in legitimate trade union activity as part of the consultation, negotiation and bargaining machinery (see section 10.4 below) although this does not have to be in paid work time
▶ Allow the rights for individuals to be elected as *trade union representatives*, or health and safety representatives (see Chapter 12) through the individual balloting procedures described by each recognised trade union
▶ Allow *paid time off* for these elected individuals to undertake legitimate trade union activities, as part of the consultation, negotiating and bargaining framework, in accordance with some kind of facilities and recognition agreement within the workplace (again see 10.4 below)
▶ Allow a payroll facility for trade union *subscriptions* to be deducted at source, although this is no longer automatically required by law and is subject to a workplace agreement
▶ Allow individuals rights to be *consulted* in the workplace on major issues affect-

ing their contract of employment, any impending redundancies, health and safety issues, all matters relating to a transfer of undertaking, either individually or through their recognised trade union as part of the consultation, negotiating and bargaining framework.

All this, of course, requires an organisation to have a positive culture towards employee relations and not to be fearful of trade unions, their members or their likely actions. The employee or industrial relations environment in the UK at the beginning of the twenty-first century is much more positive and constructive than that witnessed during the 1970s or indeed the 1980s. Politicians with a right-wing tendency will argue that this is because the Thatcher Conservative Government stripped away some of the excessive powers that trade unions had and forced them to choose either to become modern democratic institutions or die. Left-wing politicians will probably argue that this is because trade unions have steadfastly continued to represent their members' interest, and the new Labour Government has taken steps to redress some of the balance in terms of trade union powers and recognition.

The truth probably lies somewhere between the two, but it is interesting to note that the UK industrial relations scene is much more like that previously enjoyed by our EU partners, and indeed it is with some irony that one can observe deteriorating industrial relations in countries that previously enjoyed great harmony (for example Germany and Holland). "Working in Partnership" is the theme of the Labour Government and it encourages social partnership both nationally, between government and national trade union and TUC representatives, and at all levels in local government, the health sector, and in industry as a whole. Indeed, there is considerable evidence of "Working in Partnership" becoming reality in workplaces where previously poor industrial relations were the order of the day. There is no doubt that the current political backcloth has assisted in this process but there is also undeniably a different mood and tenor within employer and trade union attitudes in the current climate.

Trade union recognition

The employer, having established the rights of individuals to belong to a trade union or to be elected to trade union office, will be faced with a major policy decision: to determine whether or not it recognises trade unions for the purposes of collective bargaining and negotiation. Much here, of course, will depend on whether trade unions are already recognised in the workplace, in which case their de-recognition will be difficult to achieve given the provisions of the *Employment Relations Act*, and if they are not already it will depend on the wishes of the workforce, given the rights for trade union representation conferred by this legislation. Assuming there is either a positive decision to recognise or it has arisen as a result of a workplace ballot, there are a number of issues to be dealt with:

QUESTIONS

I Which trade unions are to be recognised? There is no legal limit placed on the number of trade unions that need to be recognised, and much will depend on the nature of the employer's business and the sector they operate in. Some industries and professions have a tradition of single union representation (for example doctors and the BMA), and some a tradition of multi-union representation.

2 What aspects of employment policy are to be the subject of collective bargaining? Although the law says that trade union rights apply to pay, conditions, disciplinary, grievance, redundancy, health and safety and transfer issues, the employer may choose to extend the collective bargaining remit to cover a much wider panoply of issues depending upon the nature of the organisation. Progressive employers have a wide remit covering the organisation of work, business planning and development, and all aspects of workplace activity.

3 What rights to time off are to be given? The law requires employers to give elected trade union officials reasonable time off to fulfil their duties, but there is no prescription. Much again, therefore, depends on the nature of the employer and their resources.

4 What will be the union representatives' role within the workplace? Having determined the amount of paid time off to be given to trade union officials, there will need to be some agreement with them about how this role is to be organised and represented.

This latter point leads us into the issue of how the organisation intends to take the matter of individual and collective rights and form it into some kind of recognition and facilities agreement for trade unions. A typical facilities and recognition agreement would state:

- the names of the recognised trade unions
- the aspects of employment policy included within collective bargaining
- the rights to time off to be given to elected officials
- the methods and procedures by which stewards are elected and re-elected
- the methods and procedures by which stewards are organised in the workplace and represent their interests.

Because this document is important and underpins the relationship between the employer and trade union representatives, it is usually important to have it signed and dated as a formal statement of agreement. Once this is in place it is then possible for the employer to turn their attention to the development and maintenance of an appropriate consultation, negotiation and bargaining machinery to allow employee relations to function properly in the workplace.

10.4 Consultation, negotiating and bargaining

Whatever the level of trade union recognition in the workplace, the organisation needs to establish some process for consultation, negotiation and bargaining on a range of issues. As outlined above, the issues included in this collective bargaining framework will vary from the statutory minimum to a much wider spectrum. Indeed, this definition of the collective bargaining territory will dictate much about the machinery that is put in place to support it. There is no right solution: what employers need to do above all is select machinery and processes that are effective, that work for their situation and are agreeable to their recognised trade unions. For the purposes of this book, three "model" scenarios are described.

Statutory model

The statutory model will allow the minimum work to be done to support *statutory requirements* for consultation, negotiation and bargaining. Whatever the number of recognised trade unions, stewards and the nature of the recognition and facilities agreement, there will probably be no more than one or two work groups or committees in place to facilitate employee relations work. Paramount in these will be a "Joint Consultative and Negotiating Committee" where representatives of management and trade unions (often known as the Staff Side) will meet together on a regular basis to discuss issues relating to statutory terms and conditions of employment, health and safety and matters relating to redundancies and transfers as they arise.

Such a committee would normally constitute five or six management representatives and proportionate representation from the trade unions. The committee might meet three or four times a year and would be chaired by a management representative. There would usually be a secretary for the Management Side and a secretary for the Staff Side who would be responsible for coordinating agendas and agreeing the constitution of the committee and the ground rules within which it operates. Decisions made by it would not necessarily be binding on the employer, although they will be wise to heed the outcomes. This kind of machinery provides the minimum reactive framework to deal with employer's statutory requirements for trade union recognition, was the kind of machinery that was heavily favoured in the 1970s and 1980s and is still found in smaller and less sophisticated organisations, or those where there is a very formal tradition of trade union recognition.

The good practice model

The good practice model has been the hallmark of progressive employers enjoying good industrial relations over the last fifteen to twenty years, and is adopted by many more organisations today as a less adversarial approach to industrial relations is adopted. It will have a more sophisticated machinery that will include:

- A joint consultative and negotiating committee (JCNC), being a broader forum than that described above and encapsulating a broader range of collective bargaining issues outside the statutory minimum. It might be chaired by management or staff side representatives in rotation, is likely to have a joint secretary, and will meet between four and six times a year.
- A health and safety committee consisting of management and staff side health and safety representatives to consider health and safety specific issues, often constituted as a sub-group of the JCNC.
- Sub-groups of the main JCNC which facilitate joint working between man-

agement and staff side on a range of workplace issues of common interest, trying to find joint solutions and avoid industrial conflict.

- An informal network of management/staff side consultation on specific issues to try and resolve problems as they arise and foster a good industrial relations climate and positive employee relations culture.

This model is essentially the model that builds on the government's aspiration for working in partnership outlined above, and is found in many parts of the public and private sector where there is a long tradition of trade union recognition, but a joint desire to foster progressive industrial relations.

The works council model

The Works Council Model builds on the good practice model, but goes a stage further and integrates trade union representation with wider staff representation in the workplace. Staff may, therefore, sit side-by-side with recognised trade union officials on a whole spectrum of workplace interests. Although the environment described in the Good Practice Model may still exist it will be enhanced at all levels in the workplace by informal consultation that encourages worker participation in all respects. It is the employee relations model envisaged by the EU's *Works Council Directive* and is practised by some progressive and multinational organisations.

Training

No matter which model suits the particular organisation's circumstances, putting in place proper machinery and facilities will not of itself be a recipe for positive employee relations in the workplace. So, often poor employee relations are the product of a lack of knowledge and awareness sometimes on behalf of managers, and sometimes on behalf of trade union representatives themselves. Although many of the large recognised trade unions and the TUC invest heavily in training in employment law and associated matters, many employers do not, and come into conflict simply because managers do not have the knowledge and skills to handle employee relations issues skilfully and sensitively. Training for both management and staff side is therefore an essential prerequisite for good employee relations. The subjects tackled in this training will depend on the nature of the agreements described above, but will need to cover an introduction to employment law, and the principles of good negotiating, consultation and bargaining practice that fit in with the machinery in the workplace. ACAS have a particularly strong tradition of undertaking such training and will often provide it on a joint basis for both management and staff side representatives, and this is a useful platform for joint working.

Communications

Rather like training, the best machinery in the world will not deliver good employee relations unless the wider workforce environment is conducive to it.

The principle of good communications is the key to good practice here, as all the evidence shows that organisations that communicate well at all levels enjoy better employee relations than those that do not. Indeed, it is possible to identify the major conflicts in the workplace as usually the result of poor communications or misunderstanding. Thus, again, a clear communications strategy in the organisation with the workforce as a whole, and with trade unions in particular, will go a long way to promoting a positive employee relations environment.

10.5 Disciplinary, grievance and disputes procedures

As identified above, some of the most sensitive, difficult employee relations issues to deal with are those related to discipline and grievances, with the consequence of failing to resolve them properly either being recourse to legal action or often a dispute in the workplace. In this section we will consider model procedures for handling each of these aspects.

Disciplinary procedures

Disciplinary procedures and their operation should be based on the ACAS codes on the subject. Good practice guidance within these requires an organisation to adopt four key procedures where disciplinary action may result in disciplinary sanctions or offences which could lead to terminating the contract.

Develop a disciplinary procedure

The procedure should be in writing and specify to whom the organisation's disciplinary rules apply. The procedure should provide for employees to receive natural justice in all aspects of disciplinary matters. Natural justice means knowing the case against them, the right to prepare a defence, and the right to be represented in having their case heard. The procedure should also provide for employees to be represented by a trade union official or a workplace representative (note the *Employment Relations Act* allows the employee to be represented by any trade union official of their choice in disciplinary matters). The procedure should also lay out the procedures for conducting investigations, the suspension of employees, the conduct of disciplinary hearings, a provision for appeals to be heard and a range of disciplinary sanctions, as described below.

Develop disciplinary rules

Rules help specify what is and what is not acceptable to the organisation and these should be included in the procedure and indicate particularly those matters that will be constituted as gross misconduct and may lead to dismissal. Gross misconduct would normally be described as acts of violence, theft, gross insubordination, or other actions which will place the organisation and the staff at risk.

Distinguish between conduct and capability

It is important for disciplinary procedures to distinguish between matters of conduct and capability as confusion will lead to legal challenges and poor practice. Conduct is about a failure or shortcoming in an employee in relation to the rules of the organisation, whereas capability is about their ability to undertake the work required of them dependent on their skills, aptitude or health.

Conduct investigations

It is important for the disciplinary procedure to set out a process for conducting investigations. An objective investigation of the facts of the case are a key principle of natural justice. It therefore follows that those investigating matters should be objective and not involved in any hearing of a disciplinary nature that may result. The investigation should be thorough but conducted as quickly as possible. Suspension of an employee under investigation may be justified where their continued presence in the workplace might jeopardise the investigation or may be in their own interest due to the matters at stake. In these circumstances suspension should normally be on full pay as no guilt should be assumed until a full hearing has decided on the case.

Operate rules fairly

This is a truism that is nonetheless difficult to operate in practice. It means that the manager in charge of a case needs to keep an open mind at all times, ensure a separation between the stages of investigation and hearing, and keep the employee against whom the allegations are made, informed at all times.

Establish a range of disciplinary sanctions

There are normally four or five stages in a range of disciplinary sanctions available. These start with oral warnings and work their way up to summary dismissal. A full hierarchy of potential sanctions is shown at Figure 10.1.

Allow appeals to be heard

It is a fundamental principle of natural justice that an employee who is disciplined has the right of appeal against the finding. This will normally apply to the more serious level of sanctions such as a final written warning and always in cases of dismissal or summary dismissal. Grounds for appeal would include representation that the original sanction was too harsh; the disciplining manager was not objective; the hearing was unfair; or new evidence has come to light. The appeals procedure should spell out at what levels of disciplinary sanction appeals will be allowed, who will hear the appeal, and what the timescale for lodging and hearing appeals will be.

As described in this model ACAS approach, it is vital that the organisation distinguishes between matters of potential misconduct and incapability. Incapabil-

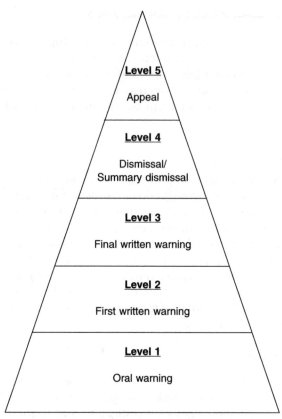

Figure 10.1   Hierarchy of disciplinary sanctions

ity by definition will have to be managed over a longer timeframe, ensuring that monitoring is put in place to try to identify the reasons for poor performance, whether the gap can be bridged (through training, guidance and support), allow the issuing of warnings to encourage and improve performance, and only ultimately resort to the sanction of formal disciplinary action and/or dismissal. A disciplinary flow chart for managing poor performance is described in Figure 10.2. In the case of dismissals on grounds of ill health, it is particularly important that reference is made to the employee's GP or the occupational health service. Their advice should always be sought before any ill-health dismissal is contemplated, remembering that it is perfectly legal for the employer to dismiss whether or not they believe the absence to be genuine, so long as they can show that it will not be possible for the employee to reasonably meet the requirements of the job on an ongoing basis.

Grievance procedure

Grievances are in essence a complaints procedure for staff relating to issues in their employment. As with the disciplinary matters, it is important that a proce-

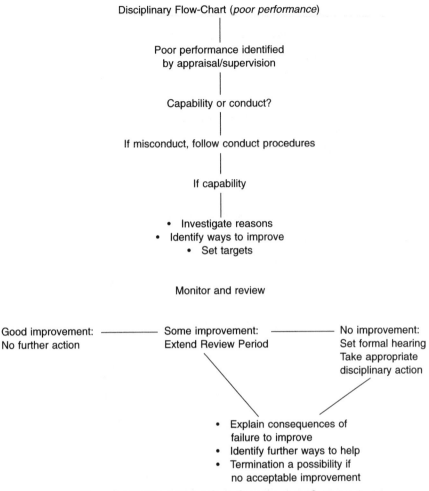

Disciplinary Flow-Chart (*poor performance*)

Poor performance identified
by appraisal/supervision

Capability or conduct?

If misconduct, follow conduct procedures

If capability

- Investigate reasons
- Identify ways to improve
  - Set targets

Monitor and review

Good improvement: ———— Some improvement: ———— No improvement:
No further action   Extend Review Period   Set formal hearing
                                                           Take appropriate
                                                           disciplinary action

- Explain consequences of
  failure to improve
- Identify further ways to help
- Termination a possibility if
  no acceptable improvement

Figure 10.2   Disciplinary flow chart (poor performance)

dure should be established in accordance with ACAS provisions and should provide for:

- Informal resolution of grievances at the lowest possible level.
- Scope for progression to a higher level where no resolution is possible.
- Objective assessment of the facts from both employee and manager.
- The right for the employee to be represented.

By definition the grievance procedure will have a close relationship with and interact with other organisational procedures such as the disciplinary procedure. These relationships should therefore be identified and codified in the grievance procedure saying when it will apply as opposed to the other procedures referred to. Those organisations that adopt whistleblowing procedures under the provisions of The *Disclosure of Information Act* will need also to identify how griev-

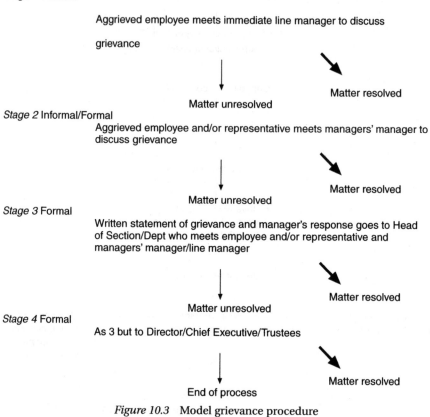

Stage 1 Informal

Aggrieved employee meets immediate line manager to discuss
grievance

Matter unresolved

Matter resolved

Stage 2 Informal/Formal

Aggrieved employee and/or representative meets managers' manager to
discuss grievance

Matter unresolved

Matter resolved

Stage 3 Formal

Written statement of grievance and manager's response goes to Head
of Section/Dept who meets employee and/or representative and
managers' manager/line manager

Matter unresolved

Matter resolved

Stage 4 Formal

As 3 but to Director/Chief Executive/Trustees

End of process

Matter resolved

Figure 10.3   Model grievance procedure

ances will be distinguished from acts of whistleblowing. A model grievance procedure is described at Figure 10.3.

Disputes machinery

The third aspect in this trilogy of formal employee relations procedures is
that which relates to disputes. In the event of a dispute with a trade union or
staff (either individually or collectively) organisations may need to establish
some sort of procedure to resolve disputes at an early stage and promote
good employee relations. It is to be hoped the negotiating, consultation and
bargaining machinery described above will go a long way to ensuring that any
disputes are kept to a minimum, and that the proper operation of disciplinary
and grievance procedures in themselves will minimise any recourse to a formal
dispute. However, it is good practice to have such an outlet within an organisation as a place where aggrieved trade unions and all staff can go when all else
has failed.

ACAS will usually agree to provide conciliation in such matters and can advise on the setting up of model procedures to assist employers dependent upon their circumstances. The main factors to be considered in the creation of a good disputes procedure will be the possibility for resolution at the earliest possible stage (as with grievance procedures), and of ensuring that all other measures have been exhausted before it is triggered. It will also need to be objective and impartial, and may require representation from outside the organisation, perhaps including ACAS in some formal capacity. Again the operation of the disputes machinery should be included in training for managers and trade unions as part of the promotion of a positive employee relations culture.

10.6 Problem areas

QUESTION:
My organisation had a very bad experience in terms of trade union representation in the 1970s. We had strikes and all kinds of unrest in the workplace and the unions were de-recognised in 1982. Frankly, the prospect of inviting them back in is terrifying even though I know the law may require it. What can we do to ensure there is responsible employee relations in the future?

ANSWER:
Your organisation's experience was sadly not uncommon in British organisations in the 1970s and clearly led to a backlash which encouraged the Conservative Government to legislate to reduce the powers of trade unions. But the bad experience of the past should not necessarily dictate your feelings about the future. Trade unions themselves have reformed considerably and are much more democratic, open and socially responsible organisations than they were thirty years ago. They too are operating in a different environment, and need to be commercially aware and astute to gain proper influence in the workplace. As you say, their recognition may be a fact of life for your organisation dependent upon the strength of employee feeling. It is much better therefore to try and foster an open and cooperative attitude rather than a climate of suspicion and fear. The key principles outlined in this chapter should help go some way to overcoming these fears. So, identify clear rules on individual and collective rights; establish a clear employee relationship machinery, and above all encourage training for both your managers and trade union representatives. ACAS are very well placed to advise on these matters.

QUESTION:
I appointed a new receptionist just over a year ago, and I am afraid he has turned out to be something of a disaster. He is surly and difficult in his attitude and more importantly the quality of his work is poor. I am not quite certain though how to deal with this matter in a disciplinary context. Is this a poor performance/capability issue or is it about conduct and how should I approach it?

ANSWER:
You are quite right to ask this question as an initial point for determining how to tackle this case. You need to ask yourself first of all whether the employee has the skills and aptitudes

to undertake the work you require of him or whether he has these skills and aptitudes but is just obstinate and difficult. Employers are sometimes nervous of pursuing the incapability route because by definition it is a longer process requiring them to identify deficiencies, counsel the employee and give him/her an opportunity to improve, providing warnings along the way. However, it is important to separate the issues clearly and decide whether this is about incapability or conduct before proceeding down a disciplinary route. If you have clear evidence that he is breaking your organisation's rules through his rudeness and surly attitude, then you can proceed down the misconduct route.

Remember to investigate the facts, collect the evidence, and conduct a disciplinary hearing if this is justified. Remember also to consider an appropriate sanction dependent on the severity of his actions and the evidence that supports this or otherwise. From what you have said it is unlikely that there would be grounds for gross misconduct and summary dismissal in this case, and the level of a written warning may be appropriate. Also remember that misconduct does not have to be progressive. Just because you may give the employee a low level warning, it does not mean that if he commits an act of gross misconduct next week you have to proceed to the next stage. You can jump into the procedure at any level if misconduct is the issue. Whichever process you decide to pursue, make sure that you stick to your procedure and act reasonably. Further details on handling the termination of a contract of employment are described in Chapter 4.

QUESTION:
I have been asked by my director to handle a grievance involving an employee who reports to him. Frankly I am rather uncomfortable about doing this because I do not really know what the issues are and I think I am only being asked to handle it because the director regards this particular employee as a nuisance. What should I do?

ANSWER:
The first thing you should do is refer to your organisation's grievance procedure if you have one, and make sure that the grievance is heard at the appropriate stage. Remember that the key principle behind grievances is to ensure that they can be resolved and this begs that they are heard at the lowest level within the organisation. You need first to ascertain, therefore, who this employee reports to and if this is to the director, then I am afraid he must deal with this matter himself in the first instance and cannot pass this off to you to deal with.

Encourage him to hear the grievance if this is the case and ask him to keep an open mind and listen to the issues. He then needs to determine whether or not it is within his gift to resolve the matter and provide real solutions to the employee's grievance, or indeed whether the grievance has real substance. If it does, and the director does not resolve it, then it is likely that your procedure will provide for it to be heard at another level, and it may get to chief executive or board level which may cause the director some embarrassment. So it is in his and the organisation's interests to hear this grievance openly, fairly and genuinely to provide resolution without discharging the responsibility to somebody else.

10.7 Activity

Miss G, a secretary in your office, is continually late for work. Matters have got worse to the point where you, her line manager, have decided you cannot let it go on any further. Would you:

- Call her in and give her a disciplinary warning under your disciplinary procedure.
- Dismiss her from your employment.
- Call her in and tell her to buck her ideas up and not to be late again.
- Call her in for a discussion to find out why she is being late and investigate the reasons behind it.

If despite warnings and help her attendance fails to improve, at what point might you consider her dismissal from the organisation?

10.8 Checklist

- ► Employee(or industrial) relations is concerned with the maintenance and development of workplace communications, consultation, negotiation, bargaining with staff, trade unions, and staff associations.
- ► It is an area in which the law has increasingly regulated practice.
- ► Trade union power was at its height in the 1970s but was greatly curbed during the 1980s and early 90s.
- ► The *Employment Relations Act* confers important new rights on trade unions to allow representation and recognition in the workplace.
- ► In terms of trade union activity, issues relating to individual rights, trade union recognition and representation are considered.
- ► The machinery and systems to support these rights are also examined in terms of approaches to negotiation, consultation, and bargaining.
- ► Training, communication, and the fostering of a positive employee relations climate are of equal importance.
- ► Disciplinary, grievance and disputes procedures are examined as part of the employee relations framework.

☑ 11 Redundancy, reorganisation and transfers

11.1 Introduction

Although all of the territory connected with the termination of a contract of employment is potentially difficult from a HRM point of view, some of the most complex and difficult aspects to manage are those connected with redundancy, reorganisation and transfers. The pattern of employment has changed so much over the last twenty years that the nature of organisations and the boundaries between them are changing at a pace and with a complexity never seen before in the UK.

Long gone are the notions of lifetime employment with one employer, whose core business and trading name remain unchanged for thirty or forty years. Even those who are lucky enough to remain working with one organisation often find that the nature of the business will change considerably or the parent or holding company will change its name or status during the life of their employment. With so much emphasis on reducing organisational costs, maximising effectiveness and competitiveness, companies in the private sector and public sector organisations are constantly seeking ways to improve their efficiency. So mergers and acquisitions, transfers and reorganisations, are very much the bywords of organisational life as we enter the new century.

So what are the implications for the Human Resource Management professional? Put simply, there is tremendous scope for things to go wrong both from an employment law perspective and in terms of handling people properly, unless there is a very clear frame of reference and good practice is adhered to at each and every stage of the reorganisation, transfer or redundancy process. Although making people redundant from their employment remains one of the least pleasing aspects of HR work it is a fact of life for the Human Resource practitioner today and the one major benefit to have come from this aspect of employment changes over the last twenty years is that there is now a significant body of knowledge about what constitutes good practice in managing this difficult and sensitive aspect of HRM.

In this section we examine some of the key legal requirements for managing redundancy, reorganisation and transfers; look at the good practice requirements relating to each topic in turn; and explore some of the inter-relationships between these distinct facets of change management. The good news from the HRM point of view is that the practitioner who can successfully manage in this complex and demanding arena will usually win a reputation for being highly effective and will prove to be a highly valuable resource to organisations who would otherwise be vulnerable, both in terms of potential litigation and in damage to their industrial and human relations. It is also true to say that these aspects of change management in organisations are now something of an industry in themselves, and are proving to be essential skills for good Human Resource managers across the board.

11.2 Legal framework

The *Redundancy Payments Act 1965*

This Act introduced the right of employees who lost their jobs in certain circumstances to receive a payment from their employers irrespective of whether they had another job to go to. The Act was amended by the *Employment Protection Act 1975* and these provisions in turn were re-enacted in The *Employment Protection (Consolidation) Act 1978* and are now consolidated in the *Employment Rights Act 1996*.

The Act requires certain preconditions to be met for the individual to qualify for redundancy payment, including: that they must be an employee of the organisation; that they must have been continuously employed for a period of two years ending on what is known as the relevant date (the relevant date is when a contract of employment is terminated); and that the reason for termination of the employment was redundancy. For the purposes of the Act redundancy is defined as a cessation of the business for the purpose of which the employee was employed, or that the kind of work the employee is required to carry out has ceased or is diminished or is expected to diminish. It also follows from this definition that the employee must have been dismissed on grounds of redundancy to qualify for a redundancy payment. They are not considered to have been dismissed if they are renewed or re-engaged in their employment within four weeks of the original contract of employment ending, or if they are offered employment by an associated company or organisation which would otherwise invalidate their redundancy payment.

The *Redundancy Payments Act* and its successor pieces of legislation also include exemptions from the right to a redundancy payment on the following grounds:

- Employees who have attained the normal retiring age, usually 65 years of age.
- Employees who have been offered employment on the same terms and conditions as their original employment or are offered suitable alternative employment and in either case have unreasonably refused the offer.
- Employees who have been dismissed on grounds of misconduct.
- Employees who are employed under a fixed term contract of 2 years or more where dismissal consists of the expiry of that term without it being renewed.

The time limit for payment of redundancy payment after the *relevant date* is normally a period of 6 months and all issues relating to the redundancy will normally have been expected to be resolved during that period unless a claim for unfair dismissal has been lodged with an employment tribunal during that time and has yet to be heard. The issue of *suitable alternative employment* is key to the legislation and issues of good practice which are dealt with below, as an employee who is dismissed by reason of redundancy loses their right to redundancy payment if they unreasonably refuse an offer of suitable alternative employment. To constitute an offer of suitable alternative employment, the following conditions must be met:

- The offer of employment must be made by the original or an associated employer (and by implication would offer the employee continuous employment).
- The offer must be made before the ending of the previous contract of employment.
- The offer may be oral or in writing.
- The offer must take effect either immediately on the ending of the employment under the previous contract or after an interval of not more than 4 weeks thereafter.
- The offer must be either on the same terms and conditions or offer suitable employment in relation to the employee (the latter term means that the employment must be relevant to the previous nature of employment with the organisation).

If the terms and conditions of the renewed or new contract of employment offered differ, an employee has a right to a statutory trial period of 4 weeks, beginning from the ending of the previous employment, in which to decide whether the alternative employment is suitable for them. The idea is to provide employees who are so redeployed the opportunity to find out whether they are suited for the work or indeed whether the employer finds the match between the job and the employee satisfactory also. If at the end of this period the employee accepts the alternative employment, they are deemed not to have been dismissed on grounds of redundancy. If, however, as a result of the trial period employment does not continue, then termination on grounds of redundancy still applies and a redundancy payment will be due.

The legislation goes on to stipulate the amount of redundancy payment that an employee who was terminated on grounds of redundancy would be eligible for. This is dependent on the employee's age, length of continuous employment and their gross average salary. Figure 11.1 attached provides a ready reckoner for calculating redundancy payments in accordance with these statutory provisions. It should be noted here that all the above provisions, including the entitlement and calculation for redundancy payments, are the statutory minimum. Many employers choose to provide entitlements over and above the statutory entitlements, and have more generous rules relating to length of service entitlement, redundancy payments, and in some cases even the length of continuous service required to qualify for such a payment.

Age in years	2	3	4	5	6	7	8	9	10	11	12	13	14	15	16	17	18	19	20
20	1	1	1	1	—														
21	1	1½	1½	1½	1½	—													
22	1	1½	2	2	2	2	—												
23	1½	2	2½	3	3	3	3	—											
24	2	2½	3	3½	4	4	4	4	—										
25	2	3	3½	4½	5	5	5	5	5	—									
26	2	3	4	4½	5	5½	6	6	6	6	—								
27	2	3	4	5	5½	6	6½	7	7	7	7	—							
28	2	3	4	5	6	6½	7	7½	8	8	8	8	—						
29	2	3	4	5	6	7	7½	8	8½	9	9	9	9	—					
30	2	3	4	5	6	7	8	8½	9	9½	10	10	10	10	—				
31	2	3	4	5	6	7	8	9	9½	10	10½	11	11	11	11	—			
32	2	3	4	5	6	7	8	9	10	10½	11	11½	12	12	12	12	—		
33	2	3	4	5	6	7	8	9	10	11	11½	12	12½	13	13	13	13	—	
34	2	3	4	5	6	7	8	9	10	11	12	12½	13	13½	14	14	14	14	—
35	2	3	4	5	6	7	8	9	10	11	12	13	13½	14	14½	15	15	15	15
36	2	3	4	5	6	7	8	9	10	11	12	13	14	14½	15	15½	16	16	16
37	2	3	4	5	6	7	8	9	10	11	12	13	14	15	15½	16	16½	17	17
38	2	3	4	5	6	7	8	9	10	11	12	13	14	15	16	16½	17	17½	18
39	2	3	4	5	6	7	8	9	10	11	12	13	14	15	16	17	17½	18	18½
40	2	3	4	5	6	7	8	9	10	11	12	13	14	15	16	17	18	18½	19
41	2	3	4	5	6	7	8	9	10	11	12	13	14	15	16	17	18	19	19½
42	2½	3½	4½	5½	6½	7½	8½	9½	10½	11½	12½	13½	14½	15½	16½	17½	18½	19½	20½
43	3	4	5	6	7	8	9	10	11	12	13	14	15	16	17	18	19	20	21
44	3	4½	5½	6½	7½	8½	9½	10½	11½	12½	13½	14½	15½	16½	17½	18½	19½	20½	21½
45	3	4½	6	7	8	9	10	11	12	13	14	15	16	17	18	19	20	21	22
46	3	4½	6	7½	8½	9½	10½	11½	12½	13½	14½	15½	16½	17½	18½	19½	20½	21½	22½
47	3	4½	6	7½	9	10	11	12	13	14	15	16	17	18	19	20	21	22	23
48	3	4½	6	7½	9	10½	11½	12½	13½	14½	15½	16½	17½	18½	19½	20½	21½	22½	23½
49	3	4½	6	7½	9	10½	12	13	14	15	16	17	18	19	20	21	22	23	24
50	3	4½	6	7½	9	10½	12	13½	14½	15½	16½	17½	18½	19½	20½	21½	22½	23½	24½
51	3	4½	6	7½	9	10½	12	13½	15	16	17	18	19	20	21	22	23	24	25
52	3	4½	6	7½	9	10½	12	13½	15	16½	17½	18½	19½	20½	21½	22½	23½	24½	25½
53	3	4½	6	7½	9	10½	12	13½	15	16½	18	19	20	21	22	23	24	25	26
54	3	4½	6	7½	9	10½	12	13½	15	16½	18	19½	20½	21½	22½	23½	24½	25½	26½
55	3	4½	6	7½	9	10½	12	13½	15	16½	18	19½	21	22	23	24	25	26	27
56	3	4½	6	7½	9	10½	12	13½	15	16½	18	19½	21	22½	23½	24½	25½	26½	27½
57	3	4½	6	7½	9	10½	12	13½	15	16½	18	19½	21	22½	24	25	26	27	28
58	3	4½	6	7½	9	10½	12	13½	15	16½	18	19½	21	22½	24	25½	26½	27½	28½
59	3	4½	6	7½	9	10½	12	13½	15	16½	18	19½	21	22½	24	25½	27	28	29
60	3	4½	6	7½	9	10½	12	13½	15	16½	18	19½	21	22½	24	25½	27	28½	29½
61	3	4½	6	7½	9	10½	12	13½	15	16½	18	19½	21	22½	24	25½	27	28½	30
62	3	4½	6	7½	9	10½	12	13½	15	16½	18	19½	21	22½	24	25½	27	28½	30
63	3	4½	6	7½	9	10½	12	13½	15	16½	18	19½	21	22½	24	25½	27	28½	30
64	3	4½	6	7½	9	10½	12	13½	15	16½	18	19½	21	22½	24	25½	27	28½	30

Statutory redundancy pay entitlements (based on weeks of statutory redundancy pay)

Figure 11.1 Redundancy payments statutory ready reckoner

The *Trade Union Reform and Employment Rights Act 1993*

This legislation imposed far-reaching obligations on employers to notify both recognised trade unions and employees directly affected about the likelihood of forthcoming redundancies and the reasons for them. It is a very important piece of legislation governing the handling of redundancies and places strict requirements on employers. The legislation requires that where an employer is proposing to dismiss at least 20 employees on grounds of redundancy in a particular establishment, within a period of 90 days or less, they must consult about the proposed dismissals with trade union representatives or other representatives of the employee or the employees themselves.

This consultation must begin at the earliest possible opportunity and must not be a sham. For the purposes of this consultation, the employer must disclose in writing:

- the reason for the impending redundancy;
- the number and description of employees whom it is proposed to dismiss as redundant;
- the total number of employees of any such description employed by the employer at the establishment in question;
- the proposed method for selecting the employees who may be dismissed;
- the proposed method of carrying out the dismissals;
- and the proposed method for calculating the amount of any redundancy payment, statutory or otherwise.

The consultation must also include a dialogue about ways of avoiding dismissals to try and reduce the number of employees to be dismissed and mitigating the consequences of the dismissal. It therefore follows that employees and all their representatives must have the opportunity to explore the reasons for the dismissal and to try and provide other options for consideration. Where an employer is proposing to dismiss more than 100 employees at any one establishment within a period of 90 days or less, the consultation must begin at least 90 days before the first of those dismissals takes effect. In any other cases in which consultation is required, consultation must begin at least 30 days before the first of those dismissals takes effect.

The *Transfer of Undertakings (Protection of Employment) Regulations 1981 (TUPE)*

This legislation describes far-reaching rules for the protection of the employee's rights upon the transfer of their employment from one undertaking to another. The legislation is known in shorthand as *TUPE* and has since been amended by the *Trade Union Reform and Employment Rights Act 1993* and a number of European directives, most significantly The *Acquired Rights Directive*, which are now consolidated into UK law. This is a complex piece of legislation and some of the terms within it need careful definition for it to be understood. For the purposes of the original 1981 legislation, a transfer was defined as including any trade or business. At this point, therefore, the regulations did not apply to any undertaking that was not commercial by nature.

As this exclusion was inconsistent with the EU's *Acquired Rights Directive*, the UK government had to introduce legislation to ensure that *TUPE* principles applied to all forms of organisational transfers, and hence the amendment to legislation included in the *Trade Union Reform and Employment Rights Act 1993*. The regulations also cover the transfer of part of an undertaking, meaning a unit which is to some extent separate and self-contained from the remainder of the main organisation or enterprise of which it is part. This has prevented organisations from disposing of part of their main business without protecting the employment rights of the employees who transfer with it.

For the purposes of the legislation, transfer means the sale, merger or disposition of a business or an organisation from one party to another, where the original business and identity is carried on by the new owner or transferee. There is a significant body of case law that has been used to determine what constitutes such a transfer, which will be referred to later in this chapter. The most significant aspect of the legislation is that the employees of the transferor (the original organisation) automatically become from the moment of the transfer employed by the new organisation (or the transferee) on the terms or conditions which they enjoyed with the original employer. The employment to be transferred and protected here concerns the terms and conditions and the contract in force immediately before the transfer takes place. This prevents the new employer unilaterally changing terms and conditions of employment or making staff automatically redundant as a consequence of the transfer, and if they do so they will be liable to a claim of unfair or constructive dismissal which is likely to be automatically found.

As well as the contract of employment and the terms and conditions of employment contained within it transferring from one employer to another under *TUPE*, collective agreements made between the transferor and trade union also automatically transfer to the transferee. The collective agreement may relate to working practices or some other aspects of terms and conditions of employment that are incorporated into the contract, and may include recognition of a trade union itself which similarly would also transfer under the legislation. *TUPE* also recognises the role of trade unions and employees in terms of the consultation requirements which are analogous to those required in a redundancy situation. Regulations which are now incorporated alongside *TUPE* require employers to undertake early consultation on the following aspects of an impending transfer:

- The fact that a relevant transfer is to take place.
- When it is to take place.
- The reasons for it.
- The legal, economic and social implications of the transfer for employees.
- The measures which the employer envisages taking in relation to those employees (as the transferor).
- The measures the employer intends to make for those employees who are automatically transferred (as the transferee).

As with the redundancy legislation, transferees and transferors who fail to undertake appropriate consultation may be subject to a claim to a tribunal, with compensation payable where a breach of the law is found.

TUPE also makes it clear that any termination of a contract for a reason associated with a transfer of an undertaking is likely to be automatically unfair and invite a claim of unfair dismissal against either or both the transferee or the transferor. The only grounds on which either a transferee or a transferor are likely to be able to successfully resist such a claim is if they can show there are very strong economic, technical or organisation reasons requiring changes in the workforce that have enforced a termination of contract, leading to a redundancy. So if, as a result of a transfer, the transferee can show that they would be unable to remain a viable business with all the employees transferred on their current terms and conditions of employment, then some more redundancies may be justifiable but the grounds will need to be compelling. The same rules apply to the variation of contracts of employment by the transferee after the act of transfer.

Although *TUPE* protects the terms and conditions and contracts of employees and collective agreements at the time of transfer, this does not mean to say the transferee cannot seek to vary the contract after the event. In these circumstances, normal rules for an employer seeking to vary a contract of employment apply, with the employer needing to demonstrate a strong economic, technical or organisation reason for varying contracts of employment. It is worth noting here that there is no minimum time limit within which employers cannot seek to make such a contractual change. There is a commonly held misbelief that employers have to protect a transferring contract of employment for a minimum period of at least 6 months or 1 year before they can seek to make such a variation – no such time limit applies subject to a valid economic, technical organisational reason being found.

11.3 Handling redundancies

Given this onerous legislative framework, it follows that the handling of redundancy situations requires a sound procedural approach in HRM terms if employee and employer are not going to come into conflict. Matters are not helped by the obvious fact that redundancy is of itself a traumatic experience for both organisation and individual employee. The trauma for the organisation is normally founded on the fact that redundancy is seen as a failure either in business terms or that in managing organisational change the employer has been unable to absorb its workforce or re-deploy or re-skill them so as to allow them to be retained. More often than not redundancy is a sign of commercial failure or a financial retrenchment in the organisation. For the employee, the consequences are more personally felt and often drastic. Unless alternative employment can be quickly found, or it occurs at a time in life where the employee is financially secure or of retiring age, redundancy usually brings unwelcome associations of being disowned by the organisation and concerns over livelihood and protection of individual and family wellbeing. The emotional aspects of handling redundancies, therefore, cannot be overplayed as they are often devastating and are overlooked at the organisation's peril.

Given these potential hurdles, many organisations seek to protect themselves by agreeing with their trade unions or individual employees a redundancy policy that describes both the process and procedure they will pursue in the event that a redundancy situation will occur. Such procedures are designed to take as much of the emotion out of the situation as possible, allow both employer and employee to focus on the important task of preserving employment, and maximising employment protection.

EXAMPLE

A typical redundancy policy would contain the following features:

1 Causes: the kinds of situation that will lead to a redundancy occurring (a reorganisation, transfer of location, or a major change in business).

2 Procedures for consulting with staff and trade unions: this will normally include minimum time periods that will have to comply with statutory requirements outlined above, and local arrangements for consulting (who, what, where and when).

3 Method of redundancy selection: a good redundancy practice requires the employer to define up front the grounds for selecting employees for redundancy. Selecting an individual for redundancy is automatically unfair if it is in contravention of an agreed procedure and if the grounds for selecting an individual for redundancy are not objective and without discrimination. So selection for redundancy on grounds of race, culture, gender, trade union membership or disability will be automatically unfair. Potentially fair grounds for selection will include attendance and performance records (although care will need to be taken to ensure the assessment is objective and based on true information); age and length of service (with the notion of "last in first out" as the usual fallback position for employers who do not otherwise state explicit criteria); or because of cessation of work in a particular department, skill or occupation (although here for redundancy to be fair the whole of the department would have to be placed at risk unless some other additional criteria mentioned above are also to be used).

4 Employment protection methods: many large employers are able to offer a range of alternative employment options to employees who are at risk of redundancy and policies usually spell out the means for identifying these and how employees will be notified of them. It is usual in these situations for organisations to suspend normal external recruitment and selection procedures, agency and in some cases work for contractors so that they try to preserve as much work in-house as possible in order to ring-fence for the at-risk employees. Some organisations go further and suspend all forms of recruitment and contracting to give first priority to at-risk employees, even if this requires fundamental, redeployment, re-skilling and re-training to keep them in a job. It should be noted that once these features become part of a redundancy and employment protection policy, then the employer will be judged by them at any tribunal considering a case of unfair dismissal arising from the handling of a redundancy situation.

5 Employee support and counselling: the prospect of redundancy is serious for any employee, and the good employer therefore needs to provide at-risk employees with as much information as possible about the potential risks to them and support, at the time when redundancies are likely to happen. Such information and support will include: advice about alternative jobs in the organisation they may apply for; advice on and support with financial management; outplacement support for jobs in other organisations including CV preparation; advice on interview techniques, and time off to search for alternative work; and occupational health advice and stress counselling to help individuals cope with the pressure and stress of dealing with a potential redundancy situation.

6 Notice periods and redundancy payments: if all else fails, and the redundancy becomes a reality, the at-risk population needs to be notified of the organisation's policy for making redundancy payments, whether these are just the statutory minimum or a more generous local arrangement, and the notice periods that will imply. In the latter case, the notice periods stipulated in the individual's contract of employment must be given as a minimum requirement, although it is often the case in a redundancy situation that a more generous notice period will be provided, and very often this will be paid in lieu to employees to maximise their leaving package and the time they have available to search for alternative work.

A model approach to handling a redundancy dismissal procedure is outlined at Figure 11.2. It outlines the steps necessary for the good employer to take in a logical sequence when considering a redundancy exercise and is applicable for any number of posts.

11.4 Reorganisation and managing internal change

Very often, the circumstances leading to a redundancy or a transfer of undertaking will arise because of the need for major organisational change or internal reorganisation. Indeed, such has become the pace of organisational change over the last twenty years, that managing change has become a HRM industry in its own right. Whatever the context for and reasons lying behind such change, there are a number of important principles to observe that will help, develop and enhance good HRM practice. The degree of flexibility built into existing contracts of employment will determine whether changes can be made without the need to renegotiate or declare a redundancy. A mobility clause or a broadly defined workplace may allow the reallocation of employees to new locations. Similarly if a job title covers a range of duties and there are no more specific contractual commitments, a reallocation of tasks within the range can be achieved in accordance with the contract of employment and so provide the employer with much greater flexibility.

If a job description is included as part of the contract of employment this may determine the scope available for changing duties in detail. Clauses such as "any other duties that maybe required" do not allow management complete flexibility. Tribunals are likely to interpret this as meaning that other duties consistent with the job title and of a broadly similar description to the remainder of the job description could be allocated. The job title itself will also have a bearing on the degree to which the work of the post and the individual in it can be varied.

So, for example a general manager of a production outlet may be reasonably expected to take on a range of duties connected with that function even if he/she has not previously undertaken them, but it would probably not be reasonable to suddenly expect them to become the accounts manager or HR advisor. Some contracts of employment include flexibility clauses relating to the number of hours to be worked and the time of day when hours are allocated. Whilst this does allow considerable flexibility, there is a body of case law which shows employers

```
Reasons
1. Define a policy
2. Identify reasons for redundancy
3. Explore alternatives
4. Act early
```

```
Consult
• Trade unions and staff
• Explore alternatives
• On reasons and selection criteria
• On methods for handling
```

```
Protect
1. Jobs where possible
2. Suspend other recruitment and
   contractors
3. Give priority to at-risk job-holders
4. Retrain, redeploy, reskill
```

```
Notice and payments
• Define policy on notice and payments
• Refer to contract or statutory
  minimum
• Explain in policy and to staff/unions
• Provide proper written notice
• Advice DTI as appropriate
```

```
Remember
• To provide trial periods in case of
  redeployment
• To consult early and meaningfully
• To follow your procedures
```

Figure 11.2   Model approach to handling redundancy

cannot go beyond reasonable measures and in no cases must they breach statutory provisions in varying contracts. So, for example, in the case of *Secretary of State for Employment v. Dearie* and *Cambridge County Council*, it was found that an attempt by a local authority to reduce working hours below a minimum statutory level (in this case asking an employee to waive their rights to minimum statutory entitlements) would automatically be illegal.

For all these above reasons, major changes in employment circumstances that are likely to alter pay, terms and conditions of employment, the job description, or job location are likely to lead to a change in contract of employment, in which case the model procedure for handling a variation of contract must be followed (see Chapter 3).

Reorganisation has become very much the name of the people game in the late 1990s and early 2000s in UK organisational life. The constant need to innovate and stay competitive means organisational structures and the way people are deployed within them has to be endlessly dynamic, and this usually leads to frequent bouts of organisational change. Whether the reorganisation affects job title and job descriptions, skills requirements from individuals in the job, pay and terms and conditions of employment, the nature of the employer's business, or the place of work, there is a body of good practice which will help employers avoid litigation, minimise staff discontent, and focus energies on creating a new organisational direction with the minimum of disruption.

11.5 Transfers of employment

One prominent employment lawyer recently commented that the *TUPE* regulations had created more new business for him and his colleagues than any other aspect of employment law over the last decade. Whether this is true or not, it is undeniable that the law relating to transfer of undertakings is still in flux, and has been affected by both new legislation and important case law posing tremendous practical problems for employers and personnel advisors alike. Although the 1981 *TUPE* regulations have been embodied in primary UK legislation, and the *Acquired Rights Directive* from the EU now means these are applicable to both commercial and non-commercial undertakings, much of the rest of the framework relating to transfers has been created in an incremental way making it difficult to keep an up-to-date knowledge of an already complex subject. As ever, a logical, methodical approach is required to develop good HRM practice, a summary of the steps for which are described in Figure 11.3. The key steps can be described in more detail.

Determine when TUPE applies

The first stage in assessing a transfer situation is deciding whether or not a transfer of undertaking in the meaning of the law is intended or not. In deciding whether there has been a transfer of an undertaking the critical question is whether the undertaking retains its identity and is carried on by the new employer, the transferee. In answering that question, all the factual circumstances must be considered but particular issues include:

- the type of undertaking or business concerned;
- which intangible assets such as buildings and movable property are transferred;
- the value of intangible assets at the time of the transfer;
- whether the majority of new employees are taken over by the new employer;
- whether customers are transferred;
- and the degree of similarities between the activities carried out by both the transferee and the transferor.

If the answer to the majority of these questions is "yes", then the *TUPE* regulations are likely to apply. In a landmark test case, the European Court of Justice held, determining the outcome in *Foreningn Af Arbejdsleder I Danmark v. Daddies Dance Hall 1998*, that there was a relevant transfer. In this case the lessee of a restaurant premises gave notice to its employees upon the end of the lease

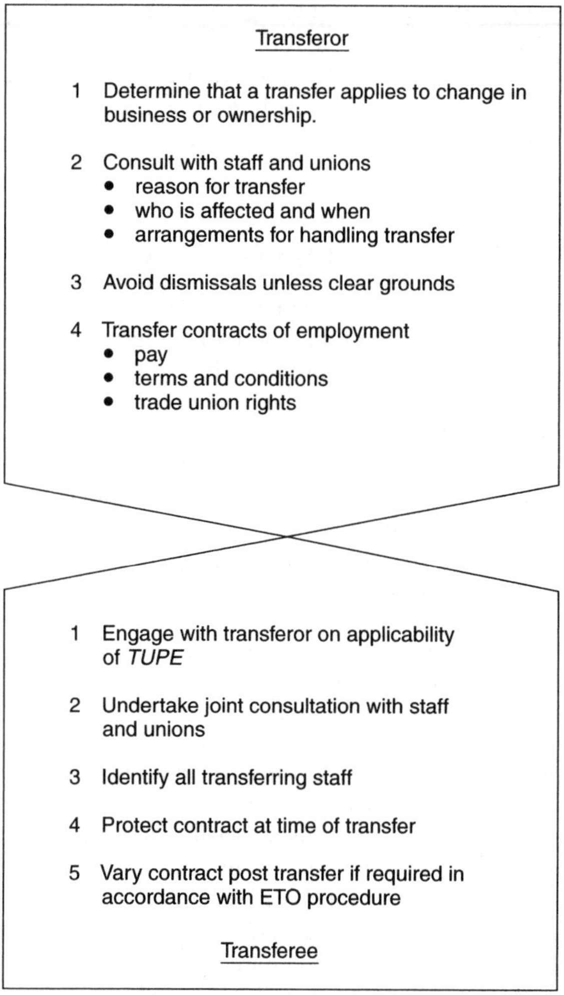

```
                    Transferor

   1  Determine that a transfer applies to change in
      business or ownership.

   2  Consult with staff and unions
      • reason for transfer
      • who is affected and when
      • arrangements for handling transfer

   3  Avoid dismissals unless clear grounds

   4  Transfer contracts of employment
      • pay
      • terms and conditions
      • trade union rights




   1  Engage with transferor on applicability
      of TUPE

   2  Undertake joint consultation with staff
      and unions

   3  Identify all transferring staff

   4  Protect contract at time of transfer

   5  Vary contract post transfer if required in
      accordance with ETO procedure

                    Transferee
```

Figure 11.3   TUPE: a methodical approach to handling transfers

and the lessor then granted a new lease to a third party which continued to run the business without any interruption. The European Court of Justice held that the identity of the economic unit was retained and therefore a transfer of undertaking had occurred and continuity of employment should be provided to the employees. *TUPE* will also often apply in the case of a contracting out of a service that was previously run in-house or where there has been a change of contractors in providing an already contracted-out service.

So for example, in the case of *Dines v. Initial Healthcare Services 1995*, the court held that a transfer of undertaking had occurred even though no assets had changed hands and the service was more or less provided on the same basis as before. All that had happened is the name of the contractor had changed. However, in considering the employment ramifications of *TUPE*, courts and tribunals are usually minded about the degree to which the undertaking transferred provides gainful employment for one or more individuals. Therefore in the case of *Betts v. Brintell Helicopters 1997*, the Court of Appeal held there was no transfer on a change of contractor providing helicopter services to a company where the new contractor took over no staff and only a limited part of the old contractor's assets.

Consultation with staff and trade unions

Broadly speaking, consultation requirements for handling a transfer are similar to those for handling a redundancy situation. In an important EU judgment, the European Court of Justice upheld a complaint by the European Commission that the UK provisions on consultation and information, previously provided in the *Trade Union Reform and Employment Rights Act 1993*, were inadequate and the UK had failed to fulfil its obligation under an EU directive on consultation. As a result of this decision, the government issued regulations (the *Collective Redundancies and Transfer of Undertakings Amendment Regulations 1995*). This requires information to be provided to trade union or staff representatives (and by implication to the staff themselves):

- about the fact that a transfer is to take place; when it is to take place;
- the reasons for it; the implications of the transfer;
- and how the transfer is to be managed.

As with redundancy consultation, both the transferor and transferee must undertake meaningful consultation and attempt to seek agreement about the measures they are taking. It follows that there must be early consultation with trade unions and staff representatives about the nature of any proposed transfer of undertaking and how this will affect employees. The representatives must have the opportunity to make their proposals and for these to be considered by the employer and responded to. All of this requires both the transferee and transferor to have good mechanisms in place to undertake early warning consultation on the details of a proposed transfer of undertaking. Information on how employees will be affected, the nature of the business to be undertaken, the place of work, and any impact on contracts of employment must be included in the consultation arrangements.

Avoid dismissals connected with a transfer

A transfer of undertaking cannot in law be treated as a dismissal. If an employee is dismissed by either the transferee or transferor and the reason for the dismissal is a reason connected with the transfer, the dismissal is automatically unfair unless it qualifies as an economic, technical or organisation reason entailing changes in the workforce. It therefore follows that there is a burden on employers to ensure that employment is protected in transferring the contract of employment from one employer to another. There are essentially three ways for employers to treat potential terminations during a transfer arrangement.

- ▶ First, for the existing employer (the transferor) to make them redundant and pay appropriate compensation on economic, technical or social grounds in advance of the transfer. Adopting a model redundancy procedure is the legally safe way for the transferor to avoid a legal challenge as a result of the transfer.
- ▶ Secondly, for both the transferee and the transferor to agree on those elements of the existing workforce that legitimately will transfer as part of *TUPE* and those that will not. This often applies when only part of an organisation transfers to another. For example, a retailing outlet may change hands, but the manufacturing and distribution arm of the larger company may not and it may be legitimate for parts of that organisation's main employment to stay with the transferor.
- ▶ Thirdly, for the transferee to make staff redundant in compliance with a stated redundancy procedure, again on economic, technical or social grounds. A dismissal post transfer simply arising from the transfer itself will not be good enough reason for the employer to be able to sustain a reasonable argument.

Transfer contracts of employment

Where the regulations do apply, contracts of employment of employees transferring to the new organisation without any dismissal taking place means that the employees will retain all their existing terms and conditions, including collective agreements with trade unions and trade union recognition rights afforded to them under the original contract of employment. The one notable exception to date is pension rights, although the law is about to be changed to cover them. In employment the new employer will be expected to make pension arrangements that are broadly equivalent to those enjoyed under the previous employment if they are not going to be at risk of a claim of constructive dismissal by the transferring of employees. This is an area of the law that is still being tested by case law.

An employee cannot object to being transferred unless they can show that a change in their working conditions is significant and to their detriment. In these cases, the onus would be on the employee to terminate their contract of employment and claim constructive dismissal showing that the new employer had effectively breached their contract of employment by fundamentally changing their terms of conditions of employment. The kinds of collective agreement that will transfer with the contract of employment are those made between the transferor and trade unions on the employee's behalf and will include as example redundancy selection agreements; disciplinary procedures; consultation and negotiation procedures; and facilities agreements.

Many devices have been used by unscrupulous organisations and employers to try and circumvent the *TUPE* regulations, and the law is now wise to these manoeuvres. Parent companies wishing to dilute terms and conditions of employment have sought to transfer staff and undertakings to arm's length companies set up as a company separate from the organisation itself although still owned by it. An associated employer is defined as being an organisation over which another employer has control and where the nature of the business or entity carried out has a similar nature or identity. The good practice principle to be observed here is that it is easier for organisations to work within the law than outside it and there are legitimate ways to alter terms and conditions of employment within *TUPE* without breaching legal requirements.

The economic, technical or organisational grounds for change in contract of employment apply with *TUPE* as with any other contractual variation situation and the smart employer will be able to justify one or more of these grounds where they are genuine. In this respect the law is quite specific in being able to distinguish between the unscrupulous employer who wishes to dilute terms and conditions to save labour costs, and the genuine employer who has to effect changes in terms and conditions of employment to stay in business or allow the organisation to operate effectively.

11.6 Problem areas

QUESTION:

I work for a large pharmaceutical company and we are planning to make a specialist laboratory technician post redundant in the near future because we no longer need this work to be undertaken, as a result of changes in technology. As this is below the 20 people threshold for notification under the consultation requirements of the *Employment Rights Act*, need our organisation undertake any consultation at all in this case? Also, what would the selection criteria for redundancy be in such a case?

ANSWER:

Although you are technically correct to say The Employment Rights Act *does not require any formal consultation to be undertaken in the case where less than 20 people are at risk of redundancy, the thrust of European directives and good practice suggest that you should still seek to consult with your recognised trade union(s) in your workplace or to whom this employee belongs, and, of course, with the employee themselves, about the background to and reasons for the redundancy. Dependent on the redundancy policy your organisation has in place (and presumably since yours is a large pharmaceutical firm you will have one), you will need to comply with the measures articulated there about seeking to protect employment and alternative employment options. From the description of this employee, they are in a very specialist post and it may be difficult to identify suitable alternative employment, although much will depend on their skills and experience and the other forms of work you have available in the company at that time. Nonetheless you should seek to consult with the employee and the trade union as applicable on the reasons for the redundancy, the likely timescale for effecting it, the notice period applicable, and the entitlement to any redundancy benefits that apply in this case, as well as any measures you can take to seek redeployment for this individual.*

In the case of a single-post redundancy such as this, the selection criteria are obvious – presumably the criterion is that there is a cessation of work in this specialism because of changes in technology. Always be careful, however, to identify that a single post truly is that, and does not belong to a wider family of posts with similar requirements, of whom the employee can claim to be part and where some wider selection criteria might need to be identified. Remember that in the absence of the organisation stipulating redundancy criteria, a tribunal or court hearing a dismissal claim arising from a redundancy will assume that "LIFO" (last in first out) will apply. This may not be what the company wishes to achieve and some positive identification of selection criteria is therefore preferable.

QUESTION:

Our organisation is going through a major restructuring at the moment, and we are stripping out a layer of management which is considered to be too expensive and does little to add value to the organisation. To be honest, part of the reason for removing this layer of posts is some of the people in them. They are commonly regarded as "dead wood", have been around for a long time, are very stuck in their ways and do not have the up-to-date skills the company requires. Nonetheless, one or two of them are good and we want to find a way of keeping them and losing the others painlessly. How should we go about this?

ANSWER:

The simple and blunt answer is you should not be using redundancy as a tool for selecting out poor performers or individuals with out-of-date skills because redundancy is by definition about a cessation of work or reduction in the posts required to carry out such work. What you are describing sounds like a hybrid between a genuine streamlining exercise and some "weeding out" of individuals who are no longer considered fit for the job. Such a mix-and-match approach is difficult to defend and highly dangerous for the company, who should be advised against it. Expressed simply, once the individuals you identified have all been put at risk it is illegal to "pick and choose" between those you like and those you do not unless there are some explicit and objective redundancy criteria to support their retention. Whilst performance appraisals, or rather negative outcomes of them, are used in some cases as a redundancy selection tool, they need very careful handling and consistent records in practice to ensure this is a defensible line. So the best HR advice is to separate the issues. If there is a genuine redundancy, select appropriate criteria to deal with the management group you have identified.

There is no legal reason why employees who have been redundant and have at least a 4-week break in their service cannot be re-engaged at a later date by the organisation in some different capacity if they have valuable skills but it is important to treat them as part of a redundant group in the interests of equity and good practice. Far better that the poor performance issues are tackled through the organisation's recognised routes of appraisal, training, support or discipline procedures if justified, rather than using the crude tool of redundancy, although it is undeniable that this happens in some organisations.

QUESTION:

I work in a large local authority, and staff morale is very low at the moment because we are about to experience our third major reorganisation in seven years. People are simply tired of it and, as the HR advisor to this latest round of changes, I am finding it very difficult to engage people in the change process. People seem to have been very scarred by previous reorganisations, which are now deemed to have been failures. How can we start to overcome some of this cynicism?

ANSWER:

This is one of the most difficult areas of HRM to tackle because, as all the established management writers in this area, including Peters, Handy and Taylor, recognise, human nature essentially resists enforced change. All the empirical research into the subject shows that change works best where the employees affected by it identify with the reasons for change, are involved in the setting of the goals which will drive the change process, and are engaged in the change implementation process. This requires a thorough ongoing communication with them and their representatives. Clearly, change that is driven by the need for cost-reduction and savings, thus placing jobs at risk, is going to be much more difficult to own than change that does not, albeit there are some good case-study examples where change has been a success despite initial resistance and cynicism. However, there is no magic formula and the threads that run through these examples of success will always have as their watch words ownership, communication and good implementation procedures.

QUESTION:

I work for a private cleaning company, which is about to take over the contract for cleaning a hospital and some previous in-house providers. We are very worried, because one of the major public service unions has strong membership amongst the existing cleaning staff who are due to transfer to us under the *TUPE* regulations. Does the organisation have to recognise this trade union given that it does not fit into our company's style and culture?

ANSWER:

The simple answer is yes, at least at the point of transfer, because trade union rights and any collective agreements they have helped negotiate form part of the transferring terms and conditions of employment under the regulations. Failure to recognise the trade union is likely to invite a claim to a tribunal by one or more employees, possibly sponsored by the trade union, which would be almost certain to succeed in such circumstances. The Employment Relations Act 1999 also gives new powers to trade unions to hold ballots amongst the workforce where there is a strong desire for trade union recognition in an otherwise non-unionised environment. So either way the odds are stacked against your company in this matter.

Organisations can seek to vary contracts of employment of transferring staff after the point of transfer on economic, technical or organisational grounds and, like any other plan to vary the contract of employment, these grounds must be sound and procedures for managing the change in contract (including consultation, seeking to gain agreement, and consulting any existing recognised trade union) must be followed if there is to be any chance of resisting future litigation. Beware though: trade union recognition is highly volatile territory and it is better for your company to recognise the potential benefits of working with trade union recognition in the spirit of modern industrial relations legislation than trying to resist the tide.

11.7 Activity

What are the major consultation requirements facing an organisation which plans to make 25 staff redundant in the near future? As the company does not have a redundancy policy, outline the steps they should take to comply with the law and good practice requirements. In the absence of any redundancy payments policy in the organisation, advise them in your answer on the redundancy entitlement that would accrue to a 55-year-old man with 30 years service.

11.8 Checklist

▶ There has been a large growth in the number of reorganisations and transfers in the workplace because of the major changes in business patterns in the last twenty-five years.

▶ Organisations with fluctuating finances are prone to redundancy situations from time to time.

▶ The law regarding transfers (*TUPE*) was originally designed for commercial and private organisations only, but was extended to cover all types of employment by the *Acquired Rights Directive*.

▶ The law regarding redundancy has been refined and extended significantly over the past twenty-five years.

▶ There are now significant consultation requirements placed on employers in handling both transfers and redundancy situations.

▶ A dismissal connected with a transfer is automatically unfair unless there is a strong economic, technical or organisational reason for this.

▶ The contract of employment in force at the time of the transfer from transferor to transferee must be honoured upon transfer (including collective agreements and trade union rights).

▶ Any subsequent changes to the contract are subject to the same rules that govern a normal variation in contract (see Chapter 3).

▶ Organisations must make clear the grounds for selection for redundancy (which must be fair and objective), the arrangements for handling redundancies, criteria for qualifying service, and policies on payments and service, to affected employees.

▶ These are best described in a redundancy policy, outlining the other measures, including employment protection arrangements, that may be provided.

⬛ ⍌ **12** Health and safety and risk management

12.1 Introduction

Health and safety at work first became a consideration as part of the framework for managing staff resources as far back as the nineteenth century. Since that time there has always been a major tension in the workplace between the needs of the employer, striving to increase productivity and output, and the welfare and protection of the employees and their need to work in a healthy and safe workplace. The nineteenth-century conflicts were stark, between the enormous hazards of the workplace, which often resulted in death, serious injury or reduced life span for employees at the behest of exploitative employers, long hours of work and heavy physical demands of the factory system in the wake of the industrial revolution. In post-war Britain the tensions increasingly became more subtle as the rights of the employees grew, supported by the strength of the trade unions, and systems of work gradually became safer and less demanding with the increased use of technology and less and less reliance on the physical labour of individuals. Indeed, contrast the workplace of 2000 with that of a hundred years ago in virtually any sector of employment and the revolution will be seen to have been phenomenal. In factories production is now very heavily automated, with machines performing the back-breaking work that the employees' predecessors would have performed in the late Victorian factory setting of 1900. The banking or office environment is similarly transformed. Whereas the pen, paper and ledger would have dominated the office environment of a hundred years ago, the streamlined office of today will often have no more in it than a computer terminal and keyboard in an air-conditioned, thermostatically controlled, pleasant office environment.

However, the physical labour risks of a hundred years ago have been replaced by new challenges to the health and safety of employees including, in working with new technology, a risk of eye strain, repetitive strain injury, back problems and of course the phenomenon of the 1990s, stress at work. Physical risks also still exist in some form in labour-intensive industries such as construction and has been all too vividly displayed by tragedies such as the Paddington rail crash in 1999. So health and safety at work and risk management (a more modern systematic approach for managing risks in the workplace) are still very much key issues for HRM at the turn of a new century. In this chapter we first consider some of the definitions of health and safety at work and then the development and importance of this area of work in the role of human resource practitioner.

12.2 Legal framework

Until the mid 1970s, the law relating to health and safety at work was primarily contained in the *Factories Act 1961* and the *Office, Shops and Railways Premises Act 1963* and their associated regulations. These acts are very prescriptive, setting out detailed requirements of what must be met and when. However, the approach to health and safety law was transformed with the benchmark legislation of the *Health and Safety at Work Act 1974*, which imposed much wider and general enabling obligations on all those concerned with health and safety at work, namely manufacturers, suppliers, employees and employers.

The *Factories Act 1961*

This Act covers three main areas:

1. General health and welfare provisions;
2. General safety provisions
3. Measures relating to young people

The health and welfare aspects of the Act cover cleanliness of the factory environment, overcrowding, minimum temperatures, ventilation, drainage, lighting, drinking water, washing facilities, accommodation for clothing and seating. The safety provisions govern: the fencing, guarding and cleaning of machinery; training young people in the use of machinery; hoists and lifts; ropes and lifting tackle; safe means of access and safe places of employment; dangerous or explosive substances; fumes, air and gas holders. Although the later *Health and Safety at Work Act* provided much wider umbrella provisions for employer responsibilities for health and safety at work, the *Factories Act* is still an important piece of legislation because of its prescriptive nature and the minimum standards it prescribes under each of the above headings.

The *Offices, Shops and Railway Premises Act 1963*

The Act was introduced to extend to these premises protection similar to that afforded for factories by its partner act. As with the *Factories Act*, the legislation covers the type of premises described in its title and the general provisions are very similar. The legislation deals with cleanliness, lighting, ventilation and minimum space provision for employees. So, as an example, there is a requirement for at least 40 square feet of floor space for each person employed or 400 cubic feet for each person if the ceiling height is less than 10 feet: these provisions still operate today. The oft-quoted minimum temperature provisions still prevail although they are frequently misunderstood. The temperature requirement is slightly higher than for those who work in factories, and the Act states that a temperature of 61°F or 16°C must be reached after the first hour of work; perversely, there is no maximum temperature provision in the Act, although most employers operate reasonable boundaries and by agreement would not require employees to work in temperatures that are excessively hot.

The *Health and Safety at Work Act 1974*

Of all the legislation that affects HRM, arguably none is more important to the wellbeing of individuals than this landmark piece of legislation. The *Health and Safety at Work Act* is an enabling law which places a general duty on employers, manufacturers and employees to maintain standards in health, safety and welfare of people at work and to protect the general public and visitors against risks to safety and to prevent pollution of the environment. Because of its enabling nature, subsequent regulations governing specific aspects of health and safety at work have been published which are enforceable as a general duty on all parties by the Act itself. So, although there has been no significant new primary legislation governing health and safety since 1974, the Act has "enabled" many changes in health and safety regulations to be introduced since that date.

EXAMPLE

1   The *control of substances hazardous to health* regulations
2   The *electricity at work* regulations
3   A multiplicity of *EU regulations* including the *Working Time Directive* 1998.

The term "so far as is reasonably practicable" recurs throughout the Act. In broad terms this phrase involves balancing the degree of risk to employees against money, time or trouble involved in minimising the risk. If the likelihood of injury is insignificant and it will be very expensive to take precautions, such precautions are unlikely to be deemed reasonably practicable. Conversely, high-risk situations require high investment to protect them, and a current example of this is the debate raging nationally about safety in the railway system in the wake of the Paddington disaster. Clearly in this scenario the risks are potentially high and the costs of preventing the risks are equally significant. A number of key duties are placed on the individual parties by the Act.

Employers' duties

Provision and maintenance of plant and systems of work that are safe and without risk to health; arrangements for ensuring safety and absence of risk to health in connection with the use, handling, storage and transport of articles and substances; the provision of information, instruction, training and supervision that is necessary to ensure health and safety at work for employees; the maintenance of any place of work under their control in a condition that is safe and without risk to health and the provision and maintenance of means of access to and egress from the place of work that are safe and without risks; the provision and maintenance of a working environment for employees which is safe without risk to health and adequate with regard to facilities and arrangements for welfare.

Employee's duties

Employees also have a duty under the Act to take reasonable care for the health and safety at work of themselves and other people who might be affected by their actions. They also have a responsibility to cooperate with employers and others to enable them to comply with the statutory duties and requirements imposed by the Act. Additionally, employees must not intentionally or recklessly misuse anything provided in the interests of health, safety or welfare in pursuance of any aspect of health and safety law.

Manufacturers, designers, and suppliers

These parties also have duties under the Act and must: ensure so far as reasonably practical that articles are designed and constructed in order to be safe and without risk to health when new; ensure that substances are safe and without risk to health when properly used; ensure that necessary tests and examinations are carried out; and provide adequate information about the use of tests and any conditions which must be observed in the use of articles or substances.

The Act requires employers who employ at least 5 employees to prepare written policy statements and provide for the appointment of safety representatives and safety committees (see below). To determine whether or not they are protecting the health and safety of employees, employers are also required to undertake *risk assessments* as a methodology for determining what the risks of a particular occupation or setting are, and how these may be reasonably managed. The reference in this chapter, therefore, to risk management is about this generic approach to managing health and safety at work, and it is now the cornerstone of good human resource practice in this vitally important area of law.

The *Fire Precautions Act 1971*

This Act lays down minimum requirements in work premises relating to fire safety. It is an offence under the Act for employers not to have a fire certificate in respect of the range of premises covered by the Act (which in turn usually relate to the nature of the business and the size of the premises). Before granting a certificate, a local fire authority will inspect the premises to satisfy itself as to the means of escape, fire fighting equipment and warning methods in place in the workplace. The Act has been updated by the publication of the *Fire Precautions Regulations 1997*, where employers are also required to comply with specific requirements in relation to fire detectors and alarms, emergency exits and evacuations, and the maintenance of equipment and devices. Enforcement is the responsibility of the Fire Authorities and these provisions remain in force today.

Health and Safety Regulations

The enabling nature of the *Health and Safety at Work Act 1974* means that other regulations have been issued which are enforceable through it. The regulations are numerous and it is not possible to cover every aspect for the purposes of this book. However, there are some key regulations that should be noted.

▶ The Control of Substances Hazardous to Health Regulations 1998.
▶ The Health and Safety (first aid) Regulations 1981.
▶ The Reporting of Injuries, Diseases and Dangerous Occurrences Regulations 1995.
▶ The Electricity at Work Regulations 1998.

Each of these regulations provide detailed guidance of the duty placed on employers and employees in relation to, for example, the provision of first aid facilities at work. They have statutory force because of the enabling nature of the *Health and Safety at Work Act* itself.

EU Legislation

The influence of EU-derived legislation in the health and safety field is substantial. The Treaty of Rome, which originally established the European Economic Community in 1957, had as one of its principle objectives the harmonising of conditions relating to the health and safety of workers throughout the European Union. This is achieved by the adoption of directives by the European Union that stipulate minimum requirements to improve workplace health and safety. They are usually implemented in the UK by means of regulations made under the *Health and Safety at Work Act*. The most significant of these is the framework directive dated 1993, which is often referred to as the "six pack". This package of directives were all adopted under the *Health and Safety at Work Act* by the UK government and include regulations that cover the:

• Use of machines and equipment;
• Use of personal protective equipment;
• Use of visual display units;
• Handling of heavy loads.

Significantly, since 1993 the UK government have also adopted the *Working Time Directive* which was fully implemented in the UK in 1999. The provisions of this directive are far-reaching for the management of Human Resources and are dealt with in detail in Chapter 6. The ancillary provisions of the directive for the protection of young people at work also regulates the hours of work and rest of children and young people under the age of 18.

12.3 Enforcement of health and safety in the workplace

Given this complex array of legislation and statutory regulations, it is important for the good employer to adopt a clear and systematic approach to the management of health and safety at work. Before we consider a model approach to managing health and safety, it is first worth considering some of the more detailed provisions of the Act itself which have a bearing on good practice in this area. The Act provides for a framework to enforce legislation.

The Health and Safety Executive

The Health and Safety Executive is responsible for enforcing the provisions of the *Health and Safety at Work Act* and does this by a programme of inspection. Inspectors are organised on a regional basis and cover all kinds of employers and premises covered by the Act.

The Health and Safety Commission

The Commission is responsible for carrying out policy changes under the Act and providing advice to local authorities and others to enable them to discharge their responsibilities. It issues codes of practice and regulations as well as having the power to make investigations and inquiries.

Powers of inspectorate

In order to ensure that the law on health and safety is being complied with, inspectors of the Health and Safety Executive have the power to: enter any premises at any reasonable time, as long as they are acting within their field of responsibility; bring with them a police officer if they believe they are likely to be obstructed; inspect the premises; carry out any examination or investigation they think necessary; order that the premises be left undisturbed while they carry out their investigation; take samples of anything found on the premises; demand to be shown any document they think necessary; require the use of facilities; interview and ask questions of anyone they consider appropriate.

Improvement and prohibition notices

As a result of their periodic inspections, Health and Safety Inspectors have the power to issue notices on the spot as a result of their visit. There is no need for them to apply to a court for permission to serve one or to await a prosecution. An Improvement Notice may be served by the inspectors if they believe the person has broken or is breaking one or more of the relevant statutory provisions regarding health and safety. This covers anything discovered that is contrary to the *Health and Safety at Work Act*, the *Factories Act* or the *Offices, Shops and Railways Premises Act*. If an inspector issues an Improvement Notice it will: state how they believe the law has been broken; specify precisely the reasons they have for holding this view; and specify a time period (which must not be less than 21 days) in which the employer is expected to remedy the situation. It should be noted that the Improvement Notice will not tell the employer how to put things right, although guidance may be given. The onus is therefore very much on the employer to comply with the requirements of the Improvement Notice in the time specified.

A prohibition notice may also be served by inspectors who believe that an activity is going on which involves or will involve a risk of serious personal injury. It is therefore by definition much more serious than an Improvement Notice. In a Prohibition Notice the inspectors will: state their belief regarding the risk of serious personal injury; state their reasons for believing this; and direct that the unsafe practice or activity must not continue. A Prohibition Notice can take effect immediately, although in some cases they are deferred for a specified time limit. It should be noted that the powers under this form of notice are wide-ranging and can lead to the closure of premises or an operation until the inspectors are satisfied that matters have been appropriately remedied.

Powers of prosecution

Failure to comply with an Improvement or Prohibition Notice, or obstructing inspectors in the course of their work or failing to carry out any activity, or failing in a general duty under the *Health and Safety at Work Act*, the *Offices, Shops and Railways Premises Act* or the *Factories Act*, may lead to prosecution. Sanctions range from fines or, in severe cases, imprisonment. The responsibilities falling on employers as a result of the *Health and Safety at Work Act* and its other associated legal provisions are therefore onerous indeed.

12.4 The essential framework

Although we will consider later in this chapter some of the good practice principles that will underpin good health and safety management at work, there are some essential elements to establishing a framework for managing health and safety that will not only ensure compliance with the law, but will also encourage the adoption of these principles.

Health and safety policy

Every employer is required by the *Health and Safety at Work Act* to prepare a written statement of their general policy on health and safety, and the arrangements for carrying out that policy which are in force from time to time. All employees must be advised what the policy is. The core components that should be in a good policy include: a general policy on health and safety in the workplace; identification of specific hazards and how they are dealt with; what management's responsibility for safety is; and how the policy is implemented. It therefore follows that the policy will say something about the arrangements the organisation has and who is responsible for managing this infrastructure.

Safety representatives

As the Act places a responsibility on both employees and employers in managing and promoting health and safety at work, the reinforcement of the employee's role is underpinned by provision for the appointment of safety representatives by trade unions. The functions of safety representatives are to carry out inspections and investigations and provide vigilance on behalf of employees to ensure that employers are meeting their statutory responsibilities and to encourage employees to support this. Safety representatives have a right to draw the attention of management or the Health and Safety Executive/Health and Safety Commission or other statutory body to matters they believe are causing them concern, and they have rights in law to be protected from action by the employer where they are acting reasonably in the exercise of these responsibilities. They usually have the backing and support of one or more trade unions and this is one of the core responsibilities that form part of the negotiating and consultation machinery for trade unions in modern employee relations practice (see Chapter 10).

Safety committees

Because safety representatives need a way of collectively representing their views, many employers decide to facilitate this by the establishment of a Health and Safety Committee. The Act itself does not specifically instruct employers to set up such a committee but it is tantamount to it, as the following extract will show:

> It shall be the duty of every employer if requested to do so by the safety representatives to establish, in accordance with regulations made by the Secretary of State, a Safety Committee keeping under review the measures taken to ensure the health and safety at work of employees as may be prescribed. (s. 2.7 *Health and Safety at Work Act*)

Where such a committee exists, the safety representatives have a right to be consulted about the membership of the committee, how it performs its role and its relationship to other bodies on which trade unions sit (such as Staff Consultation Fora and Joint Negotiating Committees).

Safety training

There is also a general requirement in the Act for employers to provide safety training along with information, instruction and supervision to ensure the health and safety of their employees. There is thus fairly wide scope for employers to determine what is appropriate to meet their circumstances, some examples of which are dealt with below.

12.5 The management of health and safety at work

There is a considerable body of good practice which exists to aid employers develop sound approaches and good systems for managing their responsibilities for health and safety in the workplace. The best guidance is published by the Health and Safety Executive, who advocate a systematic approach to ensure employers can cut through the complexities of the law and regulations and ensure compliance. This is summarised at Figure 12.1.

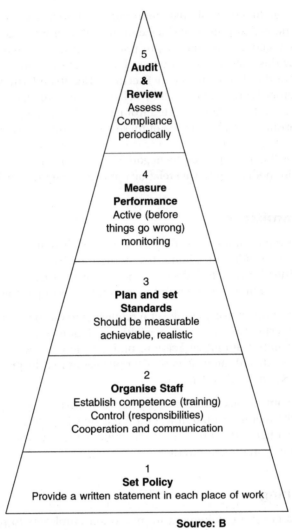

Source: B

Figure 12.1 Systems approach to health and safety management

Establishing a policy

As referred to above, a written statement of the organisation's policy is the essential foundation for good health and safety management. The policy, which should be made available to all staff, usually given either as part of or as ancillary to the contract of employment, should state who is responsible for managing health and safety. This will require naming post-holders or individuals who have certain responsibilities, although in law the ultimate responsibility rests with the chief executive or the managing director. Policies should also state the arrangements for identifying hazards and assessing risks. To be successful, a good health and safety policy should have ownership and it therefore follows that safety representatives and health and safety committees should periodically review the policy and ensure that it is up-to-date and reflects contemporary practice. At the end of the day the policy will be judged by how successful it is in providing and describing an infrastructure for managing health and safety in the workplace. So it needs to be constantly reviewed and updated to ensure it is fit for purpose.

Organising staff

To make the organisation's health and safety policy really effective, staff have to be involved and committed. This goes further than simply allowing trade unions to appoint safety representatives and to meet regularly in health and safety committees. Good organisations encourage 'a health and safety culture' where the identification, management, and prevention of risks is central to the work that everyone in the organisation undertakes. The Health and Safety Executive describe four key components to encouraging this positive 'health and safety culture'.

KEY POINTS

- ▶ Competence
  (Recruitment, training and advice).
- ▶ Control
  (Allocating responsibilities and securing commitment).
- ▶ Cooperation
  (Between individuals and groups).
- ▶ Communication
  (Verbal, written and visible)

"Competence" means that the organisation has the skills necessary to carry out tasks safely and implies that proper training and support arrangements are in place, particularly where the operation of complex equipment or where high-risk environments are involved. "Control" means having appropriate management and supervisory systems in place to make sure employees understand their responsibilities and act accordingly. "Cooperation" is connected with the involvement of staff and trade union representatives in the health and safety management process. Lastly, "Communication" is about providing information to individuals about hazards, risks and preventative measures.

Plan and set standards

One of the major problems in developing good practice in health and safety management is avoiding nebulous phrases that have little meaning or impact in the workplace. Planning should therefore include the setting of objectives, the identification of hazards, the assessing of risks and the implementing of standards in developing a positive health and safety culture. To be of use, the standards the organisation should aspire to should be measurable, achievable, and realistic. It is in this area of work that the methodology of the risk assessment comes into play. A risk assessment should describe the activities involved in carrying out a particular task and the various risks implied.

   A good simple example is that of changing a tyre on the wheel of a car. The activities include the jacking up of the car, the removal of wheel nuts; the removal of the damaged tyre; replacement of a new tyre; the re-engaging of wheel nuts; and the winding down of the car jack. Each activity has its own risks: the raising of the jack clearly involves the lifting of a very heavy vehicle with all its attendant risks; the removing of nuts involves a mechanical process that may cause injury to the individual performing the task; the removal and replacement of the tyre involves lifting a heavy object with attendant risk of back injury; and the re-tightening of wheel nuts and the letting down of the jack have their own potential hazards.

So in this situation an organisation that wanted to develop good practice would identify the risks and set standards to ensure they were managed properly. Using the replacement tyre scenario, these may include: having two jacks in place to ensure that if one fails there is additional support for the vehicle; ensuring that wheel nuts are not too tightly fixed so that they cannot be removed without undue physical effort; having two people to assist in removing and replacing heavy tyres.

Measuring performance

Once risks have been assessed and standards set, the key for the organisation is to monitor performance in health and safety to find out if it is being successful in meeting its objectives. There are two key components in monitoring health and safety at work. The first is active monitoring (before things go wrong). This involves asking questions about the standards that have been set and the assessment of their effectiveness. Reactive monitoring (after things go wrong) means investigating injuries, cases of illness, property damage and near misses and trying to learn from them to ensure that any mistakes that can be identified are not repeated. The key under this heading is the collection of information and its proper use to inform future practice. There is no use in having a serious near miss in the workplace and undertaking an investigation but then not learning from the experience.

Audit and review

To encourage the learning process described above in developing a positive health and safety culture, audits of health and safety practice provide a more complete picture than the "spot" learning that arises from the handling of individual incidents. Audits should: examine the degree of compliance with health and safety performance standards; identifying areas where standards are absent or inadequate; and collect information about underlying causes and trends.

This systematic approach to managing health and safety will go a long way towards helping employers promote good practice, and the outcomes from it will usually be manifested in changes in employment practice in the workplace. For example, the recurrence of injuries and accidents is likely to lead an employer to establish that its systems in operation are inherently risky. This may mean replacing outdated equipment or ways of working to ensure better practice. An example is the issue currently involving Rail Track and some of the attendant risks in the

British rail industry. The Paddington rail crash established that there were particular risks to do with signals and their observance by train drivers, which in the case of the Paddington crash appears to be the major cause of the collision that cost over thirty lives. The government's response to this tragedy is likely to be a change in signalling systems to ensure that the risk can be better managed. However, improved systems and ways of working do not of themselves create a safe environment. Training is essential to underpin the adoption of good practice. So, using the Rail Track analogy, it will not be enough for the government to invest in expensive new signalling systems. Train drivers and other operatives will need to be trained in their proper use and the identification of the hazards that the signals present to ensure that the complete system of health and safety operates sympathetically.

Risk assessment and management is greatly favoured by modern employers to help them identify these risks and measure the costs and benefits of tackling them accordingly. As the *Health and Safety at Work Act* of itself requires employers to take all reasonably practicable steps, a methodology needs to be devised to help employers measure costs and benefits against these risks. Continuing the Rail Track scenario, the issue open to the UK government in responding to the Paddington rail crash is therefore determining which kind of new signalling system they will invest in and what is most likely to deal with the failures identified by the accident.

Clearly, a range of options will be presented here ranging from doing nothing (with all its attendant risks and potential for adverse public reaction), to adopting a cheaper solution (which may deal with some of the risks at reduced costs), or for providing the "Rolls-Royce" solution (maximising costs but minimising risks). These trade-offs are an ongoing process for every employer, and indeed every individual in their day-to-day lives.

12.6 Health at work

Although the *Health and Safety at Work* legislation is all-embracing and deals with both health and safety issues, it could be argued that the main focus of the law is geared to safety rather than health management. In this section we consider some of the issues subject to the promotion of health at work, including smoking, drug and alcohol dependence, HIV and aids, substances hazardous to health, violence at work, upper limb disorders and manual handling. Although Stress Management can be argued to be part of the health and safety umbrella of activity, it is dealt with in Chapter 13 because of its close inter-relationship with Employee Support and Welfare schemes.

Smoking

There is a major public debate raging at present about the future of smoking at the workplace given the huge body of evidence to show that smoking is a dangerous and unhealthy practice. The law has generally not intervened in the smoking issue, but the *Health and Safety at Work Act* has been used in various test cases to require employers to adopt healthy and safe practices in relation to passive smoking. In the case of *Wharton and Morse v. Dorrington (1997)*, an employment appeal tribunal held that there was a term implied in employment contracts about employers' duties under the *Health and Safety at Work Act* in this respect. In this particular case, a non-smoker was held to have been constructively dismissed when she was required, despite her protests, to work in a smoke-affected atmosphere.

Good practice in this arena suggests employers should undertake a survey of workplace opinion about the provision of smoking and non-smoking areas at work. Some employers ban smoking altogether, which would be reasonable provided there has been prior consultation and assistance to enable smokers to adapt and that there is a reasonable notice period about the introduction of such a ban. Some employers still permit smoking in the workplace, which is usually constrained to smoking areas and, providing this is enforced (usually through the organisation' s disciplinary procedure), then an employer is likely to be able to deal with any litigation brought under the *Health and Safety* legislation about the passive smoking issue. Clearly the broader debates in society about whether smoking should be banned altogether in public places continues and may yet lead to legislation.

Alcohol and drugs

The abuse of alcohol and drugs is a feature of modern society, and it follows that a percentage of employees in the workplace are likely to suffer from drug- and alcohol-related dependency problems. The main responsibility falling on employers in HRM terms here is to ensure that they have proper policies in place to deal with any individuals who are found to have drug- and alcohol-related problems through ill-health referrals or occupational health check-ups, and to deal with preventing risks from those who are under the influence of drugs or alcohol and are in positions of responsibility. In occupations where to be under the influence of alcohol or drugs could threaten the safety of many others (airline pilots, train drivers and others), their employing organisations now undertake random testing to ensure employees are fit to operate.

In the USA, some organisations have gone much further than this and require employees to undergo drug and alcohol screening before they take up employment as part of the pre-employment health and vetting process, and it is a practice that has caught on with some UK employers in recent years. It is an issue that is fraught with dilemmas for the employer. Many individuals enjoy alcohol for legitimate recreational purposes and the issue is to what extent the employer should intrude into the individual's private life.

In terms of health and safety management, the employer's responsibilities are clear. It must take reasonably practicable steps to promote health and safety at work and the normal risk assessment methodology should apply. How risky is the task involved, and to what degree are drugs and alcohol a problem in the workplace? As long as the employer has good reasons to undertake screening and random tests, these are likely to be enshrined in the contract of employment, and breaches of rules and regulations by employees should be dealt with appropriately under disciplinary procedures where good health and safety management is jeopardised.

HIV and Aids

Aids is caused by the HIV virus. As a result, even though an individual may be HIV-positive, he/she may not develop an aids-related illness or the full blown aids condition for many years if at all. Even so, the huge increase in media attention on this illness in the late 1980s led many employers to develop medical screening facilities to test for this particular disease. Since the virus is transmitted through the mixing of bodily fluids, the risk of an individual employee contracting the disease in most normal employment situations is virtually nonexistent. It therefore follows that the employer is unlikely to be in breach of their duties under the *Health and Safety at Work Act* if they allow an individual who is HIV-positive or who has aids to continue working. Indeed it is likely to be unfair to dismiss a sufferer unless they are permanently unfit to carry out their work.

Under the *Disability Discrimination Act 1995* (see Chapter 8) an HIV infection is classified as a progressive condition and employers will have an obligation to make reasonable adjustments to the workplace to meet the needs of employees who suffer provided they can, of course, continue working. Many employers developed policies on HIV/Aids in the 1980s in response to concerns about the spread of the disease, although it is fair to say public attention is less heightened a decade later.

Substances hazardous to health

As detailed in section 12.2 above, specific regulations were published in 1994 and 1998 to deal with the *Control of Substances Hazardous to Health*. The definition of a substance hazardous to health is one that is toxic, harmful, corrosive or an irritant. Under the provisions, employers have a duty to ensure that they identify the existence and use of such substances in the workplace and that they are adequately labelled and coded to ensure individuals can be aware of the risks and hazards involved. Employers are also under a duty to take all reasonable steps to ensure that such substances are kept securely under lock and key or in suitable places (complying with the manufacturer's requirements for humidity and temperature) and that employees are issued with protective clothing when they have to use the substances for manufacturing, cleaning or other reasons connected with their duties at work. To ensure good practice in this area, most employers have inventories of hazardous substances in each area of the workplace so that these can be checked in the event of spillage, or an accident, or a health and safety inspection.

Violence at work

Rather like stress management, the management of violence at work was a phenomenon of the 1990s in the UK. The regrettable growth of violence in the workplace is linked to increases in violence in society at large and employers have a responsibility under the *Health and Safety at Work Act* to take reasonable measures to protect their staff against the potential for violence. There are certain occupations in which individuals are clearly exposed to greater risks than in others. Obvious examples include the Police Force, the Benefits Agency, and in Accident and Emergency Departments of hospitals. When an employee has been the victim of an attack in the workplace and the employer can be shown to have taken inadequate measures to prevent the risks, an employee may resign and claim constructive dismissal, as was shown in the case of *Dutton and Clarke Ltd v. Dailey* 1985.

Good practice requires employers to undertake a risk assessment of the potential for violence and to provide their employees with suitable protection. In the accident and emergency department of a local general hospital, for example, this would include the provision of security guards, barriers and training for staff to ensure that they are able to deal adequately with potentially violent patients in the course of their treatment. Violence, of course, does not just relate to acts by members of the public that cause bodily harm. Bullying and harassment at work either by members of the public or fellow employees may not cause physical harm but may have a detrimental affect on employees' morale and health and fall under the aegis of this heading. Where insufficient action is taken by an employer to stamp out the problem it is possible that they may be held liable for personal injury or even psychological damage. To deal with this employers may introduce Bullying and Harassment Policies to try and minimise the opportunities for bullying and harassment in the workplace, and to make it clear that acts of this nature are disciplinary offences and will be treated accordingly, providing training for staff to promote awareness and minimise risks.

Work-related upper limb disorders

The common manifestation of these disorders in the workplace relates to Repetitive Strain Injuries (RSI) which are usually incurred by individuals who are computer keyboard users. There is a body of evidence which shows individuals who work at computer screens using keyboards or indeed typing for protracted periods of time can incur repetitive strain injuries and employers have responsibilities under the *Health and Safety at Work Act* to minimise risks. The *Visual Display Screen Regulations 1993*, part of the EU's "six pack", are designed to help good practice in this area and focus on: appropriate use of equipment; the seating and placement of individuals using the equipment; and training to minimise the risk of strain injuries. It is also important for employers to provide access to regular eye tests and occupational health services to ensure the operatives of display-screen equipment and keyboards remain healthy and any problems can be identified and treated appropriately. Another potential response to risks in this area is by improving job design so that individuals do not continuously have to work at keyboards and computer screens, or (where they do) are afforded appropriate rest breaks.

Manual handling

Back strain and related industrial injuries have been the subject of considerable scrutiny in the arena of health and safety since the introduction of the *Manual Handling Operations Regulations 1993*. Broadly the regulations require each employer to avoid the need for employees to undertake manual handling operations involving a risk of injury. It is important for the employer to be able to show consideration has been given to ways of avoiding such operations and where they are unavoidable to undertake risk assessments to reduce the activity to the lowest level of practical risk. The use of appropriate machinery and equipment can clearly help to reduce the loads placed on individual employees in terms of handling, but some tasks will always need to be undertaken manually. So, for example, in the setting of an old people's home, although hoists and lifts may help the lifting of the elderly and infirm, there will always be a requirement for care assistants to undertake a degree of manual handling.

The requirement placed on the employer for good practice here is to undertake an assessment of the risks involved, and to provide appropriate training and resources to minimise the risks. This means ensuring that no individual has to lift loads greater than those that are reasonably sustainable, which may mean having a number of people engaged in the lifting process. Training in proper manual handling techniques can minimise back strain by ensuring that employees who regularly have to lift as part of their work are properly trained and supervised and receive appropriate occupational health support when they suffer from strains and injuries.

12.7 Problem areas

QUESTION:
I run a small engineering company of just over two hundred employees, and we have trade union recognition in the workplace. Recently, one of the two main trade unions has approached me to ask about the creation of a health and safety committee. I already provide facility time for health and safety representatives and feel this is a luxury the company cannot afford. Am I obliged to agree to the creation of a health and safety committee?

ANSWER:
The Health and Safety at Work Act *does not specifically require employers to establish a health and safety committee although it goes a long way to encouraging their existence. The important thing for your company to demonstrate will be that there is a systematic way for employees to play their part to draw your attention to any deficiencies in health and safety in your company. Given the nature of your business, it sounds as though there could be some inherent risks from manual operations, and it would therefore be wise to allow a forum for your health and safety representatives to meet with you and your fellow managers to discuss health and safety issues from time to time. Try not to look upon this as a waste of resources but rather that prevention is much better*

than cure. If the health and safety representatives identify potential risk, it would be for better to act to remedy them than wait until they lead to serious injury or worse. Also remember that breaches of health and safety are likely to result in staff absence and affect morale, as well as laying you open to a potential inspection or even prosecution. So the creation of the health and safety committee in this respect is an investment and a cost saving, not a luxury.

QUESTION:

There is a considerable debate raging at my workplace at present about the issue of smoking. A number of us who are smokers believe our rights are being infringed, because the management are planning to ban smoking altogether in the near future. There was nothing in our contract of employment about a no smoking policy when we started with the company, so would we be within our rights to take out a legal challenge on the imposition of this ban?

ANSWER:

As with most variations in working conditions, much will depend here on the way that your employer has approached the smoking issue. Remember they have to try to balance the interests of all the workforce and probably have an equally vociferous campaign going on from non-smokers who want to be protected from the risk of passive smoking. What they should have done in developing a good practice approach is: undertaken some survey of the workforce to test attitudes of everyone to the smoking issue; decided on whether or not it was therefore practicable to create separate smoking facilities; and if it was not and a ban was the only resolution (by virtue of the layout of your working premises, for example) to try and give assistance to those members of staff who wanted to stop smoking and to give you adequate notice about the introduction of the ban. Provided they took these steps, then they are likely to be judged to have acted reasonably if you were to take a challenge to a court or a tribunal on this issue.

Smoking is undeniably a health and safety issue as recent test cases have proven, and the onus on the employer is to try and protect its workforce from risks. So I am afraid that the balance of arguments are likely to be with those who wish to be protected from the harmful effects of smoke rather than those who wish to enjoy the rights to continue smoking, although the law will expect reasonable employers to try and strike some kind of balance between the two. New employees, of course, will be expected to abide by the ban which will be a condition of their employment contracts in the future.

QUESTION:

I am a trade union steward in a large local authority, and I have recently been approached by a member of staff who has been off work for some time with a stress-related illness. She has been encouraging me to try and build a case against the local authority using the precedents set by the *Walker v. Northumberland County Council* case a few years ago. This woman was employed as an accounts officer in the department collecting council tax, and had her workload significantly increased because of budget cuts. She has since gone off sick and says she is unable to return because she cannot face the workload problems. Is this test case relevant to her particular situation?

ANSWER:

The Walker case created important precedents for dealing with the issue of stress at work. However, it is important to remember the key outcomes from it. In the case of Mr

Walker, he was a child protection social worker who suffered a nervous breakdown because of pressures of work and an increase in caseload. After he recovered from his nervous breakdown he returned to work but no action was taken by the local authority to give him extra resources or reduce his workload and he suffered a further nervous breakdown which led to him having to give up work. His losses were therefore considerable and the local authority were found to be negligent in performing their duty of care under The Health and Safety at Work Act.

The situation you describe regarding your female colleague sounds slightly different. Although she claims that her stress-related illness is entirely due to workload, and indeed there may be some truth in this, much will depend on the degree to which the condition is attributable to the workplace. Are there any other factors that have created her situation in her family or domestic life? Remember her employer is only responsible for the circumstances it creates in the workplace. Is her workload unreasonable by comparison with others and has it increased to a point that is untenable? Has the employer carried out a risk assessment in this particular situation? The answer to these questions will help determine whether she has a case analogous to that of Mr Walker. Remember, however, that in his case he needed to show that he was unable to work again and had been placed in a position of risk by his employer when it returned him to a situation it knew was equally stressful. It is important to be clear in distinguishing the real facts in such cases before deciding whether or not your member has a case of similar strength.

12.8 Activity

What main features should a health and safety policy have in it to comply with good practice requirements? Based on this framework, design a model Health and Safety Policy for your organisation and contrast it with that which exists. Are there any gaps? If so, to what degree could these be detrimental to your employer's responsibilities under the *Health and Safety at Work Act*?

12.9 Checklist

▶ Health and safety has been a feature in the workplace ever since the Industrial Revolution, although the nature of the working environment and risk have changed fundamentally.

▶ The main legislative framework is provided by the *Factories Act*, the *Offices, Shops and Railway Premises Act*, and the *Health and Safety at Work Act*.

▶ The *Health and Safety at Work Act* is an enabling piece of legislation and has been updated by various EU directives.

▶ The *Health and Safety at Work Act* places responsibilities for the health and safety of employees and users of services on employers, employees, manufacturers, designers and suppliers.

- ▶ The Act is enforced by the Health and Safety Executive (HSE) with broader policy-making powers vested in the Health and Safety Commission.
- ▶ Inspectors appointed under the Act by the HSE have powers to visit premises and issue improvement and prohibition notices.
- ▶ Employers who fail to comply with these notices face financial penalties or, in severe cases, imprisonment.
- ▶ The HSE advocate a systematic approach to managing health and safety.
- ▶ This systematic approach includes establishing a policy, organising staff, planning, and setting standards, measuring performance, audit and review.
- ▶ Although much of the law concentrates on safety issues, health at work is of equal concern.
- ▶ Health issues covered in this chapter include smoking, HIV/AIDS, violence at work, and the control of substances hazardous to health.

☑ 13 Employee support and welfare

13.1 Introduction

With so much emphasis in employment law based on contractual rights and remedies, it would be easy to lose sight of some of the softer aspects of Human Resource Management such as Welfare and Employee Support which often make all the difference between the indifferent and the good employer. There has always been a conflict between the needs of the employer who wishes to push for greater efficiency output and profits, and the employee who seeks to maximise terms and conditions of employment and a conducive environment in which to work. Early Human Resource Management writers recognised the importance of sophisticated employee support and welfare systems even before they were properly ingrained in the workplace, as is so often the case nowadays. Most writers draw a distinction between those welfare facilities that provide physical benefits (improvements in holidays, terms and conditions of employment, training and development, sports and social facilities) and those which have emotional and psychological benefits (access to counselling and support facilities, improved communications, a healthy and safe environment).

This is not to say that the psychological, emotional developments are entirely new. The experiments undertaken by Elton Mayo at the Hawthorne Plant at the Western Electric Company between the wars focus very much on the development of the human relations school of Human Resource Management. The experiments run at the Hawthorne Plant centred on providing employees with better conditions, facilities and support and testing their productivity. Unsurprisingly, the studies generally showed that the greater the investment in employee support and welfare – particularly that of a psychological and emotional nature – the greater the employees' output and productivity. Thus was coined the phrase, the "Hawthorne" effect.

The growth in health and safety-related legislation through the 1960s and 1970s, most notably in the form of the *Offices, Shops and Railways Premises Act, Factories Act* and of course the *Health and Safety at Work Act* itself (see Chapter 12), gave statutory force for the first time to the employers' responsibility for furthering the cause of the health, safety and welfare of employees at work. The Hawthorne studies and the growth in employee-related support schemes led to the creation of the model of the welfare role in Human Resource Management (see Chapter 1). With the growth in regulatory legislation in the employment law in the 60s and 70s there was a tendency for the personnel function to distance itself from this welfare image in order to facilitate full acceptance of its role as a member of the management team. However, matters have now come full circle. Over the last decade there have been sophisticated advances in organisations' investment in occupational health, staff counselling, stress management and other programmes that in turn are targeted at the psychological and emotional welfare of the individual at work.

Indeed some of the buzz words of the last few years have been about the need for employers to seek out "emotional intelligence" (defined as seeking individual employees of character who can deal resiliently but sensitively with demanding and complex workplace issues) and for the "psychological contract" (which does not refer to written documents but rather describes the unwritten relationship between employee and employer at a higher psychological level particularly concerning motivation and employee development). Organisations as diverse as the armed forces, parts of the health service, the police service and major city institutions now invest heavily in employee support and welfare services developing sophisticated techniques in handling post-trauma stress (particularly relevant for parts of the health, emergency and armed forces) and stress management programmes. This section examines some of the limited legislative framework concerning this area of work, the development of good practice in counselling, stress management and employee support; and some of the difficulties in treading this delicate psychological territory.

13.2 Legal framework

As with many aspects of contemporary resource management, the primary legislative requirements governing support and welfare are relatively limited: the core piece of legislation is the *Health and Safety at Work Act 1974*. However, good employment practice and important test cases have stretched the boundaries of the law and have made employers much more aware of their responsibilities in relation to employee support and welfare over the past decade. The key legislative requirements can be summarised as follows:

The *Health and Safety at Work Act 1974*

Although this Act is dealt with in detail in Chapter 12, it is very relevant to the employer's responsibilities in relation to employees' support and welfare. Because under the Act employers have the prime responsibility for taking reasonable measures to "secure the health, safety and welfare of persons at work", a whole range of broad common law duties can be placed on employers within this definition. Thus the enabling Act has been used recently to deal with issues as diverse as:

- Smoking at work
- Stress

- Violence at work
- First aid
- Occupational health

Key test cases which are explored below have been used to define the limits of the law in each of these aspects.

The *Public Interest Disclosure Act 1998*

This new piece of legislation is relevant to the issues of employee support and welfare, because it confers important rights on employees and contractors to be able to make a protected disclosure of information about activities of work which they believe constitute wrongdoing. The Act provides statutory protection for employees (by making actions by an employer to the employee's detriment, including dismissal, automatically unfair), where the employee or contractor can show one of the following categories of wrongdoing apply:

- A criminal offence has been committed or is likely to be committed in the workplace.
- That a person has failed, is failing or is likely to fail to comply with any legal obligation to which he or she is subject.
- That a miscarriage of justice has occurred, is occurring or is likely to occur.
- That the health or safety of an individual has been, is being or is likely to be endangered.
- That the environment has been, is being or is likely to be damaged.
- That information tending to show any matter falling within any one of the preceding categories has been or is likely to be deliberately concealed.

The Act goes on to confirm various methods of disclosure for use by employees who seek to "blow the whistle", by drawing such cases to the attention of:

- the employer (usually by the use of some kind of *whistleblowing* scheme or policy).
- an appropriate legal adviser.
- a minister of the Crown where a public body is concerned.
- any other individual prescribed by the relevant Secretary of State.

An employee will be protected in law provided that they reasonably believe that the issue concerned falls into one of the above categories, that they genuinely believe it to be true and that they have acted in good faith. This new piece of legislation is an important addition to the rights of employees and clearly places a particular onus on the employers to ensure protected disclosure can happen in an unfettered manner and so aid the welfare and support of employees at work.

The *Access to Medical Reports Act 1988* and *Access to Health Records Act 1990*

These two Acts have a relevance to occupational health services and are dealt with in Chapter 7.

The *Data Protection Act 1984 and 1998*

As above, these two relevant pieces of legislation are covered in more detail in Chapter 7.

13.3 Occupational health services

So, knowing that there is a fabric of legislative protection in place to protect their interests, and promote statutory rights in terms of welfare, wellbeing and dignity at work, what kind of practical measures may exist that constitute good practice in this area of employee support and welfare? The logical starting point is the traditional role of Occupational Health in the workplace. Most modern employers now engage some form of occupational health service to provide them and their employees with a range of relevant health services. There are traditionally two main types of service provision:

1. The *directly employed* service usually comprising an occupational health nurse and/or occupational health physician (a qualified doctor) or
2. A *contracted-in* service to meet the employer's needs on an ad hoc basis.

Clearly much will depend on the size of the organisation and the employer's resources, but most medium- to large-sized organisations now have some form of in-house direct service. The more dangerous the working environment, the more work there is for the occupational health service to do in terms of both preventative or reactive services.

EXAMPLE

    1 A typical range of occupational health services will include:
       The processing of pre-employment health screening. Screening takes one of two forms normally. Either a full medical (obligatory for certain kinds of high-risk occupation such as machinery operators or drivers) or completion of an occupational health pro forma or questionnaire (checked and vetted by the occupational health service to ensure the new joiner has no major health risks).
    2 A referral and advisory service for sick and injured employees. The services provided under this heading can range from: tending to a minor graze incurred as a result of a workplace accident; referral by a manager of an individual with a recurring health problem, where they wish to seek an organisational view of the individual's ill health; or the provision of advice and support directly to the employee where they have concerns about their own fitness for work.
    3 Regular health checks, inoculations and check-ups.
       The range of work here can include programmes for giving inoculations for flu viruses, hepatitis B or other forms of inoculation or undertaking health checks for employees about to embark on overseas travel for the organisation.
    4 The undertaking of positive programmes of health promotion in the workplace relating, for example, to smoking, the use of alcohol and drugs, healthy eating and other positive health promotion campaigns.

5   Often the occupational health service will fulfil the role of welfare advice where the line or personnel manager is unable to provide it, or the individual employee wishes to seek confidential advice and a fully fledged counselling service does not exist. Indeed many of today's occupational health services are actively engaged in looking after the mental health and wellbeing of employees in the workplace where stress is now such a major factor.

13.4 Counselling services

The provision of counselling services as part of the fabric of employee support and welfare is not a new concept. Ever since the Hawthorne studies produced evidence to support the relationship between positive, emotional and psychological health and output and productivity, progressive companies and organisations have invested in the provision of such services to ensure that employees who have difficulties and problems in the workplace can receive appropriate help and support. These problems often manifest themselves in a number of different ways that affect the employee's performance and include:

- Poor timekeeping;
- Poor attendance and sickness levels;
- Poor or inconsistent job performance;
- Difficult interpersonal relationships in the workplace;
- Poor physical health;
- Dependence on alcohol, drugs or both;
- Deteriorating mental health.

Because modern employers understand that an individual's psychological and emotional wellbeing cannot be separated from their life out of work, the provision of counsellors or specialist support services is not just geared to workforce-related problems. In most organisations there are a range of individuals that an employee with problems can talk to or from whom they can seek advice. This may typically be the line manager (but confidentiality may beg that the problem is taken to a more objective individual); the personnel or HR manager (although the affinity between personnel/HR/line management often precludes this as a source of help for the troubled employee); the occupational health adviser (see above); or the specialist counsellor or welfare adviser who is either an employee of the organisation or is contracted-in to provide a specific service. The latter can provide two main forms of service, the first being advice and the second practical assistance. Modern counselling techniques go much further than merely listening to employee's problems and providing reflection or a sounding board.

A whole range of psychological interventions are available to the sophisticated counsellor at work. They include providing support when the employee has experienced a particularly stressful or traumatic incident (particularly prevalent for those working in health, police and the armed forces), often referred to as critical incident stress debriefing or critical incident stress management; or for dealing with the immediate aftermath of a particularly traumatic incident (post-traumatic stress debriefing).

But very often these interventions can be enhanced by the use of specialist referral services in the form of the Citizen's Advice Bureau, Relate, financial advisors or alcohol and drugs counsellors. The cornerstone of counselling work, be it in-house or contracted-in, is availability, access and confidentiality. *Availability* means that an employee who wishes to seek a referral, or the line manager who has agreed to do so on their behalf, needs to be sure that the service will be available and is free or modestly charged at the point of delivery. *Access* means that it is possible for an employee to make use of the service in a comfortable way without the knowledge of colleagues and within travelling distance of the workplace. *Confidentiality* means both the access route, the nature of the referral and the counselling process is strictly confidential between the employee and the counsellor. It is worth noting here that issues relating to stress and mental health are likely to fall under the remit of the *Access to Medical Records Act*, and therefore protect the notion of patient or client confidentiality.

13.5 Stress management

The concept of stress at work is not a new idea. Although it was originally viewed in terms of executive stress and seen only applying to those in senior management positions, there is a significant body of workplace research going back to the 1970s on the subject. Stress is a threat to both physical and psychological and wellbeing of employees. Glowinkowski summarised the effects of stress as follows:

> Whilst stress can be short lived it can represent a continuous burden leading to short term outcomes such as tension, increased heart rate or even increased drinking or smoking. (from a web site)

In the long term, stress is said to cause disorders such as depression, coronary heart disease, diabetes and bronchial asthma. Indeed, while stress may be a direct cause or factor in heart disease, its effects may be indirect. Stress may increase smoking and cause over-eating, which are also high-risk factors in coronary heart disease. Of course, stress at work is not just dependent on workplace-related factors and family and social aspects will all have potential impacts on the stress of individuals at work at any one time.

EXAMPLE

Stress-related illness connected with work has become a very topical issue for employers in the last decade following the groundbreaking case of *Walker v. Northumberland County Council* 1995. In this case the local authority employer was held by the High Court to be liable for psychiatric damage caused to a social worker through stress. It had failed to take reasonable steps under the *Health and Safety at Work Act* to alleviate the employee's excessive workload after he had suffered a nervous breakdown, which resulted in him suffering a second breakdown in quick succession. The risk was judged to be reasonably foreseeable in the terms of the *Health and Safety at Work Act* and the employer was therefore in breach of its duty of care. The employee received £175,000 in an out-of-court settlement.

Where such stress risks are a feature of a particular job, a risk assessment should be made in the same way as for a risk of physical injury. It is important that complaints about working conditions or workloads causing stress are dealt with quickly and thoroughly and efforts made to reduce the risk of future health problems. As well as claims for damages, it is also possible that employees who complain of excessive stress could resign and claim constructive dismissal on the basis that the employer failed in their duty of care and fundamentally breached the implied term to maintain the relationship of trust and confidence in the employment relationship. Very often stress will be the result of excessive workloads and the risk assessment will suggest one of a number of potential good practice solutions:

KEY POINTS

▶ The organisation of work, a preventative measure involving reorganisation of those aspects of work which are believed to be affecting the mental health of the employee. This may include changes that could be grouped together as organisational development, such as job rotation and individually based training and development programmes. The growth in the use of sabbaticals pioneered by progressive UK and European companies is an attempt to try and stop this kind of "burn out" process. The organisation of work, of course, may also entail the addition of extra resources to help alleviate workloads or to strictly prioritise the workload falling on an individual (as was noticeably absent in the case of *Walker v. Northumberland*).

▶ Positive health programmes, linked to the range of occupational health services available, are aimed at relieving and preventing stress and associated problems. Some approaches are not new and include the use of yoga, meditation, aromatherapy and other destressing techniques. The progressive use of occupational health in terms of health promotion and health prevention by undertaking blood tests, health check-ups and well person clinics are other attempts to promote positive health at work.

▶ Stress management training-many organisations are now running programmes designed to help both managers and employees to contain and manage stress at work. A typical stress management programme would contain a number of the following modules:

• Time management, focused on getting individuals to manage their time properly, to prioritise workloads and to minimise overload.

• Health and safety, geared to ensuring that the working environment is as healthy and safe as possible. In the information technology age, this would typically mean ensuring that regular users of visual display screens have the appropriate technology, chairs, desks and equipment at their disposal to minimise eye strain and repetitive strain injuries.

- Relaxation techniques, initiated by progressive American and Japanese companies. These techniques promote relaxation in the workplace by allowing employees the possibility to undertake physical exercise or to relax as a way of promoting good health at work. They go hand-in-hand with the provision of sports and other leisure facilities as a way of encouraging employees to engage in healthy lifestyles in the workplace. A number of major city institutions in the UK now provide free gym facilities as part of their employment package for employees to find ways of relieving stress, given the high levels of burn-out amongst traders and brokers in the financial markets of London.

- Appraisal and personal development programmes. Although at first glance such reviews may be regarded as a stressor for an employee, they are often included in stress management programmes as a way of containing and managing stress. The logic suggests that the more an employee can do to control his or her working environment and understand the facets that go to make up good performance and successful individual development, the more healthy he or she will be and the less stressed he or she is likely to become.

13.6 Employee support measures

If each of the occupational health, counselling services and stress management interventions are specifically aimed at supporting and developing good psychological and emotional welfare in the workplace, then they are often underpinned by the provision of a range of other employee support measures.

EXAMPLE

A typical range of facilities under this heading will include:

1 Provision of sports or social facilities to allow employees to socialise and relax in an environment related to the workplace. This often helps build teams and establish employer loyalty and identity and has a particularly strong tradition in major sporting circles such as football, cricket and tennis.

2 A range of welfare benefits (see also Chapter 6), including the provision of compassionate and carer's leave and access to financial assistance where employees suffer hardship or are in particular need of financial help. Other terms and conditions of employment under this heading include relocation, relocation assistance and accommodation schemes for employees.

3 The provision of a workplace nursery, child care, holiday play schemes and other support facilities geared to the employee who has family or dependent relatives.

4 Tailored training and development programmes to assist employees in their overall wellbeing and development outside strict vocational requirements of the job in question.

5 The provision of spiritual, religious and related services to employees who have a specific need (for example in cases of family bereavement).

Clearly the provision of any or all of the above will depend on the size and complexity of the organisation and its financial resources. Traditionally organisations in the finance and retail sectors are very strong in promoting employee support measures, whilst public sector employers have tended to veer away from them. There is, of course, a potential downside to the provision of these facilities. Whilst many of them have considerable evidence to show that they are a positive impact on the quality of working life, changes in employment and social patterns over the last decade or so suggest that this kind of "employer paternalism" is now outdated and can blur the boundaries between the workplace and individuals' private lives. Indeed, there is some notorious employment case law to show that employers proceed at their risk in providing entertainment and social facilities for employees. The rule of thumb here is that if the employer has organised and/or funded the event, then they are likely to have a vicarious responsibility for the conduct of their employees whilst they are engaged in the social activity. However, these negative aspects should not detract from good employment practice which begs at least a modest provision of one or more of the above employee support and welfare provisions to ensure compliance with the *Health and Safety at Work Act* and more importantly to promote a healthy workplace and a positive culture of employee wellbeing.

13.7 Problem areas

QUESTION:
Why should an employer be liable for managing the stress of employees, when the individual stress may be caused by a whole load of factors removed from the work place?

ANSWER:
In terms of strict legal obligations, an employer is not responsible for an employees' personal life and the stresses that arise from it. But drawing a distinction between the causes of stress in the interaction between home life and the workplace is difficult territory. As the Health and Safety at Work Act *places a responsibility on employers to take reasonable steps to ensure the health and safety of their employees, the most prudent approach is for employers to undertake risk assessments of jobs and working situations to try and identify major stressors. Whilst the best employment practice will be preventative (trying to avoid overtly stressful situations that may have a negative impact on employees' health), employers have an absolute responsibility to try to stop problems reoccurring where they have already been identified. The reason that Mr Walker, the former social worker of Northumberland County Council, won such substantial damages is that the local authority had returned him to an environment that had already proved to be damaging to his health because of his excessive and stressful workload. The law does not expect employers to provide sophisticated employee support and*

welfare facilities, but it does expect employers to identify risks and manage them. So the key advice in this area is:

- identify the risks
- develop measures to manage the risks
- ensure major problems are not allowed to reoccur.

QUESTION:

I want to refer an employee who has a poor attendance record to the occupational health service for a medical opinion, because the person appears to be frequently absent on a short-term basis for no good reason. Do I have to share the occupational health advisor's report with the employee once it is available to me?

ANSWER:

The Access to Medical Records Act says that individuals have a right to see the medical records that exist in relation to them. It therefore follows that a referral to an occupational health physician and the resultant opinion must be made available to the employee at some point. Good practice suggests that if the occupational health opinion in this case says that there is nothing wrong with the employee, then the occupational health advisor's letter should be shared with the employee but as part of a counselling interview seeking to get them to explain why they have so many absences. This could, of course, in turn lead to some form of disciplinary action and the occupational health advisor's letter might be used as part of the evidence. So although you may make some choice about the timing of the release of such information, it is a legal right for the employee to have access to these records in some form.

QUESTION:

I am the personnel manager for a large haulage company and we employ many kinds of HGV licence driver. We have recently had a case of a driver who failed to disclose that he had a record of epileptic attacks a long time ago. This was not picked up by our occupational health advisor in the health-screening process. Now he is in employment are we bound to redeploy him, and provide support for his health risk?

ANSWER:

In simple terms the answer is "no". Providing you have clear evidence that there was a recorded history of epilepsy with this particular driver, and he failed to disclose it in his occupational health questionnaire or in his medical, then he does not have the full capability to perform the role of an HGV driver and clearly is a potential health risk. As the matter was not picked up by the licensing authorities (in which case he would not have an HGV licence in the first place) it is safe to assume that this was kept from them as well. You would be within your rights to take disciplinary action against the employee either on grounds of their incapability (which could be gross – see Chapter 10) or misconduct (because he failed to disclose a major health and safety risk).

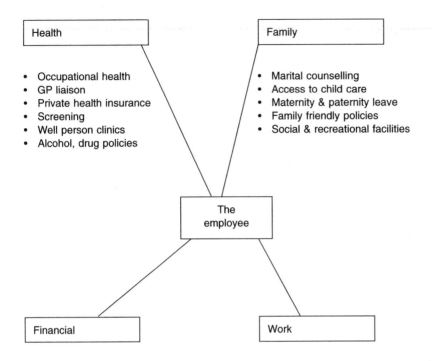

Health

- Occupational health
- GP liaison
- Private health insurance
- Screening
- Well person clinics
- Alcohol, drug policies

Family

- Marital counselling
- Access to child care
- Maternity & paternity leave
- Family friendly policies
- Social & recreational facilities

The employee

Financial

- Cheap loans
- Fair remuneration
- Financial advice & counselling
- Robust pension scheme
- Good range of welfare benefits

Work

- Rewarding job
- Good training opportunities
- Open and supportive manager
- Good workplace communications
- Developing organisation

Figure 13.1 Network of employee support and welfare provision

13.8 Activity

What legal protections exist to promote the health of employees in the workplace?

Why are organisations particularly wary of managing stress at work and what kind of measures can they employ to promote a healthy culture at work?

13.9 Checklist

KEY POINTS

▶ Employee support and welfare deals with the physical, emotional and psychological wellbeing of employees in the workplace:

- ▶ Primary legislation in this area includes the *Health and Safety at Work Act*, the *Public Interest Disclosure Act*, the *Data Protection Act* and the *Access to Medical Records Act*.
- ▶ Paramount case law includes the case of *Walker v. Northumberland County Council* 1995 which dealt with the aspect of managing stress at work and employers' liabilities therein.
- ▶ There is a significant body of good practice in terms of the provision of employee support and welfare facilities including:

  - Occupational health services
  - Counselling services
  - Stress management techniques
  - Other employee support facilities

- ▶ Employee support and welfare can be developed in a number of ways and a network of provision is illustrated in Figure 13.1.

⌄ 14 New developments

14.1 Introduction

One of the most exciting and challenging aspects of working in HRM is the ever-changing nature of the subject. The election of a Labour government in 1997 has heralded a major explosion in new employment law initiatives in the UK, and, as we will explore extensively in this chapter, the pressure for change from Europe is equally unrelenting. Add to this employment context the changes that occur almost weekly in terms of new government policy initiatives, regulations, and case law determined by courts and tribunals, and those of us who would seek to "master Human Resources" have an ever-shifting target to aim for.

There are two important aspects to developments in employment law at the end of the 1990s and at the beginning of the 2000s. First, is the accent once more on state intervention in the form of new primary legislation emanating from the UK government. If the Thatcher years in the 1980s of Conservative rule were characterised by deregulation and the rule of market forces, then the late 1990s have seen a return to central interventionism and government taking a closer and closer interest in the world of the workplace. This is evidenced by groundbreaking pieces of legislation such as the *Minimum Wage Act* and the major restoration of trade union rights through the *Employment Relations Act 1999*. It seems likely from these interventions that the balance of power in the workplace, almost exclusively with employers from most of the 1980s and 1990s, is swinging back once more in favour of employees and their representatives. Although we are never likely again to see the pre-eminence of the trade unions and the almost baronial power of trade union leaders observed in the late 1960s and early 1970s, there is no doubt that trade unionism is once more in the ascendancy. However, this is a new kind of trade unionism, based on New Labour principles of social democracy rather than the dogma of the hard left. So the accent from government and trade unions is now very much on working in partnership to deliver the government's agenda rather than industrial conflict.

The second major characteristic of this new era is the continual pressure from Europe to standardise and harmonise working practices for employees throughout the EU. We have discussed elsewhere in this book the major impact EU directives have had on Health and Safety (at Chapter 12), on Working Time (Chapter 6) and as a major influence on Equal Opportunities legislation (Chapter 8). The previous Conservative administration were not signed up to the EU Social Chapter from which they negotiated an opt out. The key difference is that the current Labour Government have opted into the Social Chapter and will therefore be required to adopt a number of EU directives that form part of this body of social legislation. Many of these aspects will be discussed in this chapter, including the newly introduced *Human Rights Act*, parental leave, the rights of part-timers and employee representation.

This is a remarkable turn around from the early 1990s when the UK economy was essentially being built on the basis of attracting business from abroad as a low-cost, low-wage labour market. In that sense the UK saw itself more as a competitor for Spain, Portugal and the lesser EU countries than France, Germany and the Low Countries. The policy of the Labour Government could not be further removed from that of their Conservative predecessors. The accent is on social justice and democracy and the equalisation of employment and practices across Europe, with the UK competing on level terms with the strongest economies in Europe and affording its workers the same benefits and rights. As this book is being written, the current Labour administration is probably at the low point of its fortunes, being in mid-term in its first period of office, but all the evidence from opinion polls and market research suggest that a second Labour term is likely building on a current majority of over 180 seats. We can therefore expect continuation of the thrust for harmonisation with our key European partners, and a modernisation and updating of employment practice in the UK to equal those on the European mainland. The UK employment market in the first decade of the twenty-first century will be a very interesting place indeed.

14.2 EU directives: the Social Chapter

Retaining a separate identity for Britain and opting out of many key EU provisions was a hallmark of the Thatcher and Major years of premiership. The Blair Government is distanced from this isolationist point of view and is wholeheartedly engaged in signing up for the mainstream of European developments. The Social Chapter was agreed by all members of the European Community, excluding the UK, as part of the Maastricht Treaty negotiated in the early 1990s. It provided that new European directives could be passed by majority voting in relation to:

- Improving the working environment and health and safety
- Working conditions
- Information and consultation of workers
- Sexual equality
- Integration of labour markets (for example fixed term contracts, casual workers and so on)

It was also agreed as part of the Treaty that majority voting would not apply to some other key issues that affected the workplace:

- Social security and the protection of workers
- Protection on termination of employment

- Worker representation
- Conditions of employment.

A qualified majority vote is obtained if 62 out of the 87 votes available are in favour of a proposal. The UK, France, Germany and Italy have 10 votes each. Spain has 8 votes, Belgium, Greece, Netherlands and Portugal have 5 votes, Austria and Sweden 4 votes, Denmark, Finland and Ireland 3 votes, and Luxembourg 2 votes. The UK is therefore in a strong position to influence the outcome of EU voting.

Five directives have already been made under the social protocol of the Social Chapter, and will be considered in this chapter. These are:

- The *Works Council Directive*
- The *Parental Leave Directive*
- The *Posted Workers Directive*
- The *Part-Time Workers Directive*
- The *Burden of Proof Directive*

Proposals for three further directives are still being debated with the EU and include:

- The National Works Council Directive
- The Sexual Harassment Directive
- The Tele-Workers Directive

The *Works Council Directive*

The *Works Council Directive* has been described by EU Commissioner, Padraig Flynn as "one of the most important measures ever taken by the European Union in the social field up to now". Essentially the *Works Council Directive* obliges businesses which are multinational within the European Union to consult and inform their workforces about issues which affect the business and workforce on a multinational level. Although the Labour Government has now signed up to the social protocol, it will be sometime before this Directive becomes effective in the UK. However, multinational businesses are already affected and other major organisations are planning to meet the *Works Council Directive* on the basis that it is the inexorable direction employee consultation issues are taking. The directive applies to multinational businesses that employ at least 1,000 people within the EU and at least 150 people in each of two different EU member states.

If an organisation qualifies, then the central management of the organisation must ensure that mechanisms for consultation and informing of the organisation's workforce are in place. Either at its own initiative, or if requested covering at least two member states, the organisation's central management must set up a special negotiating body to decide what measures should be taken to bring about the required consultation processes. If the special negotiating body and the central management of the company fail to agree a formula for this consultation machinery then the Directive allows for a compulsory Works Council to be imposed on the business. The nature and scope of the consultation in which the new works council will be engaged will depend in part on the nature of the business in which it operates, but will include consultation on:

- Major organisational change affecting the business and employees
- Major changes in terms and conditions of employment
- Matters pertaining to transfer under the *TUPE* regulations
- Matters relating to redundancies
- Matters relating to health and safety law
- Matters relating to equal opportunities monitoring.

When taken alongside the *Employment Relations Act* it is obvious that the thrust of these new arrangements will be to extend the role of employee representation and trade union rights in the workplace significantly. The message for organisations who therefore have neither trade union representation or a works council at present, is that they need to start preparing for the eventuality. In all but the smallest businesses, there is likely to be a considerable demand for staff consultation or trade union representation, and companies and businesses who have not previously embraced such an approach are bound to be affected by the thrust of these developments.

Parental leave

The *Parental Leave Directive* is one of the first measures to be agreed under the new provisions of the social protocol and chapter. The main provisions of the Directive are contained in clauses 2 and 3 of the regulations. They provide that an employee has a right to parental leave if he/she has one year's continuous service and

- is the parent of a child born after 15 December 1999 who is under 5 years old or
- has adopted after 15 December 1999 a child under the age of 18 years (this right will then last for 5 years from the date on which the child is placed for adoption or until the child's 18th birthday) or
- has acquired formal parental responsibility for a child born after 15 December 1999 who is under 5 years old.

The amount of parental leave will be 13 weeks for each child under 5 years old provided they were born after 15 December 1999. For part-time employees this leave will be in proportion to the time worked. The regulations provide that leave should be taken in periods of one week at a time. The annual number of weeks that can be taken in one instance is limited to 4 weeks per year. Part of a week counts as a full week, for example if a full-time employee takes 3 day's leave and returns to work, one week will be deducted from the 13 weeks. The contract of employment will continue whilst an employee is on parental leave and will count for the purposes of continuous service. The regulations also provide for time off for dealing with dependants. All employees will be entitled to reasonable unpaid time off to deal with dependants (partner, child, main carer, parent) when ill, and caring arrangements break down, or in case of birth, death or incident during school hours/school trip. The right will be limited to urgent cases of real need involving a dependant. An employee must advise the employer of the reason or absence as soon as is practicable and must agree the arrangements with them.

It is evident, therefore, from the agreement of this *Parental Leave Directive*, that the government is determined to introduce a body of family-friendly policies into the UK workplace. From an HRM point of view, the impact of the *Parental Leave Directive* must be included in policies for maternity leave, special leave, or other forms of absence in the workplace as they are a statutory entitlement. Employers who do not allow employees to take statutory parental leave will be subject to a claim to an employment tribunal and are likely to suffer claims for compensation as a result.

The Part-Timers Workers' Directive

The *Part-Time Workers Directive* was adopted in UK law on 7 April 2000. The regulations will have a major impact on the working lives of 6 million part-time workers in the UK who are affected. The regulations state that a part-time employee should not be treated by his/her employer less favourably than the employer treats a comparable full-time employee with regards to the terms of their contract of employment or by being subjected to any other detriment by any act or deliberate failure to act. So, for example, where a comparable full-time employee receives or is entitled to receive pay or any other benefit, a part-time employee should be entitled to receive pay or any other benefit. A part-time employee should receive or be entitled to receive pay and benefits equivalent to the comparable full-time employee, but on a pro rata basis.

The easiest example of how the regulations will work is to look at their effect on pay. As a result of the new regulations, part-time employees must not receive a lower basic rate of pay than comparable full-time employees. An employer may, however, pay a lower hourly rate where this is justified on objective grounds and an example would be a performance-related pay scheme. Clearly, if employers can show how the different levels of performance are measured by a fair and consistent appraisal system, this could justifiably result in different rates of pay between full-time and part-time employees. The concept of less favourable treatment will also apply to other key benefits in the employment contract such as contractual sick and maternity pay.

So part-time employees must not be treated less favourably than full-time employees in terms of the rate of contractual sick or maternity pay they receive, the lengths of service required to qualify for payment under contractual schemes and the length of time the payment is received. Similarly, entitlement to holiday over and above an employee statutory entitlement must be the same pro rata for full- and part-time employees in comparable jobs. Access to an occupational pension scheme, private health insurance or permanent health insurance must again be equally given to part-time and full-time employees, albeit the calculations of benefits from these schemes can be on a pro rata basis to that of full-timers. In relation to payment of overtime, it is proposed that part-time employees should receive the same hourly rate of overtime pay as comparable full-time employees, but only once they have worked for more than the normal full-time hours, as opposed to working over and above their normal part-time hours.

The concept of less favourable treatment extends beyond such contractual commitments, however. So, it will be automatically unfair to select an employee for redundancy purely because he/she is part-time. It will also be an infringement of the regulations to exclude part-timers from staff training, albeit there will be no legal obligation on employers to structure their training and practice to accommodate part-timers, although this is nonetheless good practice under equal opportunities (see Chapter 8). The remedy for discriminatory treatment on the basis of part-time working is again a claim to an employment tribunal and employers are liable for compensation taking into account that the employee's loss is as a result of less favourable treatment and that it can be proven.

So again the implications for employers and Human Resource Managers are clear. The drafting of contracts of employment, and the main employment policies in place for pay, terms and conditions of employment and other benefits, must treat part-timers as equal partners to full-timers in comparable jobs on a pro rata basis. Further details are dealt with in Chapters 3 and 6.

The *Posted Workers Directive*

The objective of this directive is to give workers who work abroad within the EU the benefit of the terms and conditions of employment of their host country. It is also intended to prevent employers in one member state from using cheap labour from another member state. It applies to all terms and conditions including pay, benefits, hours of work, rest breaks, annual holiday, maternity rights and anti-discrimination rights. There is an exception where an employee is posted to the host country for less than 8 days to install machinery or equipment but this does not apply to the construction industry. The Directive came into force in the UK in September 1999 and clearly has implications for multinational companies and those who regularly post employees to work abroad. The same imperatives apply to employers and Human Resource Managers when drafting contracts and designing pay and benefits schemes as when dealing with part-timers under the *Part-Timers Workers' Directive*.

14.3 Other employment law developments

As can be seen, the body of new employment law derived from EU social chapter directives is significant in itself but is not the end of the story. There are other EU directives in the pipeline, and developments in UK employment legislation that are likely to impact significantly on HRM. In this section we will draw together some of these new developments.

Discrimination

The government has declared it will legislate where practicable and when time permits to improve consistency in the whole arena of equal opportunities legislation (see Chapter 8). Amongst the priorities set out in a statement by the government early in 2000 was included a commitment to:

- harmonising the provisions of the *Race Relations, Sex and Disability Discrimination Acts*
- aligning the equality commission's powers, strengthening the powers of the Equal Opportunities Commission and Commission for Racial Equality to match those of the new Disability Rights Commission, removing legislative barriers to the commissions working together, and enabling them to produce joint guidance.
- combating institutional racism in all public functions via the Race Relations (amendment) Bill currently working its way through the House of Commons and extending this principle to the *Sex Discrimination Act* and the *Disability Discrimination Act* (now on the statute book as the *Race Relations Act 2001*).

It is clear, therefore, that the equal opportunities agenda is likely to become more onerous on employers and Human Resource Managers over the next couple of years. The Disability Rights Commission is clearly seen by the government as a watchdog with teeth that will rigorously enforce the powers of the *Disability Discrimination Act*, and is looking to afford equal powers to the Equal Opportunities Commission and Commission for Racial Equality in the wake of the public outcry about institutional racism following the Stephen Lawrence (Macpherson) Inquiry.

Pregnant Workers Directive

The *Pregnant Workers Directive* has been adopted by the UK via the *Employment Relations Act 1999* and updates the statutory maternity provisions referred to in detail in Chapter 6. The directive provides that female workers should have a continuous minimum period of maternity leave of 14 weeks and this must include a compulsory minimum period of 2 weeks after confinement. The directive also states that workers on maternity leave should receive an allowance equivalent to the amount the worker would receive if she was sick for 14 weeks during the period of maternity. The government's amendments to maternity regulations through the *Employment Relations Act* deal with this issue. But again it is obvious that the rights of female employees who are pregnant, or those with adoptive and family responsibilities, are a major priority for the EU and the UK government.

Employee share schemes

The government are keen to extend the concept of employee share schemes, to try to spread the enterprise culture and gain more employee commitment to the running of businesses. Proposals are likely to be contained in a Finance Bill which is due to be published shortly. It is proposed that the new scheme will allow employers to permit their employees to buy up to £1,500 worth of shares in their own company from pre-tax income which can be matched by the employer with up to £3,000 worth of shares. It will also allow the employer to give a further £3,000 worth of shares with the option of linking this to performance. So long as the shares are retained in the plan for at least 5 years, no income tax or national insurance will be levied on them. This has clear implications for HR strategies in the workplace. Employers should be looking to review their strategies, considering how they will monitor performance relative to the award of shares where they decide to participate in such employee sharing arrangements. Existing schemes should be reviewed and employment packages may need to be reconsidered to take account of the new arrangements as they emerge.

The *Human Rights Act 2000*

One of the most fundamental changes in law affecting the UK has come about in October 2000 following the introduction of this groundbreaking Act. The European Convention on Human Rights will have a major impact on the workplace and employer responsibilities now that there is primary UK legislation available. The Act will place a duty on public bodies to act in compliance with these principles and will alter the way that both the users and employees of public services are treated, and by extension will impact on all other employment relationships also. The key principles of the Act build on existing employee rights that already exist in the discrimination legislation, health and safety statute, and other provisions including data protection and disclosure measures. The aim of the legislation is, however, less on mechanistic approaches but more on trying to build an open and progressive culture in the workplace that respects human dignity and individual freedoms.

The following is a summary of the main provisions of the Act as it affects the employment relationship:

KEY POINTS

- ► *Article 6*: Right to a fair trial
  Disciplinary procedures must be fair and rigorous
  Employment tribunal procedures must promote natural justice
- ► *Article 8*: Right to family life/privacy
  Provision of flexible working patterns is needed to support parental obligations
  Employers who wish to undertake security checks must be careful that they do so in measures justified by the demands of the job.
- ► *Article 9*: Freedom of religion
  Employers' codes of conduct and dress codes must respect individual beliefs
- ► *Article 10*: Freedom of expression
  Employers must allow employees reasonable freedom of expression, for example via whistleblowing policies.
- ► *Article 11*: Freedom of assembly and association
  Employees have a right to join a union and take part in legitimate activities.

14.4 Key case law and HRM developments

As well as looking at changes to primary legislation and EU directives, the student of employment law and HR managers generally also need to consider the impact of key benchmark law cases going through the courts and tribunals and the wider impact these have on HR practice. There have been a number of significant cases recently that have an impact on contentious issues in the workplace which are currently attracting a high profile.

References

As discussed in detail in Chapter 5 there is no general obligation on an employer to provide a reference to a prospective employer for one of its past or current employees.

EXAMPLE

But as with all general rules there are exceptions, as a recent test case *Coot v. Granada Hospital* showed. The result of this case was that the European Court of Justice found that Coot was entitled to have an employment tribunal determine her claim that she had been unlawfully victimised under the *Sex Discrimination Act 1975* when Granada refused to provide her with a reference. This was despite the fact she was no longer employed by the company. As a result she was awarded £195,000 compensation. The issue here was that she could not secure alternative employment without a reference from the company who had provided references to male employees in similar circumstances. The point to note, therefore, is the interaction between important pieces of legislation with the Discrimination Acts having an overriding burden in law.

This is not to say that the reference must in every case be full and comprehensive, as shown by the case of *Bartholomew v. The London Borough of Hackney* in 1999. Bartholomew was employed as head of Hackney's Race Equality unit. He was suspended pending investigation into alleged financial irregularities and Hackney began disciplinary proceedings against him. Meanwhile Bartholomew brought a claim against the Council alleging race discrimination.

The parties reached a settlement and as a result Bartholomew withdrew his complaint and the disciplinary action automatically came to an end. Hackney was subsequently asked for a reference. The reference confirmed he had taken voluntary severance following deletion of his post and at the time of leaving he had been suspended from work because of a charge of gross misconduct, and disciplinary action had been commenced. The disciplinary action lapsed automatically on his departure from the authority. Bartholomew had an offer of employment withdrawn as a result of the reference and he made a claim for damages against Hackney. Bartholomew alleged that the Council was in breach of its duty in care and providing a reference which, although factually correct, was unfair. The tenor of the reference supplied by Hackney was therefore unfair whilst it was factually correct.

The key issues arising, therefore, are that it is important not to discriminate against any employee by refusing to give a reference and to ensure that references are accurate and strike a balance remembering that the key for the employee is finding alternative work. Advice from a lawyer should be sought if there are particularly different difficult circumstances to negotiate.

The Internet and e-commerce

The use of the Internet and Electronic Commerce has created many problems for employers and there have been a number of recent test cases that show employers have a responsibility for the actions of their employees when they use the Internet or e-mail for activities in the workplace. The key points arising from these cases show that it is important for employers who use such facilities to have a comprehensive e-mail/Internet policy in place. When implementing such a policy, employers should ensure that it is properly drawn up and communicated to all employees, specifying boundaries for using the firm's computer and equipment as well as the penalties for breaching the rules. The policy should clearly prohibit the distribution of defamatory, abusive, sexist or racist messages as well as the downloading of offensive material. The rules regarding "on-line" behaviour need to be set out too. It is particularly important to point out the perils of sending confidential messages by e-mail or Internet and the importance of having all files checked to ensure that they are free of viruses. The existence of such a policy will ensure that employers have taken reasonable care to prevent abuse and misuse of Internet facilities. So if, for example, an employee sends a defamatory message, the employer's interest can be properly protected providing the issues are identified and tackled accordingly.

More widely of course, the Internet has fundamentally and probably irrevocably altered the ways of work for the future. Internet access means that a complete redefinition of the traditional business and employment boundaries is now needed. A business no longer needs expensive premises, desks and static employees to function properly. The growth in use of home working, teleconnected distanced employees and the Internet as a medium for work makes for a new global definition of "the workplace". With this, of course, come new challenges for all aspects of HRM. How, for example, do you supervise the work of an employee you may only physically have contact with once a week? So, from recruitment to equal opportunities, the traditional approach to HRM will be tested, and no doubt reshaped, as the Internet revolution proceeds.

International labour markets

Building on the growth of "e-commerce" and the gradual breaking down of international trade barriers (particularly in the EU), the days when the HR practitioner concentrated only on the UK employment market are long gone. Although some major multinational companies have always been concerned with the employment of overseas staff, for many new businesses their marketplace is now literally worldwide.This provides a much broader context for HRM. Some the issues facing the employer of staff globally include:

- How to recruit and retain when the competition is diverse and worldwide.
- How to structure salary and benefits packages that are competitive in international economies.
- How to support staff and their families for whom international relocation and travel is a norm.
- How to train and develop staff so that they do not just have the skills for the job, but can cope with the cultural and linguistic challenges of work abroad.

International HRM therefore presents another set of challenges that are increasingly impacting not just on leading-edge commercial enterprises, but large parts of the business and service provision community as well.

Dress codes

Employers as diverse as Euro Star and the Professional Golfers Association have recently found themselves on the wrong end of sex discrimination proceedings for refusing to let women staff wear trousers. This and a general debate on what is appropriate dress code for the twenty-first century have led to a spate of issues which affects employees and employers in an HRM framework. The key for employers here is that it is reasonable for them to insist on certain dress codes, including the wearing of protective clothing and equipment as required under health and safety legislation, as long as the requirements are laid out in employment policies, and as long as the conditions of these policies are not discriminatory against any particular group. Of course, employer's dress codes can legitimately take account of protective clothing requirements which are occupationally dependent and which fall under the aegis of the *Health and Safety at Work Act.*

14.5 The future?

Whilst it is impossible to predict exactly the course of events for Human Resource Management and Employment Law in the next few years, there are some clearly defined trends that are likely to underpin such developments. The first to arise is from the EU's *Equal Rights Directive*, and the approach the European Union is taking to matters of equality and discrimination generally. Just as the health and safety directives have been used to ensure common standards in management of workplace safety across Europe over the last few years, expect the *Equal Treatment Directive* to drive and underpin a harmonised approach to equal opportunities legislation and practice throughout the community. Some of these changes will be explicit, for example through the adoption of the *Burden of Proof Directive* which will change the onus of burden of proof in discrimination cases brought before courts and tribunals. Some of it will be more subtle, such as the recent benchmark rulings concerning transsexuals and sexual orientation. But the future is clear: Europe is moving towards a set of employee rights that will ensure that direct and indirect discrimination is outlawed and the burden on employers increased in matters relating to sex, race, disability, sexual orientation, ageism and other key equality issues.

In terms of the domestic employment law scene, much of course will depend upon the shape and direction of government policy, and indeed which government is in power. If the Labour Party remain the party of government, expect a continuation in the increase of employee rights consistent with the principles of the *Human Rights Act* and building on the groundwork of the *Minimum Wage Act*, the *Working Time Directive*, the *Parental Leave Directive* and the *Part-Time Workers' Directive*. The government have already declared their intent by strengthening the *Race Relations Act* as a response to the Macpherson Inquiry and have now established the Disability Rights Commission as a powerful watch-dog analogous to the Equal Opportunities Commission and Commission for Racial Equality.

Notwithstanding their previous opposition to the Social Chapter, and a demonstrably less interventionist approach in the workplace as a whole, it will be surprising if a future Conservative government would take a completely different stance given the inexorable drive of EU directives. Indeed, during the last six months the Conservative party have changed their policy on the *Minimum Wage* and *Working Time Directives* and have now said that they will honour these provisions. However, where they are likely to depart from a Labour administration is in the further extension of some of the discrimination and employee rights legislation, and in further strengthening the power of the trade unions, which has traditionally been an anathema to a Conservative government.

Whatever the persuasion of the next government, some of these issues are finally balanced and are engendering major debates in the UK at present. The last few months have seen major crises in the UK car industry with the threatened closure of both the Rover and Ford plants in mainland Britain. These planned closures by multinational corporations are leading to a clamour for the further strengthening of UK employment protection controls and re-dundancy rights because there is a considerable body of opinion that labour protection in the UK is still a lesser priority than it is for our European counterparts. So a further strengthening of redundancy and transfer pro-tections, and the payment of compensation arising, cannot be ruled out, particularly if a Labour administration prevails in the next five to seven years.

Whatever the future policy directions, we can be sure that HRM will remain a diverse, challenging and fascinating subject for practitioners and students alike in the years to come.

14.6 Activity

Is the current Labour administration right in trying to equalise employee rights and practices in the UK with those of our major European partners by adopting the Social Chapter provisions? What are the potential costs and benefits of adopting these directives in the UK economy? Provide examples in your answer by reference to issues such as the *Working Time Directive* and the impact this has had in the UK workplace.

14.7 Checklist

- ▶ The UK domestic political scene will dictate the overall direction for UK employment law in the next decade or so.
- ▶ The impact of EU directives derived from the Social Chapter are significant now they have been adopted by the Labour government.
- ▶ The *Works Council, Parental Leave, Posted Workers, Part-Time Workers* and *Burden of Proof Directives* are considered.
- ▶ Employment law developments in the UK affect discrimination, pregnant workers and employee share schemes.
- ▶ The *Human Rights Act 2000* is likely to have a major impact on the workplace.
- ▶ Changes in HR practice are arising from the growth in use of the Internet and this in turn is expanding world labour markets.
- ▶ Some recent case law development impacts on references, the use of the Internet and dress codes.
- ▶ Likely future developments are discussed and predicted based on UK and international social and economic trends.

▼ Index

A

ACAS (Advisory, Conciliation and Arbitration Service)   168–9, 173, 178–9, 179
Access to Health Records Act 1990   106
Access to Medical Records Act 1988   106, 224, 228
Acquired Rights Directive   186, 192
age discrimination   141, 142, 148
agency workers   22
AIDS (Acquired Immune Deficiency Syndrome)   213
alcohol abuse   212–13
annual leave   *see* holiday entitlement
appraisals   108, 159–62, 163–4, 226
Asylum and Immigration Act 1996   55

B

benefits packages   100–1, 226–7
bonuses   83, 85
bullying   214

C

carers   226, 234–5
case law   9, 239
casual employment   18, 21–2, 35
childcare arrangements   102, 134, 226, 234–5
codes of practice   9
  on equal opportunities   130–3
  on health and safety   207–11
Commission for Racial Equality   130, 134–5, 136, 237
common law rights and duties   14, 77
communication with employees   73–4, 98, 173–4
  see also consultation
competence-related pay   88–9
computerised records   7–8, 111–15, 122–3, 123, 124
consensual termination agreement   50
constructive dismissal   8, 15, 39–40, 41
consultation
  on health and safety   207
  on redundancies and transfers   185–6, 189, 194, 196–8

with trade unions   171–4
on varying contracts of employment   26
with works councils   233–4
contract of employment
  and employee records   107, 107–8, 110
  and holiday entitlement   92
  legislation on   12–16, 25
  and pay and benefits   78
  in redundancies and transfers   187, 187–8, 194, 195–6
  terminating   9, 15–16, 31–52
  terms   23–5, 72
  types   17–22
  varying   15–16, 25–9, 188, 190–2, 198
contract for service   17, 193–4, 198
Contracts of Employment Act 1970   107
counselling services   223–4
courts   *see* employment tribunals

D

Data Protection Act 1984   7–8, 106, 122
Data Protection Act 1998   7–8, 106, 110, 122
disability discrimination   128–9, 136–9
  and adjustments to workplace   213
  and recruitment   54–5
  time limit for claims   43
  and training   147–8
Disability Discrimination Act 1995   8, 14, 25, 128–9, 137–8, 143
Disability Rights Commission   130, 138, 237, 242
Disabled Persons Acts 1944, 1958   127, 128, 136–7
disciplinary action
  equality of dealing   132–3
  future legislation   238
  procedures   174–6, 179–80
  record keeping   108
  warnings   33
Disclosure of Information Act 1999   129–30, 177–8
dismissals   *see* terminating contracts of employment
disputes and grievances   174–9
drug abuse   212–13

E

EAT (Office of the Employment Appeals Tribunals) 44–5
early retirement 95
e-commerce 240
employee records 105–9, 122–3
employee relations 166–81
employee share schemes 237–8
employee support and welfare 108, 189, 219–30
Employment Act 1980 80
employment agencies 22
Employment Protection Act 1975 8, 16, 80, 167, 168, 183
Employment Protection (Consolidation) Act 1978 8
    and contracts of employment 15–16, 20, 25–6, 107
    and employment tribunals 42
    and trade unions 129
    and unfair dismissal 8, 15–16, 129
    updating of 20, 80, 107, 167, 168, 183
Employment Relations Act 1999 167–8, 237
    and trade union recognition 129, 198, 231
    and unfair dismissal 33
Employment Rights Act 1996 8, 168
    and contract of employment 15, 16, 78, 147
    and employment tribunals 42–3
    and maternity rights 80, 99
    and redundancy 183
    and unfair dismissal 38, 39, 168
    and written statement 12–13, 20, 23, 147
employment tribunals 8, 42–7, 138–9, 238
    and case law 9
    future legislation 242
Employment Tribunals Act 1996 8
equal opportunities 54–5, 68, 126–44
    and employee records 108
    future legislation 236–7, 241–2
Equal Opportunities Commission 130, 133, 237
Equal Pay Act 1970 14, 54, 79, 128
ethnic minorities 65, 131, 134–6
ethnic origin *see* racial discrimination
European Convention on Human Rights 238
European Court of Justice 139–40, 192–3, 239
European Union (EU)
    directives 7, 204, 231–6, 241–2
    Acquired Rights Directive 186, 192
    Parental Leave Directive 234–5
    Part-Time Workers Directive 235–6
    Posted Workers Directive 236
    Working Time Directive 9, 204
    Works Council Directive 168, 173, 233–4
    Treaty of Rome 54, 147, 204
executive search consultants 74

F

Factories Act 1961 8, 201
Fire Precautions Act 1971 203
Fire Precautions Regulations 1997 203
fixed term contract 35, 40
flexible hours 19, 238
freedom of assembly 238
freedom of expression 238
full-time employees 18

G

garden leave 48, 51
good practice framework 10
grievances and disputes 174–9, 180

H

harassment at work 214
"Hawthorne" effect 219
hazardous substances 213
health and safety 8, 37–8, 200–18
    see also Health and Safety at Work Act 1974
Health and Safety Commission 205
Health and Safety Executive 205
Health and Safety at Work Act 1974 8, 14, 129–30, 142, 202–3
    and dress codes 241
    and employee welfare 220–1
    and employers' responsibilities 212, 215, 227–8
    and injuries 214–15
    and mandatory health and safety training 148, 207
    and violence 214
HIV (human immunodeficiency virus) 213
holiday entitlement 13, 72, 79, 91–2, 235
hours of work 13, 18–19, 91
HRM (human resource management)
    development of 2–4, 231–2
    future trends 241–2
    types of 2–5
Human Rights Act 2000 238

I

improvement orders 205–6
Income Tax Regulations 1993 80–1
induction 71–2, 153
industrial relations *see* employee relations
Industrial Relations Act 1971 42

industrial tribunals   *see* employment tribunals

information technology
computerised records   7–8, 105, 110–15
and training   146, 151, 159
and working from home   91

injuries at work   214–15, 222

Institute of Personnel Development (IPD)   53, 87, 141, 157

intellectual property   49, 54

international labour markets   240–1

Internet   113, 240

interviews   *see* recruitment

Investors in People award   72, 152, 162–3

J

JCNCs (Joint Consultative and Negotiating Committees)   172–3

job analysis   56–7

job description   13, 55–9, 190

job design   57–8

job evaluation and pay   90, 101–2

job exchange   156

job title   13

Joint Consultative and Negotiating Committees (JCNCs)   172–3

L

legislative framework for HRM   7–11

leave entitlement   *see* holiday entitlement

Low Pay Commission   79

M

Maastricht Treaty   232–3

Macpherson Inquiry   134, 136, 242

management training   154–7

manpower planning   118–22, 123–4

Manual Handling Operations Regulations 1993   215

maternity rights   98–100, 102–3, 235, 237
and pay   81, 99, 237

maternity-related dismissal   38, 102–3

MBA (Master of Business Administration) programmes   155, 163

mentoring   156–7

mergers   *see* transfers of undertakings

minimum wage legislation   8, 231
National Minimum Wage Act 1998   8, 39, 79, 87

misconduct   31, 33, 174–5

multinationals   233–4, 236, 240–1

N

National Insurance contributions   80, 93

National Minimum Wage Act 1998   8, 39, 79, 87

notice requirements   36, 40, 42, 47–8, 190

NVQs (National Vocational Qualifications)   153

O

occupational health service   70, 222–3
and medical records   106–7
referrals to   97, 98, 228

occupational pension schemes   93, 94–5

offer of employment   23, 69–70

Office of the Employment Appeals Tribunals (EAT)   44–5

Offices, Shops and Railway Premises Act 1963   8, 201

operational HRM   2–3, 118

organisations
change in   4, 60, 182–3, 190–2, 197–8
organisational culture   75, 134, 170, 174, 209, 238
role of HRM in   2–5
rules and policies   10
salary structures   87–90, 101
and training   146, 148–53, 157–9
workforce planning in   118–19

overtime   83, 85, 235

P

parental leave   234–5, 238

part-time employees   18, 235–6

Part-Time Workers Directive   235–6

pay
and contract of employment   13, 77
and employee records   110–11
legislation on   8, 78–81, 231
and recruitment   72
systems and policies   82–91, 101–2

PAYE deductions   80

pension schemes   20, 72, 92–4, 235

Pension Schemes Act 1993   92

Pensions Act 1995   92

performance management and review   108, 159–62

performance-related pay   82, 83, 84, 85, 88, 160–1, 163–4

permanent employees   17–18

person specification   56, 58–9

personal pensions   94

personnel information systems   105–18, 122–3, 124

place of work   13

policing role of HRM   3–4

Posted Workers Directive   236

post-termination restraints   49–50

post-trauma stress   220, 223–4

pre-employment screening   222, 228, 238

Pregnant Workers Directive   237
premia payments   84
private sector   2–4, 63–4, 82, 87
professional training programmes   157–9
profit-sharing   82, 85
prohibition orders   205–6
promotion, equal opportunities for   132, 142–3
psychometric tests   65–6, 131
Public Interest Disclosure Act 1998   8, 39, 141, 221
public sector
    equal opportunities   136
    HRM in   2–4
    pay   83, 86–7, 163–4
    recruitment in   63–4

R
Race Relations Act 1976   8, 14, 25, 128
    and disciplinary action   132–3
    and recruitment   54–5
    time limit for claims   43
    and training   147–8
    updating of   136
Race Relations Amendment Bill   237
racial discrimination   8, 134–6
    see also Race Relations Act 1976
record keeping   7–8, 105–6
recruitment
    costs   53, 75–6
    and equal opportunities   131
    interviews   66–9, 131–2
    legal framework   54–5
    strategies and methods   60–70
redundancies and transfers   8, 32, 34–5, 38–9, 182–99, 236
Redundancy Payments Act 1965   16, 183
references   69–70, 108, 122, 239–40
Rehabilitation of Offenders Act 1974   55, 69, 129
remuneration   *see* pay
repetitive strain injury   214
resignation, voluntary   32, 36, 40, 41
retention of employees   53–4, 71–4, 75–6
risk management   209–11, 214, 225, 228

S
salaries   *see* pay
seasonal workers   21–2
selection   *see* recruitment
self-employed status   27–8
SERPS (State Earnings-Related Pension Scheme)   93
sex discrimination   133–4, 142–3
    claims   43, 46–7
    direct and indirect   127–8

and disciplinary action   132–3
and dress codes   241
exemptions   128
legislation on   8, 14, 25, 127–8, 133, 136
and maternity rights   99
and recruitment   54–5
and references   239
time limit for claims   43
and training   147–8
Sex Discrimination Acts 1975, 1986   8, 14, 25, 127–8, 136
sexual harassment   50–1
sexual orientation   139–41, 242
shift work   19
short-listing job applicants   64–5, 131
sick pay   81, 96–8, 235
smoking   211–12, 216
staff associations   169, 173
State Earnings-Related Pension Scheme (SERPS)   93
Statutory Maternity Pay and Statutory Sick Pay Regulations 1996   81
strategic HRM   2–3, 118
stress at work   216–17, 224–6
Sunday Trading Act 1994   38

T
temporary employees   18, 21–2, 35
tenure   17
term-time employees   119
terminating contracts of employment
    legal grounds   31–3
    procedures   9, 33–6
    termination agreements   49–50
    unfair grounds   15–16, 36–9
    see also unfair dismissals
terms and conditions of employment   23–5, 72
Trade Union and Labour Relations Act 1992   129
Trade Union Reform and Employment Rights Act 1993   8, 15, 80, 167
    and discrimination   129
    and employee records   107
    on employment tribunals   42–3
    and pay   80
    and redundancies   185–6, 186, 188–90
    and transfers of undertakings   187
trade unions
    and consultation on redundancies   185–6
    and disciplinary procedures   174–6
    fluctuations in power   166–7
    and grievances   176–8
    legislation on   8, 167–8
    negotiating with   171–4

trade unions *cont.*
  recognition by employers 170–1, 172, 179, 198
  rights of employees 37, 169–70, 238
Trade Unions and Labour Relations (Consolidation) Act 1992 8, 14, 107
training 146–59
  in employee relations 173
  equal rights to 236
  in health and safety 207
  and recruitment 72
  records of 108–9
Transfer of Undertakings (Protection of Employment) Regulations (TUPE) 1981 39, 186–8, 192–6
transfers of undertakings 8, 39, 168, 186–8, 192–6
transsexuals 140–1, 242
Treaty of Rome 54, 147, 204
tribunals *see* employment tribunals
TUPE *(Transfer of Undertakings (Protection of Employment) Regulations) 1981* 39, 186–8, 192–6

U
Unfair Contract Terms Act 1977 15
unfair dismissal 39–42
  case law 9
  claims for 43, 100
  employee's rights 15
  grounds for 36–9

legislation 8
qualifying period 20–1, 33
of temporary workers 21–2
and transfers of undertakings 187–8
unsocial hours 84

V
vacancy inquiry 63–4
verbal contract 23
violence at work 213–14
Visual Display Screen Regulations 1993 214
vocational education 153
voluntary redundancy 95
voluntary resignation 32, 36

W
wages *see* pay
Wages Act 1996 78–9
Warner Inquiry (1993) 69
welfare and employee support 219–30
welfare model of HRM 3–4, 118
"whistleblowing" 8, 108, 177–8, 221, 238
workforce planning 105, 118–22, 123–4
Working Time Directive 91, 92
Working Time Regulations 1998 38, 79
Works Council Directive 168, 173, 233–4
written statement of particulars 13, 20, 23
wrongful dismissal 15, 40, 41–2

Z
zero hours 19

.